Volume 21, Number 1
(New Series)

March 1971

THE BAKER STREET JOURNAL

An Irregular Quarterly of Sherlockiana

Editor: JULIAN WOLFF, M.D.

THE BAKER STREET IRREGULARS
NEW YORK, N.Y.

**Volume 21, Number 1
(New Series)**

March 1971

THE BAKER STREET JOURNAL

Founded by **EDGAR W. SMITH**, Esq.

"Si monumentum quaeris, circumspice"

Subscription $4 a year

All communications and remittances should be sent to the Editor

Julian Wolff, M.D.

33 Riverside Drive, New York, N. Y. 10023

CONTENTS

THE IN-VERSE CANON
by Richard W. Clarke

A Study in Scarlet

Tobias Gregson, while begging his pardon,
Summoned Holmes to Lauriston Garden.
Some days later Sherlock had the straight dope
And clamped the handcuffs on Jefferson Hope.

The Lion's Mane

On the beach they found McPherson,
A badly mutilated person.
Holmes was brilliant, gathering data,
And found the villain, Cyanea capillata.

The Retired Colourman

By simple reading we can see
What a wretch was Josiah Amberley.
Without recourse to a gun or a knife
He killed Dr. Ernest and Amberley's wife.

The Veiled Lodger

Holmes did not have much to ponder
Regarding the case of Mrs. Ronder,
Whose lover named as Leonardo,
Showed cowardice and not bravado.

Shoscombe Old Place

Sir Robert spent all his money
Betting on Shoscombe Prince, his pony.
Sir Robert was able to save his face
Because his horse won the Derby race.

The Mazarin Stone

A chap with the temper of Vesuvius
Was the gent who's known as Count Sylvius.
But Holmes retrieved the stone, don't fear,
And shipped it to Lord Cantlemere.

Thor Bridge

The gold millionaire, Gibson, Neil,
For the governess did affection feel.
Holmes acted at a rapid pace
And cleared Miss Dunbar, known as Grace.

The Creeping Man

Professor Presbury's wolfhound, Roy,
Did not recognise the poor old boy
Who could climb the walls (he was very spunky)
But very nearly became a monkey.

The Sussex Vampire

Big Bob Ferguson, former three-quarter,
Had a young son, but nary a daughter.
Holmes, as usual, was on the right track
When he spotted the villain, the bad boy named Jack.

The Three Garridebs

Holmes and Watson weren't misled
To search for the last of the Garridebs.
And then no sooner than sixes and sevens,
They caught the counterfeiter, one Killer Evans.

The Illustrious Client

The lecherous Adelbert Gruner
Would come to grief later or sooner.
He received the vitriol ('twas almost a pity)
Thrown by the vindictive girl, Miss Kitty.

The Three Gables

Sherlock managed this case quite ably
By protecting the interest of one Mrs. Maberley.
He sent her a cheque with a nice kindly line
For an amount he received from Isadora Klein.

The Blanched Soldier

The former soldier named Godfrey Emsworth
Had to give people a very wide berth
Because of disease—but the doctor's diagnosis
Was not leprosy, but ichthyosis.

The Sign of the Four

Mary Morstan, lovely girl,
Every year received a pearl.
The Sholtos, Thad., Bartholomew,
Surely knew a thing or two,
And carefully, measure by measure,
Holmes resolved the Agra treasure.

A Scandal in Bohemia

In the month of March 1888,
The story too long for me to relate,
Our Sherlock Holmes was really smitten,
And the King of Bohemia sure got the mitten.

The Red-Headed League

Although Jabez Wilson did not wear a monocle,
He read the ad in The Morning Chronicle
That Ezekiah Hopkins of Lebanon, Penn.,
Founded the League of Red-Headed Men.
The work was easy and not fanatical;
He merely copied the Encyclopædia Britannical.
But once again Holmes had his day
And pinched the robber known as John Clay.

A Case of Identity

The lady on the pavement struggled with passion.
She wore her hat Duchess of Devonshire fashion.
She explained to Holmes when she made her call
That she met dear Hosmer at the gasfitters' ball.
It was our dear Sherlock that she had to thank
For exposing that villain, one Windibank.

Boscombe Valley

A dreadful deed, indeed much folly,
Occurred at a place called Boscombe Valley.
Our Sherlock explained, and that was that:
The killer—Black Jack of Ballarat.

The Five Orange Pips

The ruffians, far outside the law,
Set the pips on Openshaw.
Holmes wrote Captain Calhoun from afar,
And the Captain was drowned in the barque <u>Lone Star</u>.

The Man with the Twisted Lip

With his wife his secret he did not share.
I refer, of course, to Neville St. Clair.
But Holmes was smart and called the right tune,
Showing that Neville was also Hugh Boone.

The Blue Carbuncle

Henry Baker lost his chapeau,
Concerning which Holmes seemed to know,
And soon by a very clever ruse
He solved the problem of the goose.

The Speckled Band

In Stoke Moran lived Dr. Roylott,
And in truth he was a bad lot.
Towards Sherlock he became madder and madder,
But was done in by his own swamp adder.

The Engineer's Thumb

A villain was Col. Lysander Stark
Who lived at a place called Eyford Park.
Hatherley, with great luck it would seem,
Was saved by the very heroic Elise.

The Noble Bachelor

Lord St. Simon, man about town,
By Hattie Doran was flatly turned down.
Poor Lord St. Simon had no one to thank
As Mrs. Moulton walked off with beloved Frank.

The Beryl Coronet

Unfortunately, Alexander Holder
Thought his son was growing bolder,
And Mr. Holder will never forget
That his niece Mary pinched the coronet.

The Copper Beeches

Miss Violet Smith's report truly teaches
Us the life at the Copper Beeches.
Carlo the mastiff was an inveterate growler,
But Alice Rucastle eloped with her Fowler.

Silver Blaze

Silver Blaze was a very fast hoss
Who belonged to a chap who was called Col. Ross.
Holmes found the horse in the hands of a faker
And proved that the animal had killed Johnny Straker.

The Cardboard Box

Here is the tale of one Jim Browner.
His wife was taken by an out-of-towner.
Holmes, first in the dark, to success was soon pushing,
And explained human ears which were sent to Miss Cushing.

The Yellow Face

This is the story of Grant Munro.
The facts of the case I am sure you all know,
How Holmes was able to solve in a jiffy
All about the coloured daughter of Effie.

The Stockbroker's Clerk

This is the adventure of one Hall Pycroft
(A pity his first name was not Mycroft),
And, gentle reader, always beware
Of employment by Franco-Midland Hardware.

The Gloria Scott

Sherlock declared that he would never
Forget his old schoolmate, Victor Trevor.
Gamekeeper Hudson, a very bad actor,
In old Trevor's death was a vital factor.

The Musgrave Ritual

At Hurlstone, in Surrey, a fine feudal place,
Lived the family of Musgrave, the pride of their race,
And Brunton, going from bad to much worse,
Missed the crown that knew the head of Charlie the First.

The Naval Treaty

The treaty's loss was not for joking.
Holmes and Watson took a train to Woking.
Holmes was brilliant beyond comparison.
And nabbed the scoundrel, Joseph Harrison.

The Reigate Squires

Holmes solved problems at a very high rate.
Now we find him down at Reigate.
Poor William was shot, a very good man.
Sherlock proved the killer was Cunningham.

The Crooked Man

Sherlock Holmes inquired sharply
About the death of Colonel Barclay.
He got the whole story, as he thought he would,
By talking to Mr. Henry Wood.

The Resident Patient

Dr. Trevelyan wrote on obscure nervous lesions,
Was very much worried, and these were the reasons:
Blessington dead, and Holmes solved the riddle.
The killers were Hayward, Moffat, and Biddle.

The Greek Interpreter

This is a tale, there is only one other,
Introduced by Sherlock's own brother.
An uncomfortable sequence of events came to pass
Upon that nice Greek chap, Monsieur Melas.

The Final Problem

Although there is some disparity
About the first name of Professor Moriarty,
The world received a dreadful shock
When we had the news from Reichenbach.

The Golden Pince-Nez

And now we have a curious case
Known as the event at Yoxley Old Place.
Sherlock smoked his cigarettes,
And thereby won his hopeful bet.

The Missing Three-Quarter

Next is the story of Godfrey Staunton
(He scored from scrum when playing Taunton).
Through meadows and fields both dry and swampy
Holmes was led by the draghound Pompey.

The Abbey Grange

Sir Eustace was a veritable devil.
He never did anything on the level.
Croker's life by Holmes was saved,
And Croker married the girl from Adelaide.

Black Peter

The Sea Unicorn, with Black Peter as master,
Was a fast-moving ship, not one any faster.
The harpoon sure killed this man from the sea
Upon a dark night at Woodman's Lee.

Charles Augustus Milverton

A villain, an honest-to-goodness son-of-a-gun,
Was one Charles Augustus Milverton.
"Take that, you hound—and that!—and that!"
And Holmes and Watson never looked back.

The Six Napoleons

A journalist named Horace Harker
Really was a nosey Parker.
The busts were made by Gelder & Co.,
And the villain was known as Signore Beppo.

The Second Stain

The jilted girl used much bravado
When stopping M. Lucas (first name Eduardo).
This was a case with which Sherlock could cope,
And he restored the lost letter to Trelawney Hope.

Wisteria Lodge

Here is the Tiger of San Pedro
Who received his come-uppance near Toledo.
Sherlock's fee was beaucoup shekels
For solving the problem of John Scott Eccles.

The Bruce-Partington Plans

His name was Arthur Cadogan West;
He really and truly was one of the best.
But a villain crocked him on the bean
(By the name of Hugo Oberstein).

The Devil's Foot

Mortimer Tregennis found the devil's foot.
He made his brother mad, did a murder to boot.
But once again our Holmes did not fail—
Bagged the big hunter, Leon Sterndale.

The Red Circle

Mrs. Warren had a roomer;
Her actions caused her much ill humour.
Gennaro had a lovely wife,
And he stabbed Gorgiano with his knife.

The Empty House

With the air-gun made by Herr Von Herder
The old shikari was bent on murder,
But Sherlock floored him with a clout,
And it's a good thing brother Lestrade was about.

The Norwood Builder

The unhappy John Hector McFarlane
Despaired of his life again and again.
Now Holmes was smart; he raised Oldacre's ire
By having all hands shout "Fire, Fire, Fire!"

The Dancing Men

Of all of Holmes's villains (indeed there are many)
Not one was worse than Mr. Abe Slaney.
He designed the dancers and raised a great clamour
When he shot the owner of Ridling Thorpe Manor.

The Priory School

Young Saltire attended the Priory School
And (usually) lived up to the rules.
The German teacher got it straight in the neck,
And Holmes received a most generous cheque.

The Three Students

Hilton Soames held the chair in Greek.
It took our Sherlock less than a week
To find who had pinched the exam paper,
And Gilchrist went free despite his wrong caper.

The Hound of the Baskervilles

Holmes responded with a will
To help young Henry Baskerville.
Holmes came forward with a bound
And put an end to the dreadful hound.

The Valley of Fear

A hard-bitten man, both tough and flinty,
Was the giant known as Master McGinty.
Holmes made this case reductione absurdo
By predicting the death of good John McMurdo.

Lady Frances Carfax

Watson was ordered to go to Lausanne,
Seeking La Carfax in that lovely town.
All that Sherlock wished to hear
Was a description of Holy Peters's ear.

The Dying Detective

The person described is not a myth.
I refer to that villain, Culverton Smith.
Sherlock's part was very effective,
Pretending to be the dying detective.

His Last Bow

A sailing and a polo sport
Was the Kaiser's special spy, Von Bork.
But Sherlock did something really big
That landed Von Bork in the brig.

The Solitary Cyclist

Roaring Jack Woodley and Mr. Carruthers
Wanted dear Violet (no doubt there were others).
Woodley cried, "She's my wife, she's my kiddo."
"No," said Carruthers—bang!—"she's your widow."

Many actors portrayed the famous sleuth. Above: Basil Rathbone as Holmes
and Nigel Bruce as Dr. Watson; they played the roles on radio, in films.

THE RÔLE OF PUBLIC TRANSPORTATION
IN THE SOLUTION OF CAPITAL CRIME

by Harry W. Springer, with David A. Wallace

We have long thought that public transportation has
been given less than adequate attention in the solutions
of the capital crimes credited to Sherlock Holmes. Consequently, we engaged in extensive research, and—I may
point out—at no modest expense to our personal fortunes
and our peace of mind.

For example, we were in possession, some months ago,
of all public timetables, route maps, and other such information. This was, we believe, the first attempt to
assemble some of the more pertinent details of public
transportation during the late nineteenth and the early
twentieth centuries. With our access to computers and
computer programming, we quickly realized that the obvious answer to the problem of reducing this mass of
data (gleaned, we may add, from all parts of the globe)
to some semblance of order was to subject it to some of
the more advanced techniques of computerisation. With
the traditional thoroughness of a member of the Maiwand
Jezails preparing a learned paper of this sort, we engaged the best minds available in the data-processing
industry. These experts dissembled [!] this fantastic
mass of information onto punched cards, magnetic tapes,
and so on. Unfortunately, before the project was complete, some oaf inadvertently folded, spindled, and mutilated one of the key cards in the sequence. As a result, all of our researches into the precise scheduling
of transportation and the effect minute-by-minute variations in arrivals and departures had on the success or
failure of the solutions of some of the great crimes
went for nought. You may imagine that this was one of
the most disappointing moments in our long months of
complicated and costly research. Undaunted, however, we
knew that we would have to map out a new course. As a
result, we resorted to a technique which enabled us to
present the statistical data we painstakingly gathered
for your consideration. The technique was well known to
Holmes and is familiar to public transportation directors
generally. It is known as the science of deduction, or,
in laymen's terms, attempting to be in the right place
at the right time. It is not an exact science.

As most of you who have used public transportation,
either now or in the past, can confirm, things don't
always happen when they are supposed to. That is to say,
an omnibus, a growler, a hansom, or a smart little landau

is not always in the right place at the right time, or when the published timetable suggests that the mode of conveyance might appear.

Nevertheless, what we are attempting to prove is that without public transportation the heinous crimes of the last century could not have been solved.

Come with us, then, gentlemen: let us board a hansom and rattle through the streets to Waterloo or Charing Cross or Paddington. Holmes, as you know, never took a train at King's Cross or Liverpool Street. Our investigations never shed any light on this mystery.

If we had not had our unfortunate experience with the punched cards, we would be able to say dramatically, as Holmes did, "Come, Watson, come, the game is afoot!" Instead, we are forced to say, "Afoot the game is, Watson come—" or words to that effect.

Enough of levity. Let us now examine some of the great crimes and determine whether or not they could have been solved without the use of public transportation. Consider, if you will, Silver Blaze. In his chronicle, Watson wrote, "We had left Reading far behind us before he thrust the last one of them [newspapers which he had procured at Paddington] under his seat and offered me his cigar-case." Then followed that often-quoted calculation of the speed of the train. The conversation went on apace, and Holmes proceeded to elucidate to Watson the essential facts of the case. We need not dwell on the fact that the case was brilliantly solved. But who can argue that the Great Southern Railway was not a contributing factor, affording Holmes, as it did, a quiet carriage, thus allowing him to clear his mind and form some opinions?

From Silver Blaze, let us turn to the barque Gloria Scott. This ill-fated ship, as you will recall, was instrumental in providing Holmes with a vehicle (no pun intended) to make his talents commercially available for the first time.

The Gloria Scott, to this very day, is recorded in British maritime circles as having been "lost at sea with all hands." We know, of course, that this is not the case and that the survivors, who were convicts being transported to Australia, passed themselves off as survivors of a passenger ship when they were picked up by the British brig Hotspur. Years later, however, Holmes was able to unravel the mystery. Observe, if you will, that the name of the passenger ship was never mentioned in the narrative. Therefore, public transportation (the passenger ship) contributed to the solution of this interesting case simply because it was never involved.

Transportation takes many forms. What about the bicycle? This remarkable machine, invented by the eminent
Scottish blacksmith, Kirkpatrick McMillan, was featured
in The Solitary Cyclist. Watson does not elaborate on
whether the bicycle in this case was a penny-farthing or
whatever. You will recall, however, that Miss Violet Smith
visited Holmes and Watson in their quarters, and Holmes,
with a resigned air and somewhat weary smile, requested
the beautiful visitor to take a seat and tell them what
was troubling her. "'At least it cannot be your health,'
said he, as his keen eyes darted over her [not lecher-
ously, we hope]; 'so ardent a bicyclist must be full of
energy.'" We need not proceed further with the details
of this case. And there may be some who would not agree
that the humble bicycle can be considered public transportation. That is a moot point. A great part of the
world's population depends on this vehicle and its vari-
ants to get from place to place. Consider China, the
most populated of the world's nations. It would be
brought to a veritable standstill without the rickshaw,
and this study would be less than complete if the bicycle had not been included.

Let us leap ahead to the winter of 1895. Lestrade is
speaking: "A passenger who passed Aldgate in an ordinary
Metropolitan train about 11:40 on Monday night declares
he heard a heavy thud as of a body striking the line."

What case are we referring to? What else but The Bruce-
Partington Plans. The Plans, of course, described a submarine, a mode of transportation outside the sphere of
this report. Suffice it to say, however, that some of the
designs are incorporated into the American Polaris submarines and their counterparts, the British Dreadnoughts.
The peace of the world depends so much on these levia-
thans of the deep that security reasons prohibit us from
discussing them beyond this point.

We mention this only as an aside, because the Bruce-
Partingon Plans case is the outstanding example uncovered
in our researches concerning capital crime and public
transportation. You will remember that the body of young
Cadogan West was found just outside Aldgate Station on
the Underground system in London. Holmes deduced that
the body had not fallen from the train at this point.
(Bear in mind that the doors on the old Underground trains
were of the sliding type and were not self-closing.) He
deduced further that the dead body had been placed on the
roof of the coach and had been jolted off. Where had the
body been put on the coach top? First, at a house window
overlooking the track, and second, where the trains were

halted to allow other trains to pass—a junction in an open cutting overlooked by the backs of houses.

Holmes knew his London well. Mycroft proferred the information that Herr Hugo Oberstein, living at 13 Caulfield Gardens, Kensington, was a known spy. Sherlock, on the other hand, knew that Caulfield Gardens overlooked a cutting where the Underground had a junction, and there were halts to allow trains to go through. Holmes, then, narrowed the suspicion down to Oberstein. The plans were recovered and a megalomaniac was deprived of a master weapon with which to tyrannise the rest of the world.

You will agree that this case above all others does prove the indispensable part public transportation has played in criminology.

In closing, let us say that it is possible to go to Gloucester Road Station on the London Metropolitan Transit System and retrace the footsteps of Holmes and Watson when they went to look for the back window of Herr Oberstein's house. It is a short walk to Cromwell Road, and a slight glance to the right will reveal the very house from which Cadogan West's body was lowered to the coach's top. The railway lines themselves are no longer visible as they were, for all the vast open space has been roofed in to cover the new London Air Terminal.

And so we have come full circle: four-in-hands and barques; rickshaws and penny-farthings; steam locomotives and underground trains. Who can deny the rôle this collection of vehicular traffic has played in mankind's development?

It has been our intention to present the case of public transportation and its inestimable help in solving crimes. We hope we have achieved this objective, and we now caution you: "Drive carefully!"

Bibliography

In the Footsteps of Sherlock Holmes, by Michael Harrison.

They Startled Grandfather—Gay Ladies and Merry Mashers of Victorian Times, by W. H. Holden.

Whitaker's Almanac.

Murray's Diary.

Illustrated London News.

News of the World.

The Tailor and Cutter.

"Assisting with Bus Timetables," in National Fortune-tellers Association House Organ, The Crystal Ball.

Annual Report, Long Island Railroad.

HOLMES AND COMMUNICATION
Dr. Kohki Naganuma

Throughout the sixty stories, the telephone as one of the
means of communication appears only in six:

1) The Man with the Twisted Lip   2) The Greek Interpreter
3) The Retired Colourman   4) The Three Garridebs
5) The Illustrious Client   6) The Blanched Soldier

In other stories, telegrams and letters are the main means of
communication. This may give us the impression that Holmes preferred telegrams and letters. Taking the time into consideration
—the 19th century, when the telephone had not been developed,
and hansoms, railways, and the underground were the only means
of transportation—Holmes had to depend on letters and telegrams. However, by careful reading, I encountered many cases
where I could not be convinced as to his way of handling the
means of communication. Let us begin with telegrams.

The Devil's Foot (March 1897 case, published in December 1910):
Watson commented on Holmes: "He has never been known to write
where a telegram would serve." We can understand that he liked
a telegram, as he was always in a hurry to solve the crime.

A Study in Scarlet (March 1881 case):
On the morning of March 4th, Holmes and Watson visited the
house at 3, Lauriston Gardens to investigate the case. Leaving
there at 1 P.M., Holmes sent a long telegram to the head of the
Cleveland police, asking him to find out whether or not Enoch J.
Drebber was really married. He returned to Baker Street, and
then went to a concert, leaving Watson, who had been entirely
tired out, alone in the rooms. It was about 8 P.M., after the
supper dishes were set, that he returned. He said to Watson, "I
have just had an answer to my American telegram." This was about
seven hours after he had sent his telegram. It is difficult to
judge whether the reply came too quickly or not. As Drebber's
application for protection had been made to the Cleveland police
before Holmes's cable arrived, he might have been able to get
the answer so fast. Otherwise it would have been impossible to
investigate and wire back in less than seven hours.

The Yellow Face (April 1882 case):
A telegram from Norbury was delivered when Holmes and Watson had
finished their tea. It said, "The cottage is still tenanted. . . .
will meet the seven o'clock train and will take no steps until
you arrive." This telegram was from Mr. Grant Munro, to whom
Holmes had said, "Let me advise you, then, to return to Norbury
and to examine the windows of the cottage again. If you have
reason to believe it is inhabited, . . . send a wire to my friend
and me. We shall be with you within an hour of receiving it, and
we shall then very soon get to the bottom of the business." Is
it possible that they were able to get to Norbury from London
"within an hour"? Norbury station is about nine miles from Baker
Street. We are not told how Holmes and Watson got to the place.
At present one takes the underground at Baker Street and changes
at Charing Cross for Victoria Station, then takes the railway.
It takes approximately an hour and a quarter at best. It can be
easily imagined that they needed more time in those days, and
that it was impossible to reach Norbury "within an hour."

The telegram from Munro was dispatched on the same day that
he called on Holmes. The question is, could it have been delivered to Holmes before seven o'clock? Holmes and Watson came
back to Baker Street at nearly five in the evening. After several minutes, Munro reappeared and talked to Holmes shortly.
Then he just caught the train for Norbury at about five. As I

have mentioned, he could not get to Norbury within an hour, even at best. So let us suppose that he could get there in an hour and a quarter—the highest speed even now. He arrived there after 6:15. From 6:15 to 7:00 he saw the face and dispatched the wire. Holmes received it and got on the seven o'clock train. How on earth can all these things go on in 45 minutes? Could the telegram be delivered in less than 30 minutes? We are not able to imagine exactly how circumstances were at the time, but I'm afraid that all this is impossible.

The Cardboard Box (August 1885 case):
Holmes received a letter from Lestrade, asking for his help. The letter was delivered in the morning—from which arises our question. The Inspector wrote: "I shall be either at the house or in the police-station all day." Holmes started at once, after dispatching a wire to Croydon, where the house was. When Holmes arrived, Lestrade was at the station. Here I cannot help shaking my head. There were two stations, one at East Croydon and the other at West Croydon. The east station, which is closer to London, is the third stop from Norbury. If one can get to Norbury within an hour, he might not need much time to reach Croydon. Suppose it takes an hour and twenty-five minutes to Croydon (to Norbury, an hour and fifteen minutes); the telegram should have reached much more quickly. Lestrade stayed at the house, five minutes' walk from the station, so he could get there quickly after receiving Holmes's telegram. However, the question is whether the telegram could be delivered so promptly in those days.

The Hound of the Baskervilles (September 1886 case):
Holmes, who had stayed overnight at Baskerville Hall, went out early in the morning. He had come back when Watson got up. Two hours after breakfast (8:00 A.M.?) he arrived at Coombe Tracey station (about 10:00 or 10:30). There was a telegram from Lestrade: "Wire received. . . . Arrive five-forty." (One had to start from Paddington at 10:30 A.M. in order to reach Dartmoor in the evening.) Holmes saw the telegram at 10:00 or 10:30, but the exact time of its arrival is not known. How does this work out?
6:00 A.M. (before breakfast) Holmes dispatched telegram.
7:00–8:00 Scotland Yard received it. (Lestrade was there then?)
8:30–9:00 Lestrade wired back.
10:00–? Holmes received wire at the station.
It is very doubtful that all this could have been carried out so promptly and smoothly.

The Sign of Four (September 1887 case):
Holmes and Watson began their investigation at about 3 o'clock in the dawn. They stopped the investigation to go home in a hansom. Taverns were about to be opened for the early-morning workers. On the way home, Holmes sent a wire to Wiggins of the Baker Street irregulars, saying "I expect that he and his gang will be with us before we have finished our breakfast." It was between eight and nine that Holmes sent the wire, and I imagine that it was less than an hour later that Wiggins and the boys rushed into the room. ". . . Three bob and a tanner for tickets," said Wiggins, indicating that they had used some means of transportation. This sounds a little funny. The telegram arrived too fast in this case, much more promptly than a telephone call!
    There is another question in The Sign of Four. Athelney Jones called at Baker Street at 3 P.M. and told Watson who was taking charge during Holmes's absence, "I had a wire from him [Holmes] this morning." The wire was dated from Poplar at twelve. Here I have a few questions:
1. Jones said he had received the message in the morning, but it had been dispatched at twelve. This does not mean midnight be-

cause Holmes did not send any messages then. If it did mean midnight, Jones should have come at dawn, since the wire said, "Go to Baker Street at once." Would he have waited until 3:00 P.M.?

2. Then twelve o'clock must mean noon of the day Jones called. Holmes must have found some clue between the time he went out and noon. The sentence in the wire, "If I have not returned...," evidently indicates that Holmes was out when he sent it.

3. If Jones called at 3:00 P.M., after receiving a message that had been dispatched at noon, then his words, "I have had a wire from him this morning," are false. It is really a big mistake.

The Naval Treaty (June 1888 case):

On receiving the letter from Percy Phelps, Watson called at Baker Street (he lived in Paddington then) "within an hour of breakfas time." Holmes took "an early train at Waterloo" with Watson. (It was an hour and thirty minutes after Watson's breakfast, and before that Holmes had already been working hard on a chemical investigation. Then, why is it an early train?) In less than an ho they arrived at Woking. Phelps lived a few minutes' walk from th station. Having learned the circumstances, the two returned, and reached Waterloo at 3:20 P.M. They might have gotten on the trai at 2:20 P.M., as they were on it for an hour. Before the train left Woking, Holmes sent a few wires, inserting advertisements i every evening paper in London, and also one to Forbes of Scotlan Yard. Thus: Holmes started from Woking at 2:20; arrived at Water loo at 3:20; arrived at Scotland Yard at 3:50. The telegram migh have been delivered in ninety minutes, cutting it close. If Forbe had been out even for a short time, the telegram could not have been handed in, and he could not have seen Holmes.

There is also something strange about the wires to the newspapers. I don't know the deadline for advertisements in those days, but I think it was one or two o'clock. Holmes's advertisement was a rather long one, and it must have reached the newspaper offices at three or four. Therefore it could not have been in the newspapers that day. But Holmes believed it would be. After talking with Forbes at about 3:50, Holmes went to Downing Street and after leaving there he said, "I shall do nothing more today unless I have an answer to my cab advertisement." And he added, "I should be extremely obliged to you if you would come down wit me to Woking to-morrow by the same train which we took yesterday Evidently he expected the advertisement to appear in the evening papers, and also anticipated that he might have some replies tha day. My common sense does not let me follow this.

The Boscombe Valley Mystery (June 1889 case):

While Watson was at breakfast he received a wire from Holmes, askin him to go to Boscombe Valley and concluding, "Leave Paddington b the 11:15." Watson remarked that he only had half an hour.

1. Holmes must have dispatched a wire that morning. (The exact time is not sure.)

2. Watson said he had only a half hour, but I am not sure whethe that meant to train time, or only the time for packing. Suppose he had forty-five minutes, thirty minutes for packing and fiftee minutes for the hansom to the station. (Fifteen minutes is not sure, but the station was situated in the same district.) Then the wire must have arrived at 10:30 A.M. Watson, who had a fairl long list of patients at that time, was seated at breakfast with his wife at 10:30? Does that make sense?

3. Holmes must have been familiar with the locality around Paddington. He gave the busy practitioner only 45 minutes' notice an asked him to spare two days! If the wire had been delivered thirty minutes later, Watson could not have accompanied him.

In the latter part of the story, Holmes took out a folded paper and said, "This is a map of the Colony of Victoria. I wire

-16-

to Bristol for it last night." Holmes wired at night, and he re-received the map on the very next day! (The map must have been sent by post.) How could it be possible, however early he had wired the previous night?

Wisteria Lodge (March 1895 case):

A telegram was delivered while Holmes and Watson were at lunch. It was from Scott Eccles, Post Office, Charing Cross. Holmes wired back at once. After lunch Scott Eccles arrived, and Holmes said, "It is a quarter past two. Your telegram was dispatched about one." Well, what does this mean?
1. The telegram was sent at one from Charing Cross Post Office.
2. It was delivered at lunch time (about 1:30?). As Charing Cross is not very far from Baker Street, it seems that the gentleman could have arrived there himself earlier than the wire. I suppose he was waiting for Holmes's reply in order to learn his convenience. (What would have happened if Holmes had gone out?) Anyway, it can be said that the telegram was delivered about 1:30 at the earliest. Had it been delivered **only a little later, the subsequent** story would have become entirely different.
3. Holmes wired in return at 2:00; the wire was received at Charing Cross in the shortest possible time.
4. Scott Eccles appeared before 2:15.

How on earth could all these things be carried on at the highest speed? Might it not have been much quicker—as well as safer—to have used messenger boys or coachmen? In this case Holmes seems to have abused telegrams.

The Bruce-Partington Plans (November 1895 case):

One morning a telegram from Mycroft was received, saying that he was coming at once to see Holmes about Cadogan West. Watson found the name in the newspaper. It was that of a Woolwich Arsenal clerk who had been found dead in the Underground. Mycroft came in about five or ten minutes after the receipt of the wire. Mycroft lived nearby, and the Diogenes Club was within two miles of Baker Street. Why didn't he rush to see Holmes instead of sending a wire? He might have meant to make Holmes stay in. But suppose Holmes had been out when the wire arrived. It would have been of no use. Mycroft did not intend to wait for a reply, so he should have gone directly to Sherlock without sending a wire. Further-more, the wire was not very useful as advance notice; the proba-bility was great enough that Mycroft himself might arrive before the wire. Why did this man of wisdom, Mycroft, do such a foolish thing?

The Missing Three-Quarter (February 1897 case):

On a morning in May, the day before the rugby match between Cam-bridge and Oxford, a wire from a man named Overton was delivered. The Strand postmark showed that it had been dispatched at 10:36. Soon afterward, Overton arrived, told his story, and asked Holmes for his help. By the way, what did Overton do before he visited Holmes?
1. He wired to Cambridge to learn if anything had been heard of Godfrey Staunton. Then he had an answer that no one had seen him.
2. No reply to the wire he sent to Lord Mount-James, Godfrey's uncle. (We do not know where he lived.)
3. He visited Inspector Stanley Hopkins of Scotland Yard, who ad-vised him to go to see Holmes. (All this happened before 10:30.)
4. He dispatched a wire at the Strand Post Office at 10:36.

We cannot know when Overton got up that morning. Anyway, he had worked very hard and had done a good many things before 10:36. I doubt that he could have received a reply to the wire sent to Cambridge that same morning.

While Holmes and Watson were examining Staunton's room in

Bentley's private hotel, there entered a rustic old man who was found to be Lord Mount-James. He did not look like one who lived in London. He had started for Bentley's after he received a wire. All this took place before noon. Here I shake my head again. I cannot help thinking that the wires were exchanged too quickly.

The Retired Colourman (July 1898 case):

After Amberley's wife supposedly ran away with a doctor (taking a fairly large amount of money with them), Holmes sent Watson to investigate. Holmes went out early the next morning, leaving a note for Watson that he wanted him to be on hand at 3 o'clock. Holmes got back at three, and soon afterward Amberley came in with that telegram dispatched at 2:10 from Little Purlington, 75 miles from London. I have two questions to ask here:

1. How could Amberley get to Baker Street some minutes past 3 after having received a wire at his house in Lewisham which was dispatched at 2:10 from Little Purlington? Dispatching and delivery and the time needed for the train to Baker Street; all this happened in only fifty minutes. I am sure that it would take more time than that.

2. The wire from Little Purlington was dispatched by Holmes's agent in order to decoy Amberley. He might have had enough time to arrange this, as he went out early in the morning. However, I think the telegram was delivered too fast.

The Six Napoleons (July 1900 case):

While Watson was dressing one morning, Holmes entered with a telegram: "Come instantly, 131 Pitt Street, Kensington. Lestrade." Horace Harker's bust of Napoleon had been stolen at 3:00 A.M. The policeman on the case must have notified Lestrade. We are not sure when Lestrade was informed, but it must have taken an hour or so, judging from the distance between Scotland Yard and Pitt Street. Then, before dawn, Lestrade wired Holmes. Why did he do this? Holmes and Watson drank coffee after they received the wire, and in half an hour they reached Pitt Street by hansom. Why did Lestrade send a wire such a short distance? Could the wire have been delivered in thirty minutes in those days? Why didn't Lestrade have one of his men rush to Holmes?

The Three Gables (May 1903 case):

The telegram delivered to Holmes one morning causes my question. It said that Mrs. Maberley's house had been burgled in the night. "In the night" must mean that the telegram was dispatched the next morning. The place of dispatch was "a short railway journey and a shorter drive" from London. When was the wire dispatched so as to be delivered to Holmes early in the morning?

It is not necessary to check all the wires used in all the stories, only to say that there are many other cases in which wires were used properly. But in most cases I notice that the wires were delivered too fast. Then, how are letters treated?

The Cardboard Box (August 1885 case):

On August 1st Holmes received a letter from Lestrade by the morning post. Lestrade was at Croydon and asked Holmes to come there and help him. Three things are clear:

1. The letter was delivered by the morning post, not a messenger.
2. We are not sure when Lestrade posted it and when Holmes received it. However, he did receive it in the morning, while he was reading the morning papers.
3. Croydon is about one hour and twenty-five minutes by train from Baker Street by way of Charing Cross. I cannot understand why Lestrade wrote and posted the letter that short distance in such an emergency.

The Hound of the Baskervilles (appeared above):

At about ten in the morning, Sir Henry Baskerville, who was staying at the Northumberland Hotel, called on Holmes with a strange letter. The postmark was Charing Cross and the date of posting was the previous evening. I am not convinced that someone would have posted a letter to such a near place, the Northumberland Hotel, from Charing Cross. However, a letter mailed on the previous night might surely be delivered the next morning. Holmes said some queer things which I shake my head at. "If he were in a hurry, it opens up the interesting question why he should be in a hurry, since any letter posted up to early morning would reach Sir Henry before he would leave his hotel." It was about ten o'clock that Sir Henry reached Baker Street. Thus he might have left the hotel at nine-thirty. Who could be sure that the letter posted early in the morning could be delivered by 9:30? It would only delay the arrival of information if one used the mail for such a short distance.

The Noble Bachelor (October 1887 case):

When Holmes came home from an afternoon stroll at three, he found a letter on the table awaiting him. The sender said he would be there at four—in an hour. Here again, the question arises. At 3:30 Holmes read the letter (the time it was mailed is not sure), and he had only thirty minutes until four. What would have happened if he had stretched his legs for forty minutes more? It was rather by chance that the letter would be read by Holmes in time.

The Resident Patient (October 1887 case):

Dr. Percy Trevelyan visited Holmes to ask his help about a strange letter, saying, "Two days ago I received the letter which I now read to you. Neither address nor date is attached to it." The letter said, "He [a Russian nobleman] proposes to call at about a quarter-past six to-morrow evening, if Dr. Trevelyan will make it convenient to be at home." It is very strange that the letter which proposed the time of appointment had no date at all. One cannot know when "to-morrow" is at all.

A Scandal in Bohemia (March 1888 case):

On the twentieth of March, Watson called on Holmes. He was shown a sheet of pink-tinted notepaper, and Holmes said, "It came by the last post." Then it may have been delivered at least before 8:15. For the letter said, "There will call upon you tonight, at a quarter to eight o'clock, a gentleman who desires to consult you upon a matter of the very deepest moment.... Be in your chamber at that hour." So I may imagine that in those days letters were delivered twice a day, early in the morning and at seven or eight at night. While they were discussing the letter they heard a carriage stop, and the client entered the room. The letter had been delivered by the last post. Whenever the last post was delivered, I don't think there was much time between the arrival of the letter and the arrival of the client. The case the client brought up was, according to him, such an important one as to have an influence upon European history. I cannot understand why this client used this uncertain method to send a letter of importance. What would have happened if Holmes had been out?

The Copper Beeches (April 1890 case):

One morning Holmes tossed a crumpled letter to Watson, saying, "This note I had this morning . . . ." It was dated from Montague Place, the previous evening, and the sender said, "I shall call at half-past ten to-morrow if I do not inconvenience you." Although I do not know when it was posted, the client must have expected the letter to be delivered on the same night, since she said "to-morrow." But the letter was delivered the next morning. I think that there must have been some rule that a letter posted at a certain time would be delivered the same day. And everybody

-19-

knew this, I guess. But in the cases of the letters used in the
tales, you must notice that there were many instances in which
the writer ignored the rule.

Here I shall stop checking the letters and go into the ques-
of packages. There is only one case (The Cardboard Box) which
deals with mailing a package. [Editor's note: There is at least
one other. Holmes received a box by post from Culverton Smith,
in The Dying Detective.]

The Cardboard Box (appeared above):

According to the paper, "At two o'clock yesterday afternoon a
small packet . . . was handed in [to Miss Susan Cushing] by the
postman. . . . The box had been sent by parcel post from Belfast
upon the morning before." Miss Susan Smith lived in Croydon,
which has been previously mentioned. Belfast is in northern
Ireland. I must say that the package arrived rather quickly. In
Japan it would not arrive in such a short time, even today.

Now I want to discuss the telephone. The telephone is first
mentioned in The Man with the Twisted Lip.

The Man with the Twisted Lip (January 1889 case):

Holmes saw Inspector Bradshaw at Bow Street in a small, office-
like room, with a telephone projecting from the wall. We are
not shown the telephone in use, but we do learn that there was
one.

The Greek Interpreter (Summer 1890 case):

Mycroft, who asked Holmes to help him, inserted an advertisement
in the newspapers asking for information about Paul Kratides,
and stating that any reply should be made to X2473. Was this a
telephone number, or was it the number of a post-office box? We
cannot determine the answer. [The reply was written—Ed.]

The Retired Colourman (appeared above):

In this story the telephone first appeared in the rooms in Baker
Street. Holmes seemed to avail himself of it, judging from his
words: "Thanks to the telephone and the help of the Yard, I can
usually get my essentials without leaving this room. Also, he
said to Watson, who was to accompany the retired colourman to
Little Purlington, "Should he break away or return, get to the
nearest telephone exchange and send the single word, 'Bolted.'"
This means that long-distance calls were fairly common in those
days. Watson first made for the telegraph office, but it was
closed, and he used the telephone at the Little Railway Arms to
report the strange result of his mission to Holmes, who seemed
surprised and said, "Most singular!" This was the first time
that any telephone conversation was introduced into a story. The
voice over the telephone was "a distant voice." I guess this indicates that in those days one could not hear clearly when making
a long-distance call.

Watson intended to use a telegram at first, but he used the
telephone instead because the telegraph office was closed. This
sounds strange to us. However, in those days it must have been
quite natural. Anyway, in July 1898, when these events took
place, a telephone had been set up in 221B Baker Street.

The Three Garridebs (June 1902 case):

In this story the telephone became one of the necessities of
everyday life. Watson used the telephone directory to find a
Garrideb, and so did John Garrideb. Watson called up Nathan
Garrideb, whom the two visited at Little Ryder, where Holmes
later said, "Please give the Yard a call, Watson." Thus, the
telephone must have spread fairly widely throughout London.

The Illustrious Client (February 1902 case):

Sir James Damery asked Holmes to confirm their appointment "over the telephone to the Carlton Club," and after their discussion he gave Holmes his "private telephone call, 'XX.31.'"

The Blanched Soldier (January 1903 case):

Colonel Emsworth, who was irritated by the stubborn inquiries of Mr. James M. Dodd, ordered his butler, "Ring up the police!" The colonel's house was in a country town, Tuxbury Old Park. From this we may infer that in 1903 telephones were used not only in cities but also in country areas.

*   *   *   *

The Retired Colourman took place in July 1898. Therefore it is no wonder that Watson made a long-distance call to Baker Street from Little Purlington. In that story the telephone appeared in the Baker Street rooms for the first time. However, nobody knows when it was installed. Frank A. Waters said that there must have been a telephone there at the time of The Sussex Vampire, November 1897. The ground for this opinion is that Holmes said to Watson, "We must not let him think that this agency is a home for the weak-minded." According to Waters, "agency" must mean that an agency was listed in the telephone directory, but I don't think this is convincing enough.

The Three Garridebs and The Illustrious Client took place in 1902, and The Blanched Soldier in 1903. It is quite natural that telephones were used in those stories, as the London Telephone Exchange had already been established then. In fact, we think it strange that Holmes did not use it much more frequently.

On this point Vincent Starrett says, "Of all the analysts of that curious time one must prefer the humble John H. Watson, with his chronicle of crime and detection and his swift, kaleidoscopic record of bowler hats and 'kerridges,' of bicycles and Turkish baths, of green November fogs and baking August sunshines. Few telephones had been installed to complicate the business of life; when Holmes made haste he sent a telegram."

Waters says of the telephone: "It is to be regretted that there is so little on this modern appliance in the tales, but maybe it is better so, for we dearly treasure the gaslight era. Also, he continued to use his favourite means of communication, for in 1903 he informs Watson, 'Come at once if convenient—if inconvenient come all the same.'"

THE DARK DYNASTY: A DJINN GENEALOGY

by Philip A. Shreffler

"The world is big enough for us. No ghosts need apply."
—Sherlock Holmes, in The Sussex Vampire

"I have hitherto confined my investigations to this world. In a modest way I have combated evil, but to take on the Father of Evil himself would, perhaps, be too ambitious a task."—Sherlock Holmes, in The Hound of the Baskervilles

"I fear that if the matter is beyond humanity it is certainly beyond me."—Sherlock Holmes, in The Devil's Foot

Sherlock Holmes has been the subject of many scholarly investigations in which attempts are made to link him with the supernatural. But all the suggestions that Holmes was some Paganini of detection in league with the devil must be denied because of the Master's attitude toward demons and the like. And why, with all his supposed supernatural logical ability, would Holmes constantly allow himself to be outdone by Professor James Moriarty? Was the mathematician so much more logical and brilliant that Holmes could only bring about his destruction by brute force? The weird echoing laughter at the Reichenbach Falls would seem to bear this out. Was Moriarty quite Holmes's "intellectual equal,"[1] or was there something more about him which even Holmes was reluctant to admit—something horrible, dark, and malignant? Was Aleister Crowley really the most evil man in the world, or was it someone else?

In late January of 1847 a conjurer who called himself Bernardo Eagle appeared on the stage in York, England. Accompanying him was his eleven-year-old daughter, Georgiana. Their act was basically a telepathic one in which the daughter went into the audience and had a spectator whisper something in her ear. From the stage, Eagle would astonish the company by speaking the secret aloud. Complementing the act was, as the publicity poster explained, a complete exposé of animal magnetism, mesmerism, and a host of other occult parlour tricks. And the publicity poster (see facing page) was of paramount importance. It went on to proudly proclaim that Mr. Eagle's act put to shame the run-of-the-mill mesmerists and conjurers, for the authenticity and validity of the miracles he performed seemed unassailable. But the pièce-de-resistance of Eagle's act was that the magician himself announced that the whole thing was a hoax, a trick so clever as to be ever free of explanation by an audience, however learned. By this simple Purloined Letter tactic

of laying himself openly vulnerable to public scrutiny
did Bernardo Eagle hide his most closely guarded secret,
that his magic was indeed no hoax and that he himself
was the blackest of Black Magicians. But, unknown to
Eagle, this was not his most terrible secret, for at the
end of October in 1846 he had become the father of the
future Professor James Moriarty. That his true surname
was Moriarty and that he was to loose upon the world the
criminal genius his son was to become, the world little
suspected.

On MONDAY & TUESDAY Evenings, Jan. 25th & 26th, 1847.

FIRST APPEARANCE OF THE
NAPOLEON OF
WIZARDS,

AND THE

MYSTERIOUS LADY!

Who will give her complete Expose of Mesmerism, Clairvoyance, Animal
Magnetism, &c., for particulars of which read the following Paragraphs.

THE ROYAL WIZARD,
Mr. BARNARDO EAGLE,

Who has been Patronised by THREE CROWNED HEADS,

GEORGE IV., WILLIAM IV., AND QUEEN VICTORIA

Begs to inform the Public that his Apartments are most costly and complete, and the whole of his Arrangements on a scale
unparalleled Splendour and Magnificence.

Opinions of the Press.

From the *York Courant*, Dec. 11th, 1846.

THEATRE ROYAL.—The Theatre Royal, York, has been open during the assize week with
rather a novel exhibition, conjuring and clairvoyance, by a Mr Barnardo Eagle, accompanied
by his daughter, a little girl of eleven years of age, who is styled by her father "The Mysterious Lady," and, judging from her exhibitions, the title is not unworthily or inaptly applied.
The young lady appears on the stage, and any person in the theatre is allowed to blindfold
her, and then commences a series of the most inexplicable mysteries which we ever witness

Eagle acknowledges his and his daughter's exhibition to be a deception, the mesmeric people put forth their conjuring as true, honest facts. Miss Georgiana Eagle is blindfold
secundum artem, and her father places about among the audience gathering all sorts of
things, which the lady names without hesitation, giving the inscriptions of dates on coins
and doing other similar miracles, which to a professor of clairvoyance would be invaluable
The crowning feat, however, is the telling the thoughts of the company; and, by way of
illustration, we will just say that a gentleman in the theatre, whom we know (with other
who took the trouble to think also, to be incapable of any confederacy

The scene now shifts to the United States and to the
year 1962 when William S. Baring-Gould's famous <u>Sherlock
Holmes of Baker Street</u> was published. In this volume,
Baring-Gould made scant, but now significant remarks
about the early life of James Moriarty. The boy, we are
told, came from a west of England family influential
enough to get him a position, later on, in the mathemat-

ics department of one of England's smaller universities.[2] The question naturally arises as to what kind of influence that might have been. We have but to refer to the poster. "Mr. Bernardo Eagle, who has been patronised by Three Crowned Heads," it shouted. And the murky waters clear. A Royal Wizard could not hope to get his son into Oxford or Cambridge, but the favour of a chair at a "smaller university" would have been just appropriate.

Baring-Gould also gives us a suggested birthdate for Professor Moriarty—Hallowe'en, 1846! And the facts substantiate it. According to the press reviews of Eagle's act to be found on the poster, we know that the magician was on the road early in December of 1846. Had the boy been born on 31 October, as Baring-Gould suggests, this would allow Eagle enough time to see his son healthy and alive before he was again forced to go out and win the metaphoric bread in the most logical way for a Black Magician. But the birthday of James itself is ominously suggestive. What Black Warlock wouldn't want his son to enter the world on the eve of the greatest of the four annual witch-sabbaths? Eagle had clearly planned James's conception for early in February of 1846, and most probably magically induced the birth at the proper moment.

As a Black Warlock, the reason for the senior Moriarty's use of a pseudonym is more than obvious, but the question remains: why Bernardo Eagle? It is altogether possible that Bernardo was his given name (I hesitate to say his Christian name). It might, however, be an allusion to the soldier in Scene One of Hamlet who encounters the ghost of King Claudius. But as to the surname, there can be no mistake. The word "eagle" well suited his physical characteristics. Of course, his appearance is not pictured on the poster, but the hereditary earmarks were passed along to the professor, who was described by Holmes as possessing "rounded shoulders," "shrunken eyes," and a face which "protrudes forward" and is "forever oscilating from side to side in a curiously reptilian manner."[3] Reptilian or avian? And of course there was certainly something of the eagle in Moriarty's predatory nature.

As authorities on witchcraft will recognise, there are two basic kinds of magicians. One practices white magic and works for the benefit of his fellow man. The other practices black magic and has his own well-being and gain foremost in his mind. That Bernardo Eagle went public with his magic is a good indication of where his sentiments lay. That he covered his true craft with lies is to be expected. That he impressed his daughter Georgiana into his service and denied her a traditional education is characteristic. That he brought a son into the world on Hallowe'en is of paramount importance, for the boy was reared from the moment of his birth in an atmosphere of darkness and deceit which was to forge him into the most dangerous criminal the world has ever seen.

Sherlock Holmes must have known of the late, unlamented professor's past. Such things did not escape his notice. But, as a man of science, Holmes found it difficult indeed to hint even to himself that magic was, and is, a real dynamic force in the universe, or that Moriarty was a master of it. It is undoubtedly because he failed to make this all-important admission that he found logic useless against his foe and could only destroy him by hurling him into the seething foam of the Reichenbach. At any rate, one can readily imagine one of the original posters announcing the presence of Mr. Bernardo Eagle nestled in among the pictures of famous criminals with which the Master papered his bedroom walls.[4] And it was undoubtedly with a very clear memory and a very firm knowledge of what he was saying that Holmes pronounced Moriarty "The Napoleon of Crime."[5]

The matter of the dark Moriarty dynasty properly ends here. But there is perhaps a sinister postscript. It involves the daughter of Bernardo Eagle, Georgiana, the young witch. Surely, it is no coincidence, as D. A. Redmond has pointed out, that "eagle" is translated into German as "Adler."[6] And surely it would take an enchantress to make Holmes, who had no use for women, pronounce Irene Adler "the daintiest thing under a bonnet on this planet."[7] And surely, though born in 1855, Georgiana Eagle, through magic, could alter her appearance for the better, trumping up 1858 and New Jersey as her birthdate and -place.[8] Although the truth about thes matters will probably never be verified, is it possible that the Moriarty dynasty of crime and evil extended farther than is now generally believed? And, God, how far?

---

1. The Final Problem.
2. W. S. Baring-Gould, Sherlock Holmes of Baker Street, New York: Clarkson N. Potter, 1962, page 22.
3. The Final Problem.
4. The Dying Detective.
5. The Final Problem.
6. D. A. Redmond, "Another Gasp in re Irene," BSJ (NS) 19:41, (March) 1969.
7. A Scandal in Bohemia.
8. Baring-Gould, op. cit., p. 294.

THE PATH OF THE MASTER

by John Ball

In the cool of a certain early spring California evening I sat down with my son to discuss with him his coming manhood and some of the responsibilities which his soon-to-be-achieved maturity would entail. "You have many things ahead of you," I told him, "as well as the obvious ones of finding your place in the world, chosing the girl who is going to become your wife, and earning your Irregular Shilling."

"I have been thinking a great deal about all of those things," he said. At seventeen he had all of the vast outlook of the very young and all of the burning ambition to be up and about the business of conquering the world. "Dad, when can we go? I want some time in college first before I make up my mind finally what I want to do, and I'm a long way from picking out any one girl, you know, but as for the rest——"

I regarded him steadily for two or three seconds. "I received a letter in the mail this morning. A very important letter. It came from one of the far parts of the world."

My boy looked at me narrowly. "Would you say that it was an official letter?" he asked.

I nodded. "Very much so."

He reached over and grabbed my forearms with the sudden strength of youth. "Dad, when can we leave?" he demanded.

    *   *   *   *   *

The light rain that was drizzling down was perhaps to be expected; there had been one just like it the last time and another the time before that. "This," I explained carefully, "is Baker Street. As you know, John, the exact location is a disputed point, but if we walk together from one end to the other, we will then know that we have passed the residence."

"And the empty house across the street?"

"Of course."

At that point my boy asked a question. "Dad, why is it that there is no statue of the Master and Dr. Watson here where they lived, on the very street where they first achieved immortality?"

"That is one of those incredible oversights that sometimes appear in the affairs of men," I answered him. "It should have been done many years ago. A suitable subscription should be established very promptly; I would like to think that we could be among the first to respond."

"I hope you will forgive my saying this," John volunteered as we walked slowly up the historic street. "There are some who, in their misguided lack of understanding, might claim that——. I don't want to say it, not here on Baker Street."

"If anyone would dare to suggest that, then perhaps the best thing to do would be to recognise their limitations and call attention to the fact that in one of the principal downtown squares of Madrid there is a splendid equestrian statue of Don Quixote and Sancho."

"Admittedly fictitious personages," John said.

"Indeed so. Now when we have completed this pilgrimage, if you would be so kind as to summon a cab, we will be off to St. Barts."

At the celebrated old hospital there was some extensive construction underway; everyone was plainly harassed by it, and those who guarded the main gate had no idea where the plaque was located. We were even told that it had been removed. That possibility was too unthinkable to contemplate. Without actually receiving permission to do so, we went inside. Numerous questions later we were directed toward a sort of tower staircase built at the corner of one of the old gray buildings. Inside, we were told, there was a library where we might be able to obtain some further information.

The library on the second floor was closed and locked. So, apparently, was everything else. I went up another flight on my own to see if I could find someone, anyone at all, who might be able to offer a further word of guidance. The place appeared to be deserted. At the top I rapped on a final door which stood very slightly ajar, the only evidence in the entire building that some responsible person might be about. There was no answer to my knock or to a second. Realising that I was overstepping the strict bounds of restrained conduct, I ventured to push the door open a fraction more: there could be a corpse waiting to be discovered in some grotesque position on the floor.

There was no corpse, only a very small tower room, simply furnished, and on the wall, the plaque. I ventured inside and then stood, my head bowed, letting the aura of the greatness that had been there permeate my whole being. And, like a living phantom from another plane, I seemed to hear again the immortal words that had been spoken in that very place.

*　　　*　　　*　　　*　　　*

We had a delightful luncheon together at the Englischer Hof in Meiringen, eating at the one table which commanded a full view of the small dining room and the

street outside. Beside it, on the wall, the place of
this modest establishment on the pages of history was
identified by another of the plaques which faithful
scholars had erected for the further education of those
who might pass this way without knowing where they were.
After what could not be less than a memorable meal we
returned to our waiting car and drove the short distance
to the foot of the tram which rises from the floor of
the valley up to the popular viewpoint of the Reichenbach.

The very important plaque which marks this hallowed
place had been moved since my last visit. It had been
mounted on the wall of the summit house of the tram;
now it was displayed on the face of a monument erected
for the purpose at the lower level where all those who came
by could not fail to see it and read the history which
it set forth.

We ascended to the falls and then took off on the
foot trail which leads to the topmost point. Twenty
minutes of fair exercise brought us to a high and vaulting ledge, the precise spot where the immortal conflict
had taken place. I knew it well, as I had spent some
time there determining the precise Judo (Jiujitsu—i.e.,
Baritsu) technique which the Master had utilised to
fling his deadly opponent over the brink without himself
being forced to take the awful plunge into the blackness.
With my son beside me, I stood once more where the feet
of the Master had left their impression, gazed up at the
point where Colonel Moran had attempted murder and then
down at the raging cataract at whose dizzying depths far
below lay the grave of Moriarty. John was overcome by
emotion as he looked about him, drinking it all in and
imprinting it on his memory. When the miasma of this
solemn place had made itself completely felt, we took a
few appropriate pictures and then turned at last to de-
scend back down to the world of ordinary men. "Now, my
son," I said, we have been where many have been before
us, and generations will follow. Where we have to go
next, perhaps we will be the first."

John answered as he watched his footing on the narrow,
damp trail. "In all of the Writings upon the Writings
that I have read, I have seen nothing. I honestly believe, dad, that none have ever gone before us."

"We are not going for that reason," I told him. "We
are going because we must."

    *   *   *   *   *

During most of the preceding day we had been travelling in a very small car, one hardly equipped to deal

with the kind of roads we had asked it to cover. All of
the afternoon had been spent in a very long climb, beginning in the hot, baked plains and then crawling slowly in lower gear up tortuous roads which fought their
way up through the foothills of seemingly endless mountains. Gradually the heat had moderated as the air had
grown thinner and the tiny car had had to be put into
still lower gear. At last we had struggled up a final
grade which touched the base of the clouds and had found
ourselves in a largely native village which hung crazily
on the slope of a mountain side and needed only to turn
over in its sleep to plunge thousands of feet into the
burning valley below. At what was called a tourist cottage for any who might come by that way we had spent a
fitful night's sleep. Then we had risen early and had
prepared ourselves for the overwhelming event that was
to take place before we would again seek our beds. After
a breakfast prepared for us by a non-English-speaking
cook, we once more boarded the little car that would
take us as far as it could. After that a jeep would take
over. Higher and higher we went until the cumulus lay
below, and we were almost literally in another world.
The air was cool now and comfortable, but its thinness
was revealed by the need to breathe more deeply and to
keep physical exertion at a controlled level. Then we
reached security and stopped for some time. We answered
multiple questions, produced our identification, and
offered for inspection the special documents which had
been prepared weeks before. This was not the last of it;
we would be searched later on.

Again we took up our climb; even the jeep struggled
over the rocks with which the steep, narrow road abounded,
and it too was running in a low gear. When we arrived at
the village which was our destination, we entered into
another world. A strange and unusual language was spoken,
the people were of an entirely different culture, and
they looked at us with wonder and bewilderment. My wife,
who had bravely come the whole way with us, was the object of much scrutiny, particularly when we presented
ourselves once more for security investigation. Another
half hour saw us through these formalities; then we were
permitted to walk, carefully escorted, up a climbing
pathway to what appeared to be a large cottage suspended
on the very edge of a mountain precipice. The valley so
far below was hidden now; we were shut off so that the
mountain island on which we stood was isolated in both
space and time from the rest of earthly creation. It was
appropriate to our errand, one which was sure to be one
of the climactic events of our lives.

In an anteroom we were invited to wait briefly. During the short time available we were provided with white ceremonial scarfs and instructed in their proper use. Under the careful direction of Ven. Tenzin Geyche, impressive in the robes of his order, we were schooled in the proper protocol and rehearsed. As the minutes passed the tension began to grow, and the event before us became almost frightening.

Then we were taken to an informal reception room which was pleasantly, but very simply, furnished. Here we waited, expectancy infusing us like some potent narcotic, until, in brief procession, a group of Buddhist monks entered the room. One of them, dressed just as were the others, could not be mistaken—his radiant, gentle face reflecting his great humanity and deep spirituality. The impact of realisation came, for we were standing in the presence of His Holiness Hgawang Lobsang Yishey Tenzing Gyatso, the earthly Enlightened One, the fourteenth incarnation of Chenresik, the God of Compassion, the living changchup-sempa (Bodhisattva), the Dalai Lama of Tibet.

That we were actually being received in audience by the most inaccessible head of state in the world was incredible, but there he stood before us as with shaking hands we unrolled the ceremonial scarfs with our right hands and laid them across his extended palms. The goodness of the man was like a shining light, and in his features there burned an understanding that can never be extinguished. We were not followers of the path of which he was the world leader, but he had consented to receive us as another had been received many years before. At that time His Holiness, in his previous incarnation, had been but ten years of age, but he had known even then the true identity of the strange traveller who had managed the almost impossible feat of entering his forbidden kingdom bulwarked behind the most formidable mountains in the world. More than fifteen hundred miles of vaulting Himalayas had blocked his path, but that man none the less set foot in the sacred city of Lhasa and climbed the very long steps up to the doorway where he had been received into the Potala itself.

Then, when His Holiness began to address us, history flew out of our minds, and we were once more in a remote outpost in the extreme north of India, listening to the words of the great personage who had consented to receive us. We could only marvel at our unbelievable good fortune. Our audience was not supposed to exceed ten minutes, but His Holiness was pleased to invite us to remain longer. Tea was produced and flawlessly served, though we never saw the person who provided it. We spoke

of Tibet and the rape of the most peaceful of all nations
by the Chinese Communists. We talked of the other leaders
of the world and of the American landings on the moon.
More than an hour passed, and we were so enraptured that
we did not venture to speak of the subject most precious
to us, for a few words from His Holiness could enlighten
a world which was more than prepared for what he could
reveal.

His Holiness spoke to one of his attendants in Tibetan. The man reacted with great surprise, but when His
Holiness raised his hand in a simple gesture, he bowed
his obedience and disappeared. He returned shortly with
an art treasure of incalculable value, a thanka scroll
painting, exquisitely rendered on silk and overlaid with
the patina of centuries. It was from the treasure house
of the Potala, brought out on someone's back when His
Holiness and the few who accompanied him had made their
last-minute escape, just ahead of the Communists who had
been sent to take his earthly life. When the priceless
painting had been displayed to us it was again rolled up.
Then His Holiness took it into his own hands and placed
it in ours. The gift was so overwhelming that we could
say nothing but stammer our thanks. We left his presence
disbelieving the incredible generosity he had shown to
us. We were in a daze, but the precious thanka told us
by its reality that it was all true.

That evening in Corium House we sat and talked with a
small group of lamas and with Jayang Norbu, the young
English-speaking Tibetan who was educated in India and
whose knowledge of many things belies his years.

"You must know," he said, "that to be received by His
Holiness in audience when you are from the outside world
and not a member of the Buddhist faith is an extremely rare
event."

"We know," I replied. "I believe that in his previous
incarnation he reigned for more than fifty years and in
that time received only some three visitors from the
western world."

"True," Jayang said, and he translated my remark for
the benefit of the others.

I broke a Tibetan cookie made of tsampa and took
another sip of the buttered tea which had been served to us.

A quiet lama said something in his own tongue. I
turned politely and asked Jayang what it had been. "He
said, 'and the Norwegian,'" he translated.

Like the sudden instant impact of an electric shock
those simple words hit home. I stared at the speaker, a
man of very advanced age and obvious great wisdom, placid
in his saffron robes.

"Once more, please," I requested.

"There was one other traveller," Jayang supplied. "Such a visitor was an extremely rare event, one that is preserved in our history."

My son could not contain himself. "His name," he demanded, does he remember his name?"

The venerable lama listened to the translation, and then his ageless features reflected a hint of the light that we had seen in the face of the Living Buddha before whom we had bowed that morning. He spoke again in Tibetan.

There is little more to be said. It was our great honour to welcome the brilliant young teacher, Jayang Norbu, into the ranks of the Irregulars. He now receives the Journal regularly. If you would care to write him his address is:

> Mr. Jayang Norbu
> Corium House, Upper Dharmsala,
> Dharmsala Cantt., Kangra District,
> Himachal Pradesh, India.

Moriarty is dead. May the evil that now sweeps the land of Tibet also pass away so that in years to come men may visit the sacred city of Lhasa and in what remains of the great libraries, if anything does, find written in the archives the further story of the lone traveller who penetrated even into the forbidden borders of the Land of Snows and there found wisdom that illuminated much of his later life. And if he is living now at an age when most mortal men are long since departed from our midst, then look for the secret here in this land which was the treasure house of the mysteries of the ages.

WILL THE REAL WATSON PLEASE STAND

or

The Case for Surgeon-Major Preston

by Fred Mende

"You have been in Afghanistan, I perceive."

Some months ago, while reading a history of the Royal Berkshire Regiment, I came across the following lines in a chapter dealing with the Battle of Maiwand:

"Amongst the officers who got back was Surgeon-Major Preston who had been wounded in the early stages of the fight. There are some grounds for believing that he was the original of Conan Doyle's Dr. Watson, and certainly any Sherlock Holmes enthusiast will remember Watson's early claim to have been wounded with the 66th at Maiwand."[1]

Although I have read about such theoretical Watsonian prototypes as Major Wood, Dr. James Watson (Conan Doyle's Southsea colleague), and—as suggested by Hesketh Pearson—possibly even A. C. D. himself, the name of Surgeon-Major Preston was one which I had not encountered previously in any of my Sherlockian readings. No doubt there are those Sherlockians to whom the name is not unfamiliar, but being one who still has much to absorb in this realm, to me it was a rather intriguing find. In fact, there was enough of intrigue present to persuade me to attempt some research into the career of Surgeon-Major Preston. As a result, I am able to offer the following brief summary of his military career along with my own two-cents' worth—or rather, based upon the present rate of exchange, my tuppence worth of comment and speculation.

Alexander Francis Preston

Born 23 May 1842; A.B., M.B., Dublin 1863
Entered Army as Asst. Staff Surgeon 30 September 1863
Appointed Asst. Surgeon to the 27th Foot (Royal
    Inniskilling Fusiliers) 13 February 1866
Appointed Asst. Surgeon to the Royal Artillery
    20 July 1867
Promoted to Surgeon-Major 28 April 1876
Served in the Afghan Campaign of 1878-1880
Half pay 16 October 1881; Full pay 4 May 1882
Brigade Surgeon, afterwards Brigade Surgeon,
    Lt. Col. 30 November 1886
Promoted to Surgeon-Colonel 28 March 1892
Promoted to Surgeon-Major General 30 March 1896;
    afterwards Surgeon General

Acting Director General from 3 June 1901 to
    1 December 1901
Retired 23 May 1902
Rewarded for distinguished and meritorious
    service
Honorary Physician to the King, 1901
Died 24 July 1907

From the above record it appears that the military
career of Alexander Francis Preston was a very successful one, but it does little to shed any light upon the
statement that there are some grounds for believing that
he was the original of Watson. There is, however, one
extremely important entry, or rather part of an entry,
in his military record which I have intentionally omitted. This particular part of the entry provides us with
a most interesting bit of information which lends a good
deal of credence to the theory that Preston could very
well have been the prototype of Watson. But first let us
go back to his record for just a moment.

It will be noted that Preston went on half pay from
the 16th of October 1881 until the 4th of May 1882. Why
did he go on half pay during this period? The records do
not give us the reason, but a soldier going on half pay
in the British Army usually did so during a period of
recuperation from sickness or from wounds. With this in
mind we now come to the very important entry which should
be added to the one appearing just before that of 16
October 1881. This entry in its entirety should read as
follows: "Served in the Afghan Campaign of 1878-1880 and
was twice wounded."[2] Please note: Twice wounded.

It goes without saying that any Sherlockian worthy of
the name is familiar with the apparent inconsistency of
Conan Doyle regarding Watson's battle wound. In view of
this inconsistency the above entry quite obviously brings
up a very good question. Specifically, has this fact
anything to do with the reason why Doyle first inflicted
Holmes's Boswell with a shoulder wound, and then, later
on, with another wound in the leg or heel? If Preston
was the model for Watson, would it not be understandable
for A. C. D. to think in terms of two wounds? Could this
not, then, be an explanation as to why Watson first describes his wound, in A Study in Scarlet, as being the
result of a Jezail bullet in his left shoulder and then
later, in The Sign of Four, refers to a wound in his leg
which was also caused by a Jezail bullet? Possibly, after
all, there is a logical explanation for the enigma of the
good doctor's second wound.

Unfortunately, there is nothing to be found in the
records, at least so far, that would indicate the nature

or the anatomical location of Preston's two wounds. It
may be wishful thinking, but how singularly interesting
it would be if the wounds could be found to have been
caused by Jezail bullets in the left shoulder and leg.
Perhaps future research may some day give us an answer.

Inasmuch as the details of Preston's life and career
which this writer has been able to determine are anything
but plentiful, there quite naturally remain certain questions that are unanswerable. One aspect of the record
which is not completely resolved concerns the question
of whether Preston's wounds were both received at Maiwand. Although it is quite probable that they were both
suffered in this particular battle—the record does not
state otherwise—it cannot be accepted with absolute
certainty that this was the case. It might be said in
passing, however, that had he received only a single
wound in the Maiwand battle, it would not necessarily
disqualify him as a candidate for the prototype of
Watson.

Another unanswered question that would have an important bearing on the matter is whether or not Preston
had any personal contact with Conan Doyle between the
approximate dates of February 1882 and March 1885.[3] The
likelihood that Preston and Doyle met each other some
time during this period cannot be completely discounted,
since both were medical men, and since Preston was stationed in Dover following his return to full-pay status
in the year 1882. He remained at this particular station
through 1885 and possibly even into the year 1886. The
two men could conceivably have met some time between
February 1882 and March 1886, when Doyle first began A
Study in Scarlet. Even if it could be substantiated beyond any doubt whatsoever that there was never a personal acquaintanceship between the two men, there still remains the very logical possibility that Doyle could have
learned of Preston's exploits in the Afghan Campaign
from other sources, such as newspapers or friends.[4]

It would be most gratifying to me, indeed, could it
be definitely proven that Alexander Francis Preston was
the model for Dr. John H. Watson, but although this cannot be done at this time—or perhaps at any other time—
it should be admitted by even the most skeptical of
Sherlockians that there are several important established facts that make him at least a contender for this
distinction.   They are: (1) Preston was a medical officer in the British Army,[5] (2) he served with the 66th
Berkshire Regiment at the Battle of Maiwand, and (3)—
possibly the most important of all—he was twice wounded,
with at least one of his wounds, and quite probably both,

being received in that battle.[6] Upon these facts the
case for Surgeon-Major Preston must rest, at least for
the time being. It is not too bad a start, and, after
all, even Holmes himself began many a case with less
evidence than this.

---

1. Myatt, Frederick, The Royal Berkshire Regiment, London: Leo Cooper, Ltd., 1968.
2. The biographic index of Shadbolt, The Afghan Campaign
   of 1878-1880 reads: "Served during the 2nd campaign
   in medical charge of the 66th Regiment, taking part
   in its advance to Kandahar, and subsequently with
   General Burrows' Brigade, to Halmand. Was present at
   the action of Girishk and the Battle of Maiwand in
   which he was severely wounded while attending a dis-
   abled man in the front line of fire. Was in Kandahar
   throughout the siege. Mentioned in dispatches."
3. Doyle left England in October of 1881 in the capacity
   of ship's surgeon aboard the S.S. Mayumba, a passenger and cargo ship sailing for the west coast of Africa.
   The ship returned to England some time around the
   middle of January 1882. If a meeting between the two
   men did take place, it would most likely have occurred
   following Doyle's return. However, a contact in 1881
   would not have been a complete impossibility, provided, of course, that Preston was back in England
   before October 1881.
4. The Shadbolt book (see footnote 2) states that Preston
   was "mentioned in dispatches."
5. Mr. Crighton Sellars correctly pointed out in his
   article, "Dr. Watson and the British Army" [BSJ (OS)
   2:332-341, 1947], that if Watson's military service
   was limited to the Northumberland Fusiliers and the
   Berkshires, he was never in the Indian Army. Although
   these regiments saw service in India, they were actu-
   part of the British Army, not of the Indian Army,
   which was a separate organisation.
6. The noted British Sherlockian, S. C. Roberts, in his
   book, Holmes and Watson, states that "early in the
   course of the engagement, but not before he had,
   without loss of nerve, seen his comrades hacked to
   pieces, Watson had been struck by a Jezail bullet."
   Exactly how Roberts arrived at the information that
   Watson was wounded early in the battle, I do not
   know—it does not state this to be so in A Study in
   Scarlet—but it does coincide with the paragraph
   about Preston from the Myatt book (see first page).

*   *   *   *   *

My thanks are due to Miss E. Talbot Rice and to Mr. Boris Mollo of the National Army Museum in London for their most generous help in researching the military record of Alexander Francis Preston, and to a most gracious and kind gentleman, Major General A. MacLennan (Retd) of the R.A.M.C. Historical Museum, for his very valuable research and for obtaining the photograph of Alexander Francis Preston. Also, I must express my appreciation to Mr. Frederick Myatt and to Mr. Leo Cooper of Leo Cooper, Ltd., for permission to quote from The Royal Berkshire Regiment.

ALEXANDER FRANCIS PRESTON

A TRIFLE TRYING

by Rev. Leslie Marshall

> "Really Holmes," I said severely, "you are a
> trifle trying at times."—The Valley of Fear

Of course, Watson didn't realise it at the time, but
with the foregoing abjuration he was probably voicing
the understatement of the year (1899?).

"A trifle trying," indeed! Although the good doctor's
emphasis was on the Great Detector's tryingness, yet we
all know the Napoleonic Law: "Men are led by trifles"
(Sayings of Napoleon, q.v.).

It was, is, because the Founder of the Science of Deduction was a trifle trying that he was, is, truly eminent. Had he been overly difficult with his fellow lodger,
instead of just "at times," the patter of little horses'
feet—notably in the case of the four-wheelers—would
have been toward Queen Anne's Street (where was Dr. Watson's consulting room, anyway?) rather than in the direction of 221B, when the medic's practice lagged.

No, the Benefactor of the Race well knew the purpose
and use of being a trifle trying to his Boswell. It kept
that provider of paregoric and purveyor of panegyrics on
his toes, alert to anything which would give his notes
a fillip.

However, the learned reader of the sacred saga will
recognise that "at times" was a trifle conservative, and
that he-who-had-been-in-Afghanistan could greatly have
expanded the times had he paused to do a little summation.

Take the time when the Pundit of Probabilities lounged
on his sofa to master his ennui by a season of bulleting
from the hip that imperious V. R. on to the long-suffer-
ing Mrs. Hudson's, nee Turner, wall paper. We hear her
other paying guest exclaiming in horror, "I have always
heard that pistol practice should distinctly be an out-
door pastime" (The Musgrave Ritual).

Or recall the occasion when Mr. Holmes, rather shortly, it would seem, demanded of his bodyguard (yes, that
too) "Cut out the poetry!" (The Retired Colourman). Poor
Watson was only descanting on a "high sun-baked wall,
mottled with lichens, topped with moss . . . ." Surely
such a disclaimer was enough to try any man's soul, even
his who had suffered on a bloody battlefield so far away.

Then there was that mean trick the Nemesis of Crime played
upon his doughty representative as recorded in The Hound of
the Baskervilles. The student of the Canon will recall that

dulcet "It is a lovely evening, my dear Watson," as the latter sits "breathless, hardly able to believe his ears." However, it is to be admitted that on that occasion Miss Adler's fautor did ask forgiveness if he "seemed to have played a trick" on his plump associate.

Possibly the most trying, frustrating, and throw-up-his-hands incident in the stethoscopist's experience with his Mentor is recorded in that extraordinary tale, The Adventure of the Dying Detective. Poor Watson! His skill derided, his trust repugned, his very presence abhorred, only to find it all a pretense, aided and abetted by a grease-paint job and a reducing diet. Surely, only the magnanimity of a disciplinarian, if not disciple, could describe this episode as just a "trifle trying."

The learned reader, again, perhaps offhand, can think of a dozen other incidents which could have been in Mary's husband's mind as with severity he abjures the Queen Bee specialist as being, in short, rather difficult, but just in case it is forgotten in the cobwebs of time, the liberty is taken here of finally reminding whom it may concern of a certain incident which brought forth Dr. Watson's bitter reply.

Half-strangled, after weeks of investigation on behalf of Mr. Holmes; about to utter his last gasp, when an unshaven French ouvrier struck his assailant on the forearm, then only to be berated by aforesaid ouvrier in terms of "a very pretty hash you have made of it!" —in such a case, I say, who could forgive the Medicine Man's bitter reply, if not his satirical "Perhaps you would have done no better" (Lady Frances Carfax)?

Yes, we fear that the Keeper of the Persian Slipper was a trifle trying at times—many, many times—but well we know it was all to a great end, an end reaching into the infinity of detection.

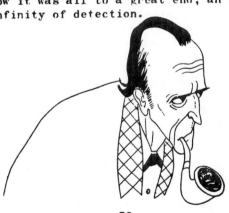

ON THE MORALITY OF ONE MR. SHERLOCK HOLMES

by Mark Levy

Leafing through the Canon, we are struck by the preponderent opportunities Holmes had to rearrange evidence, deliberately misinterpret clues, or even mastermind his own crimes. This appears to be a blatant statement, but let us conduct the dialectic as Holmes might have done. Recall, he was "the most perfect reasoning and observing machine the world has ever seen,"[1] and, almost by definition, "in his methods of thought he was the neatest and most methodical of mankind."[2] Besides, Holmes "loved above all things precision and concentration of thought."[3] So we can hardly reach an unwarranted conclusion via his methods. As a starting point, let us investigate the following heretical proposition:

Sherlock Holmes Was Immoral![4]

Now, according to Holmes, we must collect facts and see if they apply to the theory. "It is a capital mistake," said the Master, "to theorize before one has data. Insensibly one begins to twist facts to suit theories, instead of theories to suit facts."[5]

In the interest of presenting the argument methodically, we shall first pursue it along one narrow but logical channel—motivation for perpetrating criminal acts. A number of motivating forces are apparent once we accept the basic (and base) premise. Listing them in a general order of increasing morality, we can begin with Holmes's need for money. But before we condemn Holmes, we should examine this motivation's likelihood.

Money is the prime motivation criminals have for pursuing their professions; yet it seems to be least consistent with Holmes's personality (even if we confer immorality on him). Watson tells us that Holmes worked "rather for the love of his art than for the acquirement of wealth."[6] There is little evidence that Holmes was ever in a real financial bind, and yet Watson had "seldom known him claim any large reward for his inestimable services."[7] If he seldom claimed a large reward, how could his payments for Mrs. Hudson's rooms be "princely"?[8]

This inevitably leads us to the next possible motivation for Holmes to transgress the law. Considerably more aesthetically palatable, his desire for intellectual stimulation is still selfish—but not quite as vulgar as the motivation mentioned above. During the months in which little or no opportunity for first-class deduction presented itself (there were days when Holmes

was "badly in need of a case"[9]), he could have whiled
away the hours pleasantly contemplating the perfect
crime.

Watson remarked that his "companion's brain was so
abnormally active that it was dangerous to leave it without material upon which to work."[10] Dangerous! Holmes
corroborated this statement once by saying: "My mind is
like a racing engine, tearing itself to pieces because
it is not connected up with the work for which it was
built."[11] Is it possible that committing crimes, rather
than solving them, is the work to which he is making
reference? He told Watson: "I abhor the dull routine of
existence. I crave for mental exaltation."[12] Scheming a
perfect crime can be an all-engrossing hobby with which
to pass many a boring hour when one's fingers tire of
holding a violin, a pipe, a syringe, a pistol, or an old
book.

We know he revelled in "the charm of variety"[13] and
considered London "a singularly uninteresting city since
the death of the late lamented Professor Moriarty."[14]
Lamented! He once remarked to Watson: "Man, or at least
criminal man, has lost all enterprise and originality."[15]
With bitter disappointment shading his voice, he murmured: "The London criminal is certainly a dull fellow."[16]
Sadly, he noted that "audacity and romance seem to have
passed forever from the criminal world."[17]

We can picture Holmes sprawled in his chair in a con-
templative, wistful mood, envying the swashbuckling criminal life. We know that he envied Moriarty—for example,
by his remark to Watson: "My horror at his [Moriarty's]
crimes was lost in my admiration at his skill,"[18] although his description of Charles Augustus Milverton as
"the king of all the blackmailers"[19] can only be taken
as a derogatory remark—or can it?

Wouldn't Holmes have welcomed a daring change of pace
—especially if he himself were instrumental in said
change?

Another and more satisfying motivation could have been
Holmes's strategical position after he had successfully
committed a crime (preferably heinous in nature). London's underworld would soon recognise and laud him. Although he said : "There is no one who knows the higher
criminal world of London so well as I do,"[20] by committing an illegality he could secure his ties with various
criminals whose information would prove invaluable to
his subsequent investigations. In this rôle he would be
a double agent in the British tradition, giving James
Bond an English predecessor par excellence.

Any one of these suggested motivations is tenable and

can be modified to encompass Holmes's enigmatic personality.

It hinders us here to be ignorant of Holmes's extra-curricular and perhaps criminal life. We could, possibly, deduce his motivation more readily if we knew of his activities. One guideline could be his own generalisation, "the bigger the crime, the more obvious, as a rule, is the motive."[21] But that would be working backwards and therefore reproachfully, according to Holmes.

Now let us try to complete the puzzle from the viewpoint of opportunity, assuming that one of the motives listed previously is acceptable. This is a much simpler matter than it would first appear. The Master had many free moments, as evidenced by the foregoing discussion, and apparently no dearth of opportunity. Watson tells us that Holmes often travelled "under one of the numerous disguises and names with which he concealed his own formidable identity. He had at least five small refuges in different parts of London, in which he was able to change his personality."[22] Would this indicate that not only did he change his personality to conform to that of a righteous citizen of another social class, but perhaps also to that of a merciless cutthroat?

There is no doubt that if he had set his mind to it, if the motivations were strong enough, if the opportunities were sufficiently attractive, Sherlock Holmes would have had no trouble planning and executing the most diabolical, most perfect crimes in the history of the world.

This brings us to the ultimate question, and to a final channel of logical thought which will discredit all that has gone before it. Assuming the validity of our proposition, why hadn't Holmes ever actively engaged in crime? Answer: He would have been caught!

If Holmes had tried to commit a crime—a perfect crime—Lestrade, Gregson, Hopkin, et al. would soon have realised that only the Master could have efficiently pulled it off without leaving one single clue. And by not leaving a clue, he would effectively leave his fingerprints. Because of his great insight, only Sherlock Holmes could have devised and executed a perfect crime competently. After their initial wave of incredulity, the gentlemen of Scotland Yard would be forced to arrest Holmes solely on the strength of the negative evidence. So we conclude that Holmes may have been immoral after all, but being perceptive—especially in the field of crime and detection—he foresaw the eventuality of his imprisonment and decided to abstain from crime. Note: not for moral reasons, but through ratiocination.

And yet we cannot conclude that Holmes could have the slightest moral blemish. We find, instead, that there is

-42-

another point Holmes could have considered if he had wanted to commit a felony, and if he had been really immoral. That is he could easily have directed clues to incriminate an innocent party or (with his flair for sophisticated plans) he could have arranged confusing evidence. If he had been indeed immoral he would have had no compunction about performing these trivialities. Surely he knew that.

The fact that he <u>did</u> know it, and yet refrained from dabbling in a life of crime, happily disproves our original proposition. If he was not immoral, he had to be moral! Therein lies the beauty of logic. He <u>could</u> have made a superb anti-hero. Think about that. Holmes summarised our sentiments when he said: "It is fortunate for this community that I am not a criminal."23   Amen.

---

1. A Scandal in Bohemia.
2. The Musgrave Ritual.
3. The Solitary Cyclist.
4. Levy, M., "The Most Wanted Man," The Pontine Dossier, Vol. 2, No. 4, November 1969.
5. A Scandal in Bohemia.
6. The Speckled Band.
7. Black Peter.
8. The Dying Detective.
9. The Yellow Face.
10. The Missing Three-Quarter.
11. Wisteria Lodge.
12. The Sign of Four.
13. The Noble Bachelor.
14. The Norwood Builder.
15. The Copper Beeches.
16. The Bruce-Partington Plans.
17. Wisteria Lodge.
18. The Final Problem.
19. Charles Augustus Milverton.
20. The Final Problem.
21. A Case of Identity.
22. Black Peter.
23. The Bruce-Partington Plans.

The Editor is happy to announce, well in advance, a new work of scholarship which will in many ways arouse the interest of the readers of this Journal.

A Catalogue of Crime by Jacques Barzun and Wendell Hertig Taylor is a critical bibliography of detective fiction, true crime, the Sherlock Holmes literature, and related genres. It will be published by Harper and Row in late April 1971. Thanks to the intercession of Jacques Barzun (who is no stranger to these pages) and to the courtesy of the publishers, the BSJ can give a foretaste of the contents of this massive work, in all six parts of which Canonical and Conanical matters are discussed.

The authors have—and express—decided views, with which not all readers will agree. But as the motive power of scholarship is disagreement, no true-hearted Holmesian will object. Indeed, the motto of any such journal as the BSJ might well be "Long live heresy!"—though no implication is intended about the views of our colleagues that we are about to quote.

We begin our sampling from Part I—Detective Novels. Items 762 and 763 are preceded by an unnumbered biographical sketch which sets the tone of the entries following:

DOYLE, (ARTHUR) CONAN (1859-1930)

Despite the apparent length of four of his Sherlock Holmes stories (A Study in Scarlet, 1887; The Sign of the Four, 1890/91; The Hound of the Baskervilles, 1902; and The Valley of Fear, 1915), Doyle was a writer of short detective stories. Only The Hound is a whole long story: the others are novellas with an alien filling which, once read, may be left alone forever after, still leaving an interesting frame of true detection around the central melodrama. Still, in deference to outward seeming, all four tales are entered in this section. For the best text, see Edgar W. Smith, ed., Sherlock Holmes (Heritage).

762   The Hound of the Baskervilles   McCl 1902
The only perfect story among the four long ones, and one of the best in the Canon, irrespective of length. By a miracle of judgment, the supernatural is handled with great effect and no letdown. The plot and subplots are thoroughly integrated and the false clues put in and removed with a master hand. The criminal is superb, Dr. Mortimer memorable, and the secondary figures each contribute to the total effect of brilliancy and grandeur combined. One wishes one could be reading it for the first time.

763   The Sign of the Four   Lipp 1889
        or, The Problem of the Sholtos
        Also: The Sign of Four (i.e., without "the" or

The second Holmes story makes use of the Thames in an unforget-
table manner, and the detection is more active than in A Study
in Scarlet—as well as fraught with danger. For one thing,
Watson succumbs to the charms of Miss Morstan, and for another the two detectives are nearly disposed of by Tonga,
the Andaman Islander. It is also so well put together, and
the brothers Sholto are so well drawn—like their furnish-
ings—that one readily accepts the old conspiracy in India,
and even the maligning of the Andamanians.

The other two long tales are also characterized, but we
pass on to the short stories, dealt with in Part II:
2475   DOYLE, ARTHUR CONAN
        The Adventures of Sherlock Holmes   Harp 1892
The first set of twelve, almost all gems. Though popular
taste has long since fastened on spectacular ones, such as
The Speckled Band and A Scandal in Bohemia, the really
choice ones are the quieter: The Man with the Twisted Lip,
The Noble Bachelor, and The Beryl Coronet. A gratifying
overlap of taste occurs between connoisseur and plain man
about The Red-Headed League. Meanwhile Christopher Morley
points out that The Blue Carbuncle is the best Christmas
story ever written (see No. 3342). The truth is, it is impossible not to admire each and all of the twelve.

2476   The Case-Book of Sherlock Holmes   JM 1927
By universal consent these twelve stories are deemed inferi-
or to every previous collection. The reason is not in their
conception, which is often splendid, but in their execution,
which is slovenly. Doyle was tired of Sherlock Holmes, he
had picked up a great deal of American slang, and the effort
to recreate the Victorian or Edwardian scene was beyond his
strength.

Still, there are fragments of dialogue and of description
in these tales that equal or surpass anything done earlier,
and some of Holmes's most frequently quoted mots come from
these decried adventures. The three best are Thor Bridge,
The Three Garridebs, and Shoscombe Old Place, even though
the middle one is but a (second) variant of The Red-Headed
League. The worst are The Mazarin Stone and The Veiled Lodger.

Note that two out of twelve are told by Holmes and one
by a novelist-narrator who is neither Holmes nor Watson.
Apart from the cherishable bits, the only appealing thing
about the Case-Book is that its stories appeared during the
young manhood of WHT and JB, not only in The Strand but in
the Magazine supplement of the old New York World.

Comments on the Canon are followed by remarks on two sets
of apocrypha, and then on the work which by now deserves to
be called "The Play," even though it does not contain "The
Woman." First the apocrypha:

2481   Round the Fire Stories   Dday 1909; orig. 1908
If most well-read followers of the genre were asked: "In what

book by Doyle, not about S. H., can you find four tales of
detection and four more that are close to the same species?"
few would be able to name this book. Yet it does contain
such stories and nine others of crime or horror without detection. As one reads The Man with the Watches / The Lost
Special / The Jew's Breastplate / The Black Doctor, and the
rest, one marvels again at Doyle's natural gift of story-
telling and one relishes his ingrained habit of giving
clues, even when they serve narrative and are not to be used
for ratiocination.   These stories are worth reading even
around a radiator.

The Lost Special and The Man with the Watches, peripheral
to the Holmes Canon, do not mention S. H., and are not fully
satisfying, but belong to the same order of inspiration.

2482   Round the Red Lamp   App 1894
                    Being Facts and Fancies of Medical Life
A collection of short stories, several of which are as
"powerful" and as neatly turned as any in the Holmes Canon.
Not mystery or detection, though Vincent Starrett has
pointed out that one of them, Behind the Times, should be
classed with the early Holmes stories, thanks to a remark
about "Mrs. Hudson . . . my housekeeper." Excellent fiction.

And now The Play:

2487   DOYLE, A. CONAN, and GILLETTE, WILLIAM
         Sherlock Holmes   French 1922; orig. 1899
             A Drama in 4 Acts; Rev. ed. 1922
At first called "a melodrama" and given its premiere at the
Garrick Theater in New York on November 6, 1899, with Gillette in the title role. He played it again in New York in
1929 and it was still a success. Full of good scenes, but
not completely Holmesian: he is endangered by obvious things
and he succumbs to the girl Alice, on the strength of "her
ability to observe"!

We move to Part III, whose subject matter is "Studies
and Histories of the Genre." Our interest here centers on
an entry about the Agent's recollections and those of a
forgotten man, the Agent's Agent.

2939   DOYLE, A. CONAN
         Memories and Adventures   LB 1924
An endearing account of a varied and active life by a man
who belongs to the small company of writers-men-of-action.
Chapter 8 is the one that deals with his literary begin-
nings between 1885 and 1890. It records unexpected influence from Henry James; it indicates that A Study in Scarlet
was probably finished by the end of 1885, though not published till Christmas 1887; and it modestly takes credit for
the Strand's innovation of monthly stories about the same
characters (Holmes and Watson) to replace the long serial story.

Again, the decisive turn from medicine to writing occurred in London, not Portsmouth, as several interpreters

have believed. Finally, the doubts about materialism—characteristic of the 90's—which landed Doyle in the morass of spiritualism, were present early in his life and thought, not the result of anguish during the first world war, as alleged.

Chapter 21 records Doyle's brilliant detection in the Edalji case and his heroic effort to vindicate Oscar Slater. On pp. 97-100 the Barrie parody is reproduced for the first time and we learn nearby that in Spanish South America a Sherlockholmito is a clever inference suggestive of great "powers."

3003 POND, (MAJOR) JAMES BURTON (1838-1903)
    Eccentricities of Genius   C&W 1901
     Memories of famous men and women of the platform
     and stage.

The major's claim to fame is not as a soldier but as a lecture manager. The short chapter on Conan Doyle tells us that he came to the United States in 1894 and gave forty readings from October to December. In that latter month, according to a pleasant spoof, Doyle was greeted in Boston by the Cabmen's Literary Guild, one of whose members deduced Doyle's identity and itinerary from Buffalo mud in the instep of his shoe, the twisted lapels of his coat grabbed by New York reporters, and so on.

Of particular interest to all Irregulars is the contrast our scholars point out between the Agent's memory of events at one time and at another:

3343 DOYLE, A. CONAN
    "Juvenilia" in My First Book by Various Hands
                  Lipp 1894

The volume tells of the vicissitudes of the writers in getting their first work published or noticed. The accounts do not vary greatly, but the one by Doyle presents a curious feature in reference to Sherlock Holmes, the curious feature being that there is no reference to S. H. Doyle's "first book" turns out to be Micah Clarke, two years after A Study in Scarlet. The date of this report coinciding with the appearance of The Memoirs of S. H. (1894), it seems clear that Doyle was sick and tired of S.H. quite early in their career.

The other more important point is that the picture of Doyle waiting for the success of A Study in Scarlet to decide in favor of literature is inaccurate. He had been writing and selling stories to Chamber's Journal and other magazines for several years before he turned to S. H. and was earning more than £50 a year.

Part IV deals with True Crime, and Holmes is naturally referred to numerous times in the course of the learned discussions. Part V is wholly devoted to Holmes and Watson scholarship. Much of its contents will be familiar to these readers, but there are notable summaries and estimates.

Here is something a bit out of the way:

3346   GARDNER, (THE REV.) RALPH

"Baker Street and the Bible" in
The Hibbert Journal, April 1952

The Cambridge (Eng.) theologian takes up Sherlock Holmes
and the historical Jesus as manifestations of the power of
literature to induce the emotions of belief. Not that he
doubts the existence of an historical Jesus, but that he
sees historicity as unimportant in comparison with the
faith generated by the written and spoken word. Holmes and
Watson, known to be fictitious, arouse admiration and discussion and generate the sense of their actuality. The point
is not that they once lived, but that they live now, like
Christ in the believer's mind. The critic does not, however,
point out the causes of the readiness to believe.

In addition, the critics obviously consider as a form of
"study" and criticism, certain adaptations (e.g., parodies)
and dramatizations from the Canon, as hereunder:

3350   HARDWICK, MICHAEL and MOLLIE

Four Sherlock Holmes Plays   Murray 1964

These authors make the excellent point that the S. H. stories
naturally fall into acting scenes, and they are careful to
keep as much as they can of the original dialogue, also
inherently dramatic. They acquired practice in doing radio
skits for the B.B.C., then produced these one-act affairs
out of: "The Speckled Band," "Charles Augustus Milverton,"
"The Mazarin Stone," and "The Blue Carbuncle." The last is
the best.

Finally, in Part VI (Ghosts and the Supernatural) we
meet the Agent in his latter-day avocation; but the authors
of A Catalogue of Crime agree with Irregulars that a more
fitting close to this anthology is their biographical tribute to:

SMITH, EDGAR W(ADSWORTH), 1894-1960

b. Bethel, Conn.; educ. New York Univ.; enlisted in 1917
after a short secretaryship at J. P. Morgan's. Staff work in
War Dept., then for the rest of his life with General Mo-
tors, of which he became Director of International Trade.
... editor of the B.S.J. (q.v.) and scholar-publisher
extraordinary in Holmesian lore, E. W. S. had a light touch
and the right instinct for subjects in the Canon worth exploring or fantasticating about.

It should be added that Messrs. Barzun and Taylor's Catalogue (896 pp., 3476 entries) is equipped with an unusually
full apparatus of ancillary information—a comprehensive
Introduction, giving a rationale of the genre and distin-
guishing its subclasses; a glossary of terms commonly mistaken; selected "Gems from the Literature" at the beginning
of each part; and endpapers consisting of a mysteriously
inspired and thought-provoking Taxonomy of the Phylum Detective and Mystery Story.

1971 B.S.I. ANNUAL DINNER—POST MORTEMS
Ezra A. Wolff, M.D.

Once again we've come to the season
When B.S.I.'s, parting from reason,
> Derive from their tomes
> About Sherlock Holmes
Conclusions that Doyle would call treason.

To the present, no one ever saw
In the Canon much sex in the raw,
> But the ghost of Doc Freud
> Must be overjoyed
By the findings of John Bennett Shaw.

I am forcibly constrained to pray
And to hope that the <u>Rue Boulanger</u>
> And the ill-disguised stench
> Of the foul, fractured French
Of Will Oursler are not here to stay.

Irregulars feel they walk tall
In The Players' austere, hallowed hall,
> For combining their mystery
> With **theatre** history
Brings out the ham in them all.

May I be permitted to say
In my own most inadequate way
> I am now very sure
> (After Investiture)
About doggerel having its day.

THE PLAYERS

The Scion Societies

THE BAKER STREET IRREGULARS

Julian Wolff, M.D., Commissionaire,
33 Riverside Drive, New York 10023.

The Irregulars' annual dinner was held at The Players on 8 January and was attended by 100 thirsty enthusiasts. Especially notable among those present were Alfred Drake, President of The Players; Brooks Atkinson, the greatest and most scholarly of all critics; Fred Dannay, Investitured Irregular and half of the Ellery Queen team; and the Chaplain of the Irregulars, our own non-conformist clergyman, Rev. Leslie Marshall ("A Scandal in Bohemia"), who returned to the fold after many years' absence.

It was truly a great evening from beginning—the toast to the woman, Dorothy Stix (Mrs. Thomas L. Stix, Jr.), by Bill Jenkins— to end—the reports of the Scion Societies, followed by the usual informal discussions.

Of course, all of our customs were strictly observed, and the Conanical and Irregular toasts were drunk. The Constitution and Buy-Laws, as well as the Musgrave Ritual and Sherlock Holmes's Prayer, were read, and the Sherlockian songs of Jim and Bruce Montgomery were played and enjoyed. Greetings from individual Irregulars and Sherlockian societies in this country and abroad were read; newcomers were introduced; and we stood on the terrace to have our last quiet talk with those Irregulars who had broken from the ranks during the past year. Nor must we omit to mention those elegant keepsakes that we received through the courtesy of several Irregulars. The one from Lew Feldman (see Inventory) was most magnificent, and Fred Dannay generously supplied each of us with the Feb. EQMM, containing Michael Harrison's masterpiece. Deserving members were honoured, and unusually good talks were heard. These were delivered by Alfred Drake, whose address revealed him to be a real Sherlockian scholar; Thomas L. Stix, who spoke of the close re- lationship between The Players and the Irregulars; Rev. Leslie Marshall, who showed us that the stage had lost a fine actor when he entered the ministry; Will Oursler, who demonstrated his great ability as a linguist, far beyond our capabilities to com- prehend; and John Bennett Shaw, who delivered a most amusing talk in the modern style, showing evidence of much research and truly specialised knowledge, but, unfortunately, unpublishable.

*　　　　　*　　　　　*　　　　　*

THE FIVE ORANGE PIPS
of Westchester County

The 1970 meeting was held on 20 November at Baskerville Hall, the home of Benjamin Clark. The others in attendance were our founder and senior member, Richard W. Clarke, Dr. Calvin Plimpton, Henry C. Potter, Evan Wilson, and Julian Wolff. Thayer Cumings, Alastair Martin, and Frank Waters found it impossible to attend.

It is repetitious to remark that the hospitality of our host was truly magnificent, but this time he outdid himself. The qual- ity of the solid and liquid refreshment provided has probably never been surpassed.

A paper of most serious Sherlockian scholarship was given by each member, with Richard Clarke's being acclaimed as the clou of the collection.

As usual, the evening concluded with profound Sherlockian discussion (the rules of the order prohibit any mention of non- Sherlockian topics), and all agreed that it was the best meeting of any Sherlockian society ever held. (We obey the word of the Master, who does not agree with those who include modesty among the virtues.)

Clifton R. Andrew, Founder

Correspondence: Miss Lisa McGaw,
                392 Central Park West, New York, N.Y. 10025.

35 Irregulars and their friends, most of them from out of town, attended the luncheon at Keen's on 8 January, the day of the Irregular dinner. The occasion is always a most enjoyable one, since it is the best opportunity we have to become closely acquainted with fellow Sherlockians, especially those from faraway places. That is why the attendance continues to grow and those who have attended make every effort to return each year.

*   *   *   *

THE HOUNDS OF THE BASKERVILLE (SIC)
of Chicago

20 October was the date of the annual meeting, which drew a record crowd of 69 Irregulars to the Baker Street Pub. Time-honoured toasts opened the festivities, and they were followed by a fine dinner of roast pheasant.

Bob Mangler chaired the programme and presented membership certificates to Jack Schrandt and Ed Fladeland. Bob Hahn read excerpts from Vincent Starrett's MS. of his essay on "The Private Life of Sherlock Holmes," commissioned by Mirisch Productions, and then conducted the tripos for budding members.

Herb Tinning then commented on his paper, "The Singular Exploits of John H. Watson, M.D., in the Arctic Regions, 1892-93" and distributed copies of the paper. George Armstrong performed on the bagpipes, and there was a quiz for the women. The prize—the 2-volume Annotated Sherlock Holmes—was won by Julienne Stahl.

*   *   *   *

HUGO'S COMPANIONS
of Chicago

Correspondence: Robert W. Hahn,
                938 Clarence Ave., Oak Park, Ill. 60304.

A total of 37 were on hand for the first meeting of the academic year, held in the Baker Street Pub on 19 November. There were the traditional toasts, followed by a beef dinner. Several announcements followed, including one about the Sherlock Holmes Birthday Dinner, 6 January 1971. The election of officers (all the incumbents were unanimously re-elected) concluded the meeting.

*   *   *   *

THE SIX NAPOLEONS
of Baltimore

Correspondence: Steve Clarkson, Harker,
                69 Straw Hat Road, Apt. 1-D,
                Owings Mills, Md. 21117.

27 of the faithful gathered at the Baltimore Bar Association on 2 December 1970 to toast the woman and to delve into the dark mystery of Cyanea Capillata. Following the repast, the Harker reported on interim correspondence, and Ralph Edwards gave an erudite presentation on surds and conic sections. Peter Blau made an announcement about a Silver Blaze Handicap to be run at Bowie on April tenth.

The highlight of the evening was a dual presentation by Doctors Burnett and King, both knowledgeable in the phyla of jellyfish. Projecting colour-plates of Cyanea and Portuguese men-of-war, Dr. Burnett spoke on the toxic effects of their stings and responded in learned fashion to questions.

The quiz, won as usual by Philip Nathanson, was followed by a lively discussion of the evening's Adventure and related bits of esoteric Sherlockiana.

[Note: The meeting of the Napoleons reported (on page 245 of the December 1970 BSJ) as having taken place in December, actually took place on 8 September.]

* * * *

THE PRIORY SCHOLARS
of Fordham

Correspondence: P. Christian Steinbrunner,
62-52 82nd St., Middle Village, N.Y. 11379.

On Sunday, 10 January, the Scholars presented a special showing of one of the rarest of all Sherlockian films, the long-lost 1932 Fox classic, "Sherlock Holmes," with Clive Brook as the Master and Reginald Owen as Watson.

* * * *

THE SUB-LIBRARIAN SCION OF THE BSI
in the American Library Association

Correspondence: John Bennett Shaw,
1917 Fort Huron Drive, Santa Fe, N.M. 87501.

The fourth annual meeting took place on 30 June 1970 in the Detroit Hilton. Some 30 members representing the library profession and The Amateur Mendicants were present. John Bennett Shaw presided, and at the head table were Mrs. Shaw, Mr. and Mrs. Howard Haycraft, Russell McLauchlin, Bill Rabe, and Mr. and Mrs. Harry Hartman.

A most erudite paper was given by David Skene Melvin, of London, Ontario, in which he at long last laid to rest any conjecture about the why of the three James Moriartys. The charming Francine Morris (head of the new Scion in Texas) read a paper on horses and Holmes. (The chairman, a licensed mortician, was eager to listen, thinking that it was hearses and Holmes.) James Stokley then gave a slide talk. The food and drink and talk were unsurpassed, and again it was the best of some 600 library meetings held during the convention that week. Next year—Dallas.

* * * *

MAIWAND JEZAILS
of Wayne, Nebraska

Correspondence: Richard Lesh, Commandant,
505 E. Tenth Street, Wayne, Nebraska 68787.

On 24 October 1970 the Jezails mustered in Wayne, and once again the flying column from Omaha was transported via the crack Public Service coach, the Charing Cross Special. After preprandial rituals and Canonical toasts in the Victorian townhouse of Robert Johnson, the group transferred to the Sherlockian Room on the Wayne State campus and enjoyed an excellent menu.

Reports relative to the Maiwand monument were delivered by Don Reed and Ken Kopta. Alden Aust, assisted by Edwin Clark, reported on the newly discovered "Cannabis Papers." David Wallace was scheduled to deliver a paper, "Holmes, Watson, Churchill—Three Great Victorians," but he regretted that the British Official Secrets Act prohibited his reading this product of his research.

The Commandant was honoured for his years of service, and Paul Johnson received the coveted Commandant's Award.

After adjournment, the society repaired to the Robert Johnson manse, where a film of Sherlockian interest was viewed. Also on display was a splendid collection of medals connected with the Afghanistan campaigns.

THE CREW OF THE BARQUE LONE STAR
of North Central Texas

Correspondence: Miss Margaret F. Morris, Third Mate,
472 Westview Terrace, Arlington, Texas 76013.

The fall cruise was held Friday, 6 November 1970, sailing
from the Farmer's Daughter pier in Fort Worth. Crew members enjoyed a period of liquid fellowship while awaiting the Austin
group (thereafter designated as "Chips off the Old Barque").
Quiz honours were taken by Dr. Jesse Shera, and then twelve
members and a guest enjoyed a steak dinner during which toasts
were offered by Sam Lewis and Emory Estes. Greetings from absent
members and friends were read by Third Mate Morris.

John Bennett Shaw, ever helpful to new Scions, was scheduled
to speak but was unable to be present. Sandra Myres very ably
filled in by reading Mr. Shaw's enlightening paper, "The Cult
and Culture of Sherlock Holmes." The crew then offered toasts to
Mr. Shaw and Dr. Myres. After some discussion of a birthday dinner, the cruise ended with the ceremonial signing of the log.

*　　　　*　　　　*　　　　*

THE PRIORY SCHOOL
of New York

Correspondence: Andrew Page, Saltire,
3130 Irwin Avenue, Bronx N.Y. 10463.

On 3 January a second official meeting, attended by 7 members, was held at the house of Saltire. First, Canonical chronology in relation to The Sign of Four and The Stock-Broker's
Clerk was discussed, and then our official publication, Side-
lights on Holmes. It should be ready in March, and orders are
now being taken. Afterwards, a quiz on The Priory School was
given and was won by Joe Peralta. Then discussion centered
about the possible publication of a book, A Compendium of Canonical Quotations, some time in November. The meeting was topped
off by Basil Rathbone's reading of The Speckled Band.

The first official meeting was held at the same place, and
was a most informal one, with discussion travelling from subject
to subject, including the entrance examination, the Constitution,
and the forthcoming publication. The main event was a discussion
of the Holmes-Moriarty hypothesis.

This Scion is open to all Sherlockians. It meets about twice
a month, and all visitors are welcome. Out-of-state Sherlockians
are accepted as Members-in-Correspondence.

*　　　　*　　　　*　　　　*

BAKER STREET UNDERGROUND
of Ithaca

Correspondence: Richard M. Warshauer, Politician,
101 Klinewood Road, Ithaca, N.Y. 14850.

The Underground held its last meeting on 16 December 1970.
The Politician presented a paper titled "My Friend Wilson Har-
grave," which suggested an interesting counterpart in history
for the American policeman. Discussion among the members followed the paper, and also the usual toasts.

*　　　　*　　　　*　　　　*

Miss Rose Vogel (1041 Camelot Gardens Drive, St. Louis, Mo.
63125) announces that she and Steve Clarkson are going to be the
co-founders of a new corresponding Scion. There is no restric-
tion as to age or sex. Anyone interested should write to her.

HONOURS

The following were awarded the Irregular Shilling at our meeting on 8 January:

Robert Fish (in absentia), with the Investiture of "Barker, My Hated Rival."

Raymond de Groat (in absentia), with the Investiture of "Harraway."

Robert Brodie, with the Investiture of "The Gloria Scott."

Ezra A. Wolff, with the Investiture of "Sir James Damery."

August Derleth (in absentia), with the Investiture of "Inspector Baynes, Surrey Constabulary."

*　　　　*　　　　*　　　　*

THE MORLEY-MONTGOMERY AWARD
Awarded by Lew D. Feldman

This prize, Lew Feldman's cheque for $100, is awarded to the author of the best paper in The Baker Street Journal during the past year. As usual, the voting was close, but the final choice of the judges was Edward A. Merrill's "Holmes and Brunton: Civil Engineers," which appeared in the March 1970 Journal. Michael Harrison's "Why Didn't I Check Montague Street?" and Otis Hearn's "Thoughts on the Bust of Miss Mary Morstan," both of which were printed in the December 1970 issue, received Honourable Mention. (This is just as good place as any to reveal that Otis Hearn is a nom de plume of Walter N. Trenerry, a famous Minneapolis attorney.)

*　　　　*　　　　*　　　　*

Thomas M. McDade (250 North Street, White Plains, N.Y. 10602) announces a new contest:

"To encourage the art of belles-lettres a prize of $25 is offered for the best letter of not more than 500 words on any **one** of the following subjects:

> "1 - A letter from Dr. Watson to The Times (London, of course) protesting the figures of himself and Holmes as displayed in an exhibit at Madame Tussaud's Wax Works.

> "2 - A letter from Mrs. Hudson to her sister in Cornwall giving her version of events described in The Empty House.

> "3 - A letter from Sherlock Holmes to the Guggenheim Foundation applying for a grant to study drug addiction in London.

"Entries should be sent to Thomas McDade, and they must not be mailed later than 1 November 1971. The winning letter will be read at the 118th Anniversary Dinner, and will appear thereafter in The Baker Street Journal."

WANTS AND OFFERS— see p. 61 also

William R. Smith has the manuscript of the late A. Carson Simpson's unpublished 9th Sherlockian Study, and he graciously (and most generously) offers to send a copy to any interested Sherlockian. His address: 230 S. 15 St., Philadelphia, Pa. 19102. (Suggestion by the Editor: Include 12¢ in stamps with your request.)

Jack Tracy writes that his monograph, Conan Doyle and the Latter-Day Saints [a truly excellent production—Ed.], may be had for $1 by writing him at 955 East Boone, Frankfort, Ind. 46041.

LETTERS TO BAKER STREET

From Jack Tracy, of Frankfort, Indiana:

The December BSJ arrived on Pearl Harbor Day. I'm happy to say it was no bomb.

My congratulations on the December number—"one of the most remarkable ever penned." Michael Harrison was lucid and masterful, as usual, even if he does feel he deserves "to be kicked from here to Charing Cross." Brodie, Clarkson, and Narunsky were delightfully fresh. Lieberman's analysis I found "utterly satisfying." And Otis Hearn was magnificent; his essay was an absolute pearl (or two); I thought I would bust. And please—more unmitigated bleat from Lady Abigail. The only disappointment was "The Relationship of a Physician and a Master," which was long on Canonical references and short on drawing conclusions from them. Please, sir—I want some more.

* * * *

From Arthur H. Ihsen, Fairview, Erie County, Pennsylvania:

The printing in the Journal is getting too small for my eyes—at least the latter half of the September 1970 Journal. I would rather have less quantity and better printing.

[Editor's note: Discussion is invited.]

* * * *

From Martha McGhee, of Atlanta, Georgia:

Your magazine still holds great interest for me and my fellow Holmesian enthusiasts. We are a loosely organised group whose only common interest is a devouring interest in things British in general and Sherlockian in particular. In the Scots tradition we have set up a BSJ lending library; one copy circulates through the mailboxes and school lockers of six or seven thrifty souls . . . . I am the librarian for our group and have enclosed the subscription for another year—for four forlorn issues which will travel the rounds until they fall apart from sheer exhaustion. There are probably few subscriptions to the BSJ so well thumbed—or so well appreciated.

* * * *

From Daniel J. Morrow, of Blackwood, N.J.:

This is a footnote to the interesting article in the Dec. 1969 Journal, "Was There More to Watson Than Met the Private Eye?", by Benjamin Clark. Mr. Clark has, of course, made some very astute observations concerning The Engineer's Thumb. For example, it is true that many of Sherlock Holmes's cases, still in the famed tin dispatch-box, are unsolved cases. He admits as much in MUSG, and we read about the "boo-boos" again in YELL, THOR, VEIL, FIVE, and SOLI. But ENGI may not fit completely into the unsolved category. It may be that at least one of the counterfeiters in ENGI was brought to justice by the Master. Mr. Clark correctly points out that it is one case in which Holmes contributes nothing in the shape of a solution.

However, near the beginning of Shoscombe Old Place, Holmes tells Watson, ". . . Since I ran down that coiner by the zinc and copper filings in the seam of his cuff they [Scotland Yard] have begun to realize the importance of the microscope." Watson tells us that The Engineer's Thumb occurred in the summer of '89. If William Baring-Gould's date of the "coiner case," May 1902, is correct, it appears that only three years elapsed from the coiners' escape from Eyford to the time Holmes discovered zinc and copper filings in a suspect's cuff.

Surely the Master has partly resolved the case of the Engineer's Thumb.

* * * *

From W. A. Hoerr ("The Famous Card Scandal of the Nonpareil Club"), of Baptist College at Charleston, Charleston, S.C.:

Our college library has just acquired Irving Wallace's The Sunday Gentleman (Simon and Schuster), a collection of his articles on unusual persons. The book was ordered because it contains a reprint of his 1948 piece for The Saturday Review of Literature, "The Incredible Dr. Bell." Each of the articles has an appended "What Has Happened Since"; this "WHHS" deals with the feud between Wallace and Adrian Conan Doyle over Bell as a model for Holmes.

But to the point. There were two bonuses: "Monsieur Bertillon" and "The French Sherlock Holmes." The latter was Dr. Edmond Locard, who, among his other accomplishments, wrote a learned paper on the identification of tobaccos by a study of the ashes! Of even more interest, however, is the fact that Sir Arthur Conan Doyle visited Locard in his Lyons police laboratory, apparently in 1911 or 1912. In Locard's private crime museum Doyle gasped when he saw a large photograph. The subject had been Doyle's chauffeur for two months in London. He was one Jules Bonnot, recently executed for committing twelve brutal murders. When not busy with murder, M. Bonnot had engaged in arson, forgery, counterfeiting, robbery, and kidnapping.

Wallace quotes Locard, "It was quite a coincidence. That is why I always say that I caught the man who might have abruptly ended Sherlock Holmes's career."

I am not aware that I have ever run across this anecdote; perhaps it may be new to other Sherlockians also.

[Editor's notes: Many Irregulars, of course, are acquainted with The Fabulous Originals (New York: Alfred A. Knopf, 1956), also written by Irving Wallace (a subscriber to the Journal, incidentally). Chapter II, "The Real Sherlock Holmes," has to do with Dr. Bell. And one more coruscation: An interesting extract from Dr. Locard's obituary appears on page 242 of the December 1966 Journal (Vol. 16, no. 4).]

* * * *

From Irving Fenton ("The Singular Tragedy of the Atkinson Brothers"), temporarily (we hope) in Florida:

H. B. (Pete) Williams ("Old Abrahams") wrote me about a magazine called Sibyl Leek's Astrology Journal. In the January issue there is an article titled "Who Was the Real Sherlock Holmes?", by Walter Breen. After reading this I wept for shame that I had ever learned to read:

"The chart shows Sagittarius rising, with Mercury (sextile MC); Sun conjunct Jupiter in Capricorn, Square Moon in Aries—and trine Uranus in Taurus, which is loosely conjunct Pluto . . . ," and so on.

The author concludes astrologically, if ungrammatically, "The remaining alternative, then, is that whoever Conan Doyle had in mind in writing about Holmes must have had not only these characteristics . . . but the same birth data."

I was all shook up.

One should not read two world-shaking articles on the same day. (I had just finished Michael Harrison's "A Study in Surmise", in the EQ February issue.) However, a hot bath, some Equanil tablets, and a shot of cocaine should restore me.

*   *   *   *

From Lord Gore-Booth, G.C.M.G., K.C.V.O., President of The Sherlock Holmes Society of London:

29 The Vale,
London, S.W.3.

Jan. 12th, 1971.

Dear Julian,

I am horrified to have to confirm to you that the telegram from The Sherlock Holmes Society Dinner on Tuesday, January 5th, will have failed to reach you in time on Friday, January 8th.

The news of this came to me in the form of an enquiry on Saturday morning, January 9th, from the International Telegraph branch of the British Post Office who said they had a message from New York to the effect that the address '33 Riverside Drive' did not exist. I was very angry indeed, and was fortunate enough (unusually) to be able to lay my hands at once on a letter from you and to read the address to the man who had called me. He was first worried lest I was rebuking him, but I told him that this was not the case and that he should send a fierce rocket to his opposite number in New York saying that this gentleman had let him and me down and indeed owed me a few dollars compensation.

So would you accept all apologies from the Society for failing to reach you. If all else fails, we will investigate the possibility of sending next year's message by the hand of a Baker Street Irregular (London style) provided that you will hand him on arrival, with due ceremony, an irregular quarter.

Would you mind circulating this letter to everybody who was present at your dinner; if your budget will not stand this terrible burden, I will seek to meet it from an irregular account maintained top secretly by the correspondent in the United States of Mawson's Bank acting on the instructions of Mycroft Holmes.

Yours with renewed apologies,
[signed]   Paul G-B

The telegram:

SHERLOCK HOLMES SOCIETY THANK YOU AND IRREGULARS WARMEST AND RECIPROCATE GREETINGS THIS PROPITIOUS WEEK GORE-BOOTH

BAKER STREET INVENTORY

AUSTIN, BLISS
A Baker Street Christmas Stocking
Pittsburgh, Pa.: The Hydraulic Press, 1970.
This issue of "Holmesian trivia" has to do with the serial
publication of The Valley of Fear in this country—in the
Associated Sunday Magazines. Inserted as a bonus is a col-
oured reproduction of a Boston Sunday Post Sunday Magazine
cover depicting the characters in the tale.

BLAU, PETER E.
A Brief Census of the Manuscripts of the Canon
Pittsfield, Mass.: The Spermaceti Press, 1971.
Distributed as a keepsake at our annual dinner in January,
this booklet contains a listing of the manuscripts, their
location (if known), and an excellent bibliography. It is
certainly the best work on the subject to date.

BERG, STANTON O.
Sherlock Holmes: Father of Scientific Crime Detection
The Journal of Criminal Law, Criminology, and Police Science,
Vol. 61, No. 3, September 1970.
A thorough discussion of Holmes's methods, revealing that
many of them were original, and telling of the many criminolo-
gists who have paid tribute to him. The author generously
offers to send reprints of this desirable and truly worth-
while monograph to readers who send him a stamped and self-
addressed envelope. His address is: 6025 Gardena Lane N.E.,
Minneapolis, Minn. 55432.

GREENE, HUGH, editor
The Rivals of Sherlock Holmes
New York: Pantheon Books, 1970; $6.95.
A good collection of thirteen tales, examples of the feats
of Holmes's contemporaries—proving to our satisfaction
that the rivals of Sherlock Holmes are also-rans.

HARRISON, MICHAEL
A Study in Surmise
Ellery Queen's Mystery Magazine, February 1971.
As a result of his scholarly researches this great Sherlockian has produced a rare item indeed—a really new
major discovery in the Sherlockian field. His new theory
about the origin of Sherlock Holmes is well documented.

HARTMAN, HARRY
The Holy Quire
Culver City, Calif.: Luther Norris (3844 Watseka Ave.),
1970; $4.00.
A collection of Sherlockian papers (some of which have
appeared in this Journal) in the author's unique style.

PECK, ANDREW JAY
The Date Being—?
N.p., c. 1970.
Sub-titled "A Compendium of Chronological Data," this
monograph consists of an Introduction containing a discussion of the great chronologists, their methods, and
their conclusions, followed by much useful chronological
data arranged in tables. The result is a most useful production showing evidence of much diligent scholarly re-
research. (Available for $3 from the author at 2968 Perry
Avenue, Bronx, N.Y. 10458.)

RENNIE, DRUMMOND
   Is Holmes Watson?
      The Lancet, 19 December 1970.
      This is a paper of amusing, rather than serious scholar-
      ship, but the knowledgeable author (who lives in the
      United States, by the way) does reach a satisfactory con-
      clusion: "Watson is not Holmes: both are still alive."

                *   *   *   *

   Sir Arthur Conan Doyle Archives is a typographical gem, distributed by Lew Feldman as a keepsake at our dinner on 8 January.
It is a four-page folio folder listing items from what is correctly described as "The largest and most important selection
of material relating to the life and work of Sir Arthur Conan
Doyle ever offered at one time." Lew David Feldman invites inquiries for prices and further information. His address is:
139 East 63rd Street, New York, N.Y. 10021.

   Another dinner keepsake is a small folder from John Bennett
Shaw with some information about Mrs. Hudson and photographs
of that lady and Mr. Hudson.

   By the time this reaches our readers, Charles E. Lauterbach's
Baker Street Ballads will be available from Luther Norris for $3.
(Address: 3844 Watseka Avenue, Culver City, Calif. 90230.)

   A Modest Sherlockian Monograph, produced by Robert H. Schutz
on his private press, is a folder (with illustrations) treating
of the much discussed Sherlockian sanitary facilities.

   From Andrew Page we learn of two Sherlockian pieces: (1) "The
Three Students," by Ellery Queen, in Playboy, March 1971. (2)
"Sherlock Holmes Lives Again," in Clipper Magazine, published by
Pan American Airways (and abridged in Reader's Digest for Febru-
ary 1971).

   From Amsterdam, Cornelis Helling has sent BK Journal of 5
October 1970, containing an unsigned illustrated article, "Sherlock Holmes Leeft Weer Op" (Sherlock Holmes's Revival). Even in
the Dutch text it is not difficult to see references to The Baker
Street Irregulars and the Sherlock Holmes Society in Nederland.

   Michael and Mollie Hardwick's The Private Life of Sherlock
Holmes has recently been published in England by Mayflower
Books. It is the book of Billy Wilder's United Artists film of
the same name—and, needless to say, has no connection with
Vincent Starret's work with the same title.

   Four new Sherlockian records, specially dramatised for the pur-
pose by Michael and Mollie Hardwick, have been produced in Eng-
land by Discourses, 34 High Street, Royal Tunbridge Wells, Kent.
DCO 1210 The Speckled Band and The Blue Carbuncle.
DCO 1211 Charles Augustus Milverton and Black Peter.
DCO 1212 A Scandal in Bohemia and The Dying Detective.
DCO 1213 The Illustrious Client and The Mazarin Stone.
The price is 25/6d. (£1.27) each.

   Prefaces without Books, by Christopher Morley, dedicated to
Lew David Feldman, contains Morley's prefaces and introductions
to thirty books, selected by Herman Abromson. We all recognise
Chris Morley as the Master of the English language, and this book
contains some of his best writings—for us, of course, the choice
is "In Memoriam Sherlock Holmes," the introduction to the omnibus.
The book is sold for $4.75 by The University of Texas Press, 102
W. 20th Street, Austin, Texas 78712.

   Christopher Morley; An Exhibition is the well produced catalogue of the Morley exhibition held at Hofstra University, 27
May through 31 August 1970. (See page 250, December 1970 BSJ.)

*   *   *   *

PERIODICALS RECEIVED

THE BAKER STREET CAB LANTERN, No. 8, 1970. Edited and distributed in a limited edition of 221 copies by Ted Bergman, Storkvägen 10, 18135 Lidingö, Sweden, for the purpose of scholarly research. Contains articles in English and Norwegian.

THE MYSTERY READER'S NEWSLETTER, Vol. 4, No. 1, October 1970. Edited by Mrs. Lianne Carlin, P.O. Box 113, Melrose, Mass. 02176.

THE PIPE SMOKER'S EPHEMERIS, Spring-Autumn: 1970. Edited and published by Tom Dunn for The Universal Coterie of Pipe Smokers—in which many Sherlockians are interested, judging from the letters.

SHERLOCKIANA, Nr. 3-4, 1970. Edited by A. D. Henriksen for Sherlock Holmes Klubben i Danmark. Much information (in Danish) about books and other Sherlockian matters.

*   *   *   *

EXTRA-CURRICULAR ACTIVITIES

Henry Lauritzen's Christmas book for 1970 is, once more, a real delight. With its discussion of stories and authors and a checklist of detectives—all in Danish, of course—it is a most useful manual, with many good illustrations. Oh yes, the title is Mester Detektiver under Lup.

Commissioner Eric H. Silk of the Ontario Provincial Police, a Sherlockian and a Journal subscriber, is recognised as a great criminologist, and he has written the Foreword to A Century of Crime, by Marjorie Freeman Campbell (Toronto and Montreal: McClelland and Stewart, Limited, c.1970). This is of great interest to aficionados of true crime, since it is devoted to Canadian cases about which not much is written in this country.

Bryson Kalt has written a 128-page monograph titled The Mother's Guide to Child Safety (Grosset and Dunlap). It can be obtained from Parade Magazine, 733 Third Ave., New York 10017, for $1. Evidently Ted Bates lost a fine advertising man when Bryson decided to become an author.

Morris Rosenblum has two accomplishments to report: His Heroes of Mexico is in print, and his Heroes of Israel (New York, Fleet Press Corporation; $5.00) is now being published. Morris writes: "It will amaze you how I got a reference to Sherlock Holmes into both these books."

The Times Literary Supplement, London, 30 October 1970, reported the publication of the late Anthony Boucher's The Compleat Werewolf (W. H. Allen).

The 12 November 1970 issue of The Field, "The country newspaper every Thursday," contained John Linsenmeyer's learned paper, "Trespass in the Chase," which has to do with the legal aspects of foxhunting.

Luther Norris has published (for the Edgar Wallace Society) a book of Edgar Wallace's verse, The Mission That Failed, Wallace's first published work and one of his rarest.

Everett Hoffman's poem, "Lions on the Beach," appeared in The New York Times of 24 October 1970.

*   *   *   *

SPECIAL ANNOUNCEMENT: W. T. Rabe writes that he cannot guarantee to publish the Commonplace Book and Sherlockian Who's Who & What's What. Subscribers were notified by mail, and refunds were mailed in December. Those who have not received refunds should write him at 909 Prospect, Sault Ste. Marie, Mich. 49783.

Wants and Offers

Helan Halbach (P.O. Box 613, Santa Barbara, Calif. 93101) has acquired the plates from which William Gillette's play, Sherlock Holmes (Doubleday, Doran, 1935), was printed. The plates were part of the Doyle estate, having been purchased from the Gillette estate. They include Starrett's Introduction as well as Steele's Notes and his illustrations, and they are complete and in usable condition. She invites correspondence from those interested, and requests that a stamped and addressed envelope be sent for reply.

Katherine Karlson (4051 Eve Drive, Seaford, N.Y. 11783) is looking for August Derleth's The Return of Solar Pons.

Andrew Page (3130 Irwin Ave., Bronx, N.Y. 10463) wants The S.H. Journal, Vols. 1-5; Baker Street Gasogene, Vol. 1; Baker Street Pages, 1-25; Morley's Sherlock Holmes and Dr. Watson; Blakeney's Sherlock Holmes: Fact or Fiction?; The Exploits of Sherlock Holmes; Profile by Gaslight; Seventeen Steps to Baker Street; Gavin Brend's My Dear Holmes; Christ's Irregular Guide; All issues of Studies in Scarlet, and any Solar Pons books. He offers Introducing Sherlock Holmes, edited by Edgar W. Smith.

Norman S. Nolan (68 Crest Road, Middletown, N.J. 07748) says he is "willing to buy or to trade various Sherlockian and other detective-fiction items for BSJ (NS) selected issues—Vol. 1-9."

Father Francis Hertzberg (Our Lady's, Shalmarsh, Prospect Hill, Hr Bebington, Wirral, Cheshire, England) offers 20 bound volumes of The Strand, mostly pre-1900, and each containing 5 or 6 Holmes stories, at $7.50 each. He also has very early cigarette card sets of Conan Doyle characters at $6.75, and some other items of Sherlockian interest upon which he invites correspondence.

William McCullam (Fairmont Road, Newbury, Ohio 44065) offers Old Series BSJ, Vol. 2, 1947, library bound, excellent, for $20.00, including postage.

Charles W. Roberts (2425 Greenwood, Pueblo, Colo. 81003) would like to correspond with Sherlockians in U.S. and abroad.

Robert H. Schutz (1912 Ardmore Boulevard, Pittsburgh, Pa. 15221) writes: "...the Collier Collected Edition (Red Cloth with Gold Lettering) appeared in a 6-volume and in an 8-volume set. I need several of these to complete both sets and will welcome offers to sell or trade. Have some lovely single editions to trade, some with dust-wrappers."

Glenn J. Shea (5 Pine Hill Road, Jewett City, Conn. 06351) wants Sherlock Holmes: A Drama in Four Acts, by Doyle and Gillette; 221B: Studies in Sherlock Holmes, edited by Starrett; The Incunabular Holmes and Introducing Mr. Sherlock Holmes, both edited by Smith; Holroyd's Baker Street By-Ways; Doctor Watson and Holmes and Watson, both by Roberts; A Sherlock Holmes Almanac, by Petersen; The Sherlockian Atlas, by Wolff; and The Misadventures of Sherlock Holmes, edited by Queen.

Ron De Waal writes re the Stowe-Day Foundation William Gillette Exhibit, held at The Nook Farm, Hartford, Conn., birthplace of Gillette, 18 October 1970 through 31 January 1971. The catalogue is available at 50¢ from the Stowe-Day Foundation, 77 Forest Street, Hartford, Conn. 06105. And it is interesting to note that the exhibit included many items from the collection of James Keddie, Jr., Cheetah of The Speckled Band.

(More on page 54)

From the Editor's Commonplace Book

The first running of the Silver Blaze (Southern Division) will be held at Bowie Race Track on Saturday, 10 April, under the auspices of The Red Circle, of Washington, and The Six Napoleons, of Baltimore. Details are available from Peter E. Blau, 2201 M Street NW, Washington, D.C. 20037.

* * *

The Metropolitan Toronto Central Library S.H. Exhibition, announced at our dinner on 8 January, and opening on 9 January, evidently is a great success. (It will continue to 14 February.) Judge S. Tupper Bigelow reports that there was an S.R.O. crowd at the opening.

* * *

Incidentally, it was the same Judge Bigelow, who did so well at the exhibition, who dismissed the assault charges against the American lawyer, William Kunstler. Oh well, you can't win them all.

* * *

An illustration from Country Life of 6 November 1969 reveals that the jews'-harp may not be a musical instrument at all, but it is difficult to believe that garroter Parker was a remarkable performer upon the drag-rake.

1.—FROM FRONT TO REAR: DRAIN CUTTING IMPLEMENT, DRAG-RAKE (OR JEW'S HARP), DITCH HOOK, DUNG RAKE, HORSE RAZOR AND JET (OR JUT)

*   *   *

Herman Herst, Jr. ("Colonel Emsworth, V.C."), a world-
famous philatelist, was awarded Honorary Life Membership,
the first ever given, by the America Stamp Club of Great
Britain; his book, <u>Stories to Collect Stamps By</u>, won a bronze
medal at the London International Stamp Exhibition last
September; and his private stamp, issued while the post
office in Shrub Oak was closed, was recently reproduced in
the stamp column of <u>The New York Times</u>.

*   *   *

Mrs. Diane Swanson reports that University Extension,
University of California, Berkeley, is preparing the second
annual Oxford-Berkeley Summer programme, and she believes
that this may be of interest to Irregulars. Full details
may be obtained from her at Public Information Office, University Extension (415 642-3112).

*   *   *

Some reminders:
The deadline for the Journal is about six weeks before the
date of issue. (<u>E.g.</u>, the deadline for June is 15 April.)
To obtain the discount, orders for the Journal reprints
being produced by AMS Press (see December 1970 BSJ, p. 256)
should be sent to AMS Press before 31 March.
Copies of Don Redmond's <u>Cumulated Index to The Baker Street
Journal</u> (1946-1969) are available from the BSJ Editor at $5.

*   *   *

<u>Abstracts of English Studies</u>, September 1970, contains
abstracts of the articles in the June 1970 BSJ. (See items
161-168, and 287.)

*   *   *

And here is another Sherlockian bookplate:

WH🔍DUNIT

RICHARD W. CLARKE ("The Copper Beeches"), the head of R. W. Clarke & Company, stockbrokers, is a scholarly Sherlockian stalwart of long standing, and the sparking plug of our senior Scion, The Five Orange Pips, of Westchester County.
The Meadows, Holly Branch Road, Katonah, N.Y. 10536.

HARRY W. SPRINGER, an ardent Sherlockian, is a member of the Maiwand Jezails and President of the Omaha Transit Company.
1329 South 93rd Street, Omaha, Nebraska 68124.

DAVID WALLACE, a member of the Maiwand Jezails, is an engineer with Minneapolis-Honeywell. The results of his researches have appeared in this Journal on previous occasions, last in March 1969.   7711 Poppleton Plaza, Omaha, Nebraska 68124.

DR. KOHKI NAGANUMA ("The Curious Incident of Sherlock Holmes in Japan"), formerly Vice-Minister of Finance and Chairman of the Fair Trade Committee, is President of Nippon Columbia, Ltd. He has made many outstanding contributions to our literature.
15-1 Higashi-Gotanda 3-Chome, Shinagawa-Ku, Tokyo, Japan.

PHILIP A. SHREFFLER, an organiser of the Noble Bachelors Scion Society, majored in English and American literature at Washington University in St. Louis. He last appeared here in September 1969.   Rte. 1, Box 268, Union, Missouri 63084.

JOHN BALL ("The Oxford Flyer"), the famous author (In the Heat of the Night, etc.), is President of the Los Angeles Scion Society and a Master Copper-Beech-Smith of The Sons of the Copper Beeches, of Philadelphia.
16401 Otsego Street, Encino, California 91316.

FRED MENDE, who has bachelor's and master's degrees from Northwestern University, teaches instrumental music in the Charlotte-Mecklenberg, N.C., school system, and also performs on the trumpet. In addition to his great interest in matters Sherlockian, he is a serious student of history.
1214 Tarrington Avenue, Charlotte, N.C. 28205.

REV. LESLIE MARSHALL ("A Scandal in Bohemia"), our own Chaplain and non-conformist clergyman, has distinguished himself as a scholarly Sherlockian and a faithful Irregular over a period of many years.   Box 386, St. Petersburg, Florida 33731.

MARK LEVY, who studied astro-physics at the Polytechnic Institute of Brooklyn, is 22 years old and was unmarried when last heard from. As a physical scientist, he loves Holmes for his lack of emotion, and finds that Holmes's powers of ratiocination are assets in other fields, besides detection.
88-19 189 Street, Jamaica, New York 11423.

EZRA A. WOLFF, M.D., F.A.C.S. ("Sir James Damery"), is a distinguished poet who dabbles in surgery. His annual post-prandial poem each January is becoming an Irregular Journal tradition.
108-23 Jewel Avenue, Forest Hills, N.Y. 11375.

Duke of York's Theatre

ST MARTIN'S LANE WC

Proprietors ... ... Mr & Mrs Frank Wyatt
Sole Lessee and Manager ... ... CHARLES FROHMAN

CHARLES FROHMAN PRESENTS
A DRAMA IN FOUR ACTS
BY A. CONAN DOYLE
AND WILLIAM GILLETTE
ENTITLED

SHERLOCK HOLMES

BEING A HITHERTO UNPUBLISHED EPISODE
IN THE CAREER OF THE GREAT DETECTIVE
AND SHOWING HIS CONNECTION WITH THE

STRANGE CASE OF MISS FAULKNER

CHARACTERS IN THE PLAY	COMPANY APPEARING IN THE CAST
SHERLOCK HOLMES	WILLIAM GILLETTE
DOCTOR WATSON	KENNETH RIVINGTON
JOHN FORMAN	EUGENE MAYEUR
SIR EDWARD LEIGHTON	REGINALD DANCE
COUNT VON STAHLBURG	FREDERICK MORRIS
PROFESSOR MORIARTY	GEORGE SUMNER
JAMES LARRABEE	FRANCIS CARLYLE
SIDNEY PRINCE	QUINTON McPHERSON
ALFRED BASSICK	WILLIAM H. DAY
JIM CRAIGIN	CHRIS WALKER
THOMAS LEARY	HENRY WALTERS
"LIGHTFOOT" McTAGUE	WALTER DISON
JOHN	THOMAS QUINTON
PARSONS	G. MERTON
BILLY	CHARLES CHAPLIN
ALICE FAULKNER	MARIE DORO
MRS. FAULKNER	DE OLIA WEBSTER
MADGE LARRABEE	ADELAIDE PRINCE
THERESE	SYBIL CAMPBELL
MRS. SMEEDLEY	ETHEL LORRIMORE

THE PLACE IS LONDON
THE TIME TEN YEARS AGO

FIRST ACT—DRAWING ROOM AT THE LARRABEES'—EVENING

SECOND ACT—Scene I—PROFESSOR MORIARTY'S UNDERGROUND OFFICE—MORNING
Scene II—SHERLOCK HOLMES' APARTMENTS IN BAKER STREET—EVENING

THIRD ACT—THE STEPNEY GAS CHAMBER—MIDNIGHT

FOURTH ACT—DOCTOR WATSON'S CONSULTING ROOM KENSINGTON—THE FOLLOWING EVENING

SCENERY BY ERNEST GROS   INCIDENTAL MUSIC BY WILLIAM FURST

INTERMISSIONS

Between the 1st and 2nd Acts, 9 minutes
Between the 2nd and 3rd Acts, 7 minutes
Between the 3rd and 4th Acts, 8 minutes

MATINEE every Saturday at 2.15 o'clock

BUSINESS MANAGER—JAMES W MATHEWS   ACTING MANAGER—ROBERT M EBERLE
STAGE MANAGER—WILLIAM POSTANCE   MUSICAL DIRECTOR—JOHN CROOK

ICED TEA AND COFFEE can be had of the Attendants

lume 21, Number 2　　　　　　　　　　June 1971
ew Series)

ONE-HUNDREDTH ISSUE

THE

BAKER STREET

JOURNAL

An Irregular Quarterly of Sherlockiana

Editor: JULIAN WOLFF, M.D.

THE BAKER STREET IRREGULARS

NEW YORK, N.Y.

Volume 21, Number 2
(New Series)

June 1971

ONE–HUNDREDTH ISSUE

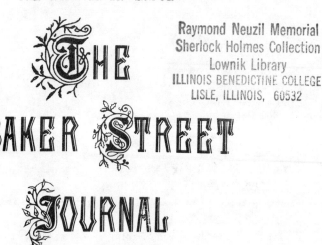

THE BAKER STREET JOURNAL

Founded by EDGAR W. SMITH, Esq.

"Si monumentum quaeris, circumspice"

Subscription $4 a year

All communications and remittances should be sent to the Editor

Julian Wolff, M.D.

33 Riverside Drive, New York, N. Y. 10023

CONTENTS

THE EDITOR'S GAS-LAMP
ONE HUNDRED ISSUES

Many readers will be surprised to learn that they are holding the one-hundredth issue of The Baker Street Journal—and justifiably so, for it is not often that a publication of this type is able to achieve that milestone.

The Journal began in 1946 with the Old Series, edited by Edgar W. Smith and published by Ben Abramson, and it ran through three complete volumes (12 issues) before it got into trouble. Vol. 4, No. 1, did make its appearance, but, due to publishing difficulties, the rest of the volume never was issued, and its last three numbers became known as the missing three quarters. There is a rumour that the galley proofs of Vol. 4, No. 2, do exist, and this may well be true, since Edgar did have them just before publication of the Old Series was discontinued.

Incidentally, although the Old Series had a masthead

Edgar W. Smith - Editor

Ben Abramson, Publisher

THE BAKER STREET JOURNAL

An Irregular Quarterly of Sherlockiana

JULY, 1946

ASSOCIATE EDITORS
W. S. Hall, Christopher Morley,
Dr. Julian Wolff, Ellery Queen, Lee Wright

HONORARY ASSOCIATES
H. W. Bell, Vincent Starrett

GRAPHIC ACCOUTREMENT
Paul McPharlin

3 West 46 Street, New York 19
TELEPHONE: BRyant 9–6561

1775 Broadway, Room 1703
New York 19, New York

* By Subscription only. Four Numbers $5.00

listing Associate Editors, Edgar did all the editorial work. The duties of the Associate Editors consisted of meeting quarterly for two hours of eating and drinking at Billy the Oysterman's and looking over the galley proofs of the next issue.

In 1951 Edgar Smith revived the Journal, and it began to appear in a more modest format as the New Series. He remained as editor until he died in 1960. Then the duties devolved upon the present editor.

And here is how our one hundred issues are made up:

Old Series, Vol. 1, No. 1, through
Vol. 4, No. 1, inclusive   13 issues
New Series, Vols. 1-20, and Vol. 21,
Nos. 1 and 2   82 issues
Christmas Annuals, 1956-1960, incl.   5 issues
                                  100

It is pleasing to note that the circulation has grown. There were about 200 of New Series Volume One printed, I believe. Some time later this was reprinted. Since then our list has gradually grown, and over 1000 copies of the March 1971 issue were sent out.

    *   *   *   *   *

As shown by this sample letterhead prepared in 1945, there was a slight change in the title of our publication before it actually appeared.

The Baker Street Quarterly

3 WEST 46TH STREET, NEW YORK 19

EDITORIAL OFFICE: ROOM 1800, 1775 BROADWAY

(1775 Broadway was the address of what Edgar liked to call the Franco-Midland Hardware Company, of which he was a vice-president.)

    *   *   *   *   *

And a short anecdote may be of interest: Ben Abramson once received a letter from The Estate of Sir Arthur Conan Doyle claiming that his publication of the Journal violated copyrights that the estate held and referring him to the estate's solicitors, Vertue and Churcher. Ben composed a reply which concluded by referring the estate to <u>his</u> solicitors, Lox and Bagels.

SEVENTEEN STEPS
by Barbara Hodan

I have often tread these steps to spend
an evening among friends
And to share for a time the light of familiar
faces.
Here I have come, weary from my world,
To be admitted with the absent ceremonies
of friendship
And settled by the fire, warm in the ease
of close company;
A partner in the dramas of this room
Where the late editions lie scattered,
Strangely ordered in their constant disarray,
As are the books, the chemicals, the papers
and cuttings;
All the accumulations of a man's life within
an arm's easy reach.
Tonight the air hangs with the heavy smoke
of the evening's pipes,
And only the strike of the clock and the
crack of the fire break the silence.
For the Master, drawn deep into his chair, is
far into a world
Which turns about some problems of curious
interest,
And for us nothing beyond that exists.
Yet it is not always so when I come.
Sometimes there is good talk and music,
With a little wine and perhaps a cold partridge
on the sideboard.
But, inevitably, some nights the bell rings;
In a moment our caller, having climbed the steps,
will enter,
And then the story begins.

SHERLOCK HOLMES ON THE SCREEN
by Roy Pickard

As many as 127 films, more than those made about all the other fictional detectives put together, have so far been made about the exploits of Sherlock Holmes. Germany, France, Italy, and Denmark, as well as Britain and America, have all produced films about the famous detective, and since 1903, when the first Holmes film was released, more than thirty actors have played him on the screen. Only Tarzan (some 40-odd films to date) of contemporary fictional heroes has in any way rivalled his popularity.

Yet when all this is said, it is astonishing to discover that Holmes has never yet been portrayed satisfactorily on the screen. The essence of his character seems to have eluded even the most talented actors, and although many have caught his eccentricities and sharpness of mind well enough and have rung out the world-famous "Elementary," none have quite managed to reflect the quieter, more intense side of the man's personality. The detective's moods, his drug-taking, and his delight in grappling with an intellectual problem have usually been passed over, or at best only fleetingly referred to.

Basil Rathbone and Arthur Wontner are perhaps the two screen actors who have come closest to most people's conception of Holmes, although the latest actor to appear in the rôle (Robert Stephens, in The Private Life of Sherlock Holmes) has an excellent chance to surpass them both.

The stories about the residents of 221B Baker Street had been in print only sixteen years when the movie makers decided to transfer their activities to the screen. The first known Holmes film, Sherlock Holmes Baffled, was produced by the American Mutoscope and Biograph Company in 1903. Other films, among them Adventures of Sherlock Holmes (1905), the Italian Rival Sherlock Holmes (1908), and Sherlock Holmes in the Great Murder Mystery (1908) quickly followed.

The most ambitious of all the early attempts to film the adventures of the great detective came from Denmark in 1908, in a film entitled simply Sherlock Holmes, an original story which, although not based on any particular Conan Doyle tale, did at least have the notorious Professor Moriarty as its chief villain. In this film Forrest Holger-Madsen played Holmes, as he did in eleven subsequent Danish one-reelers.

Germany and France (which produced eight one-reelers during 1912-13) were among the other countries to show an interest in Holmes in the pre-World War I period.

William Gillette, a stage actor who had first played Holmes in 1899, made a big impression when he appeared in Essanay's Sherlock Holmes in 1916. This was a screen version of his own play. This picture, like the original play, centred on the battle of wits between Holmes and Moriarty and included two new characters not originally created by Doyle— a young boy assistant called Little Billy, and a young woman by the name of Alice Faulkner (played by Marjorie Kay) who was inserted as a romantic interest for Holmes.

Noted author Booth Tarkington was reported to have said to Gillette: "I would rather see you play Sherlock Holmes than be a child again on Christmas morning." When he retired Gillette had played Holmes over 1300 times during his career.

The next well known actor to play Holmes was John Barrymore. In 1922 he appeared in Moriarty (called Sherlock Holmes in America), another version of Gillette's play and the most

ambitious Holmes film made up to that time. Despite some basic
improbabilities in the plot, such as Holmes's actually getting
married, the film had several things to recommend it, not
least an imaginative use of make-up disguise. One ingenious
scene had Holmes disguised as Moriarty coming face to face
with the real villain played with gusto by Gustav von Seyffer-
titz. The film included some authentic location shots of London and was directed by Albert Parker. Roland Young played
Watson, and others in the cast included Louis Wolheim and William Powell, who made his debut as a heavy in the picture.

The Times (of London), in its review of the film in January
1923, took exception to the romantic scenes. "Holmes," the
paper said, "eventually falls into the heroine's arms in a
passionate embrace. This Sherlock Holmes is made human and
(presumably) picture theatre audiences will be satisfied. But
the happy ending in this case rather spoils the character of
the hero who, from Sir Arthur Conan Doyle's novels, would seem
to be a rather unlikely lover." The Times went on to praise
Barrymore's performance, remarking that the actor "manages to
make of Holmes a convincing figure, even when he is overcome
by the pangs of love. The part would be so easy to overdo, but
his consistent restraint is the more praiseworthy."

The first English-speaking version of The Hound of the
Baskervilles also appeared in 1922, but director Maurice Elvey, although he drew a not unimaginative performance from
Eille Norwood, missed most of the opportunities that this
terrifying and superbly constructed story offered.

Elvey and Norwood continued to work together on the Holmes
stories and were director and star of fifteen two-reelers
made in 1922. All the films were based on short stories and
included A Scandal in Bohemia, The Empty House, The Copper
Beeches, The Solitary Cyclist, The Red-Headed League, and The
Man with the Twisted Lip. All told, Norwood appeared in over
25 Holmes films between 1921 and 1923.

For his performances as the famous detective, Norwood earned
acclaim from no less a person than Doyle himself, who said of
the actor: "He has that rare quality which can only be described as glamour which compels you to watch an actor when
he is doing nothing. He has the brooding eye which excites
expectation."

The last silent Sherlock Holmes (Carlyle Blackwell, in
Richard Oswald's German Der Hund von Baskervilles) and the
first speaking Holmes (Clive Brook, in The Return of Sherlock
Holmes) both appeared on the screen in 1929. The latter film,
which was based on The Dying Detective and His Last Bow and
updated to modern times, centred once more on the clash between Holmes and arch-criminal Moriarty, the aspect of the
Holmes stories that has intrigued film-makers most. A great
part of the action takes place on an ocean liner and evolves
from a murder committed at the wedding of Watson's daughter.
H. Reeves-Smith was Watson, and Harry T. Morley made an excellent Moriarty. The film itself, however, was one of the
least distinguished of the Holmes movies.

In 1931 Arthur Wontner made the first of his five appearances as Holmes when he starred in Leslie S. Hiscott's The
Sleeping Cardinal (also known as Sherlock Holmes' Fatal Hour),
a somewhat clumsy attempt to combine the short stories, The
Final Problem and The Empty House. Reviewing the film when it
opened in London in March 1931, The Times complained of "a
lack of coherence in the development of the action" and found
that "although Wontner certainly looks the part, his voice,

-71-

which is unduly harsh at times, works against him." The paper
then went on to praise the actor by remarking that "he has to
carry the film more or less on his own shoulders and thanks
to him it is possible to forget the preposterousness of the
plot in the pleasure of watching the authentic Holmes at work."

Picturegoer also praised Wontner's rendering, calling it
"wholly convincing, even to the smallest mannerisms."

Moriarty in the person of Norman McKinnell again featured
in the plot, and other leading characters included Mrs. Hudson (Minnie Rayner) and the stolid Inspector Lestrade (Philip
Newland), the rather clueless Scotland Yarder who was forever
calling on Holmes for advice. Ian Fleming played Watson, as
he did in the subsequent Wontner films.

The early thirties saw a flood of Holmes pictures. Wontner
played the character again in both The Sign of Four (Rowland
V. Lee, 1932) and The Missing Rembrandt (Leslie S. Hiscott,
1932), an adaptation of Charles Augustus Milverton; Raymond
Massey made his one and only appearance as Holmes in The
Speckled Band (Jack Raymond, 1931); and in 1932 Robert Rendel
appeared in a second British version of The Hound of the
Baskervilles.

Another Holmes film made during this period was Fox's
Sherlock Holmes (1932), a William K. Howard production which
had Clive Brook making his second appearance in the rôle,
and which was based on both the Gillette play and the Doyle
short story, The Red-Headed League. Holmes and Moriarty
clashed just as vehemently as they had done on previous occasions, but the updating of the story meant that the film
lacked the atmosphere of 19th-century London, so essential to
the over-all success of the stories.

Picturegoer was not as happy with this film or with Brook's
performance as they had been with The Sleeping Cardinal a
year earlier. It found that "instead of incisive deduction
and clever detail, there is all the paraphernalia of melodrama, with thrills of a popular order," and that Clive Brook
presented "a bumptious, obstinate character rather than a
brilliant one." Ernest Torrence as Moriarty received good
notices, however.

Sherlock Holmes was a short film running for just 61 minutes. It opened at the Coliseum, Charing Cross Road, on 25
March 1933 as the second half of a double bill. The main at-
traction was Marlene Dietrich in Blonde Venus. Prices for
the programme were quoted as 1/- to 3/9, with no seats over
1/6 before 1:30.

Reginald Owen, the actor who had played Watson in the William K. Howard production, changed rôles a year later when he
played not the worthy doctor but Holmes himself in A Study in
Scarlet. He thus became the only actor ever to play both characters on the screen.

Although A Study in Scarlet carried the title of the first
Holmes novel, it bore little or no resemblance to the original
and was just a run-of-the-mill thriller. Alan Mowbray played
Lestrade, Tempe Pigott was Mrs. Hudson, and Warburton Gamble
featured as Watson. Edwin L. Marin directed.

Arthur Wontner and Ian Fleming returned to the scene briefly in the mid-thirties in The Triumph of Sherlock Holmes
(1935) and Silver Blaze (1936), and about this time Germany
also showed renewed interest, making some three Holmes films
(Der Hund von Baskervilles, Die graue Dame, Der Mann der Sherlock Holmes war) in quick succession.

Basil Rathbone, the man whom—despite Peter Cushing's recent

long-running TV series—most people associate with Sherlock
Holmes, made his debut in the part in 1939, when Twentieth
Century-Fox produced the seventh (and best) version of The
Hound of the Baskervilles. This was a fairly lavish production
and was set in the correct period. Grahame Greene, who was
then the film critic of The Spectator, found the period sense
one of the film's most redeeming features. He wrote: "The
atmosphere of the unmechanised Edwardian flurry is well caught:
the villain bowls recklessly along Baker Street in a hansom
and our hero discusses plans of action in a four-wheeler. The
genuine Holmes London, too, is neatly touched in through the
cab-windows—the long trailing skirts and the Sargent hats;
and if Dartmoor is a rather Gothic landscape, so it was in
the original book."
    Greene was less happy with Rathbone's performance, however,
commenting that "What is wrong, surely, is Mr. Rathbone's
reading of the great character: the good humour (Holmes rarely
laughed) and the general air of brisk good health (there is
only one hushed reference to the depraved needle)."
    The Hound of the Baskervilles was a success with both pub-
lic and critics alike. Apart from a seance sequence that was
not in Doyle's story, it followed the original novel closely.
Its opening sequence on a deserted moor with a man running in
terror from the unseen beast and its climax with Holmes going
out alone into the foggy night to track down the "hell hound"
really caught the suspense and mystery of Doyle's story.
There was also a finely realised scene, admirably shot in
silhouette by Leon Shamroy, of an escaped convict being attacked and forced back over a cliff by the ferocious animal.
    Nigel Bruce made the bluffest of Watsons, and Lionel At-
will and John Carradine, two of Hollywood's most talented
heavies, appeared as suspects. An additional bonus in the cast
list was Mary Gordon, who played Holmes's housekeeper to perfection.
    Delighted with the film's success, Fox rushed their new-
found detective team into The Adventures of Sherlock Holmes
(1940). This was supposedly based on the Gillette play, but
deviated from the original by deleting (for the better) the
romantic Miss Alice Faulkner and centring for most of the time
on Moriarty's attempts to commit the super-crime of the century, i.e., steal the crown jewels from the Tower of London.
The film's set pieces were the pursuit of the heroine by a
club-footed killer through a park at night and the fight to
the death between Holmes and Moriarty (played on this occasion
by George Zucco) on top of the Tower. Like its predecessor, it
made a brave attempt to create period atmosphere; top hats and
bustles, oil lamps, hansom cabs, and of course foggy streets
being much in evidence. Perhaps the film's most intriguing
feature was its creation of a secondary villain, a South American thug who killed people with a Patagonian bolas, a weapon
consisting of three long strands of rawhide, each tipped with
a leather-covered lead ball.
    Between 1942 and 1946 Rathbone and Bruce appeared in some
twelve Holmes movies, all of which were made at Universal, who
in February 1942 had acquired the screen rights to Sherlock
Holmes from the Conan Doyle estate. None of the twelve were as
ambitious as the two Fox films, and the studio made the grave
error of updating the stories to the twentieth century. They
also devised several original, below-par screenplays, and only
on the odd occasion did they turn to a Doyle original for
their material. Sherlock Holmes Faces Death (1943), from The
Musgrave Ritual; Pearl of Death (1944), from The Six Napoleons;

and House of Fear (1945), from The Five Orange Pips, were
among those that were adapted from Doyle's short stories.
   In this Universal series of films, ten of which were directed by Roy William Neill, Holmes came up against Nazi
spies, jewel thieves, hypnotists, Eastern heavies, femmes
fatales, and even Moriarty, who, like his famous adversary,
had been reincarnated from the dead. Reginald Denny, George
Zucco, Miles Mander, and Gale Sondergaard all took their
turns as heavies. Moriarty was played by Lionel Atwill (Sherlock Holmes and the Secret Weapon, 1942) and Henry Daniell
(The Woman in Green, 1945).
   When the Rathbone-Bruce partnership came to an end in 1946,
film-makers virtually abandoned Sherlock Holmes as a screen
character, assuming, no doubt correctly, that he had been
over-exposed in the Universal series. Only The Man with the
Twisted Lip (1951), a 35-minute British second feature with
John Longden as Holmes and Campbell Singer as Watson, was
made between 1946 and 1958.
   Hammer Films, a studio famous for their lurid horror productions, was responsible for bringing the detective back to
the screen when they made yet another version of that most
filmed of Holmes stories, The Hound of the Baskervilles (1958).
   There were high hopes for this production, but, although
it included all the familiar props, the atmosphere was completely missing, and the vicious dog described by Doyle as
"that foul, fearsome thing, a great black beast, shaped like
a hound, yet larger than any hound that ever mortal eye rested
upon," was not the least bit foul or fearsome, and its appearance was a distinct anti-climax.
   Peter Cushing, the actor who has played Holmes more than
any other in recent years, captured some of the sharpness of
mind and moodiness of the detective, but for a change it was
the actor playing Watson who was more convincing—Andre Mor-
rell under-playing effectively and making the doctor an intelligent if dogged person.
   The most enjoyable feature of the film was the entirely
irrelevant performance of Miles Malleson as a bumbling old
bishop who collected tarantulas. There was also a fascinating
use of a different pipe to accompany each of Holmes's moods
and problems, e.g., the Tanganyika meerschaum for the most
difficult problems; the briar (filled with shag tobacco from
an old slipper) for furious activity; the long-stemmed rose-
wood for meditative moments; and the cherrywood, smoked during moods of irritation and bad temper.
   The Holmes films of the last decade—they include a couple
of German productions starring Christopher Lee and an odd
little piece called The Double-Barrelled Detective Story
(1965), about Holmes solving a case in the old West—have
generally been an undistinguished bunch. Only A Study in Terror (1965), an intriguingly original film which pitted the
Master against no less an opponent than Jack the Ripper (he
discovers his identity of course, but keeps his name a secret
to save an aristocratic family embarrassment), has in any way
caught the "feel" of the Doyle stories. The seedy atmosphere
of London's vice-ridden East End during the 1880's was well
caught, and the screenplay was often witty and amusing.
   John Neville appeared as Holmes, Donald Houston as Watson,
and Frank Finlay played Lestrade. Robert Morley enjoyed himself for a few minutes as Sherlock's brother, Mycroft, a character rarely played on the screen.
   The most recent film devoted to the great detective is of

course Billy Wilder's The Private Life of Sherlock Holmes (1970). This reveals events that Watson thought wiser not to include in his writings in The Strand Magazine. It has caused controversy in some quarters, not least among dedicated members of The Sherlock Holmes Society of London, by daring to suggest that Holmes and Watson may have enjoyed a homosexual relationship. In point of fact the suggestion is nothing more than a wickedly funny joke allowing Wilder and his co-scriptwriter I. A. L. Diamond to indulge in some of their wittiest scriptwriting in years.

The homosexual inference comes when a retiring Russian ballerina (Tamara Toumanova) offers Holmes a Stradivarius if he will spend a week with her in Venice and help her conceive a child with her body and his brains. In order to extract himself from this embarrassing situation Holmes pleads that, like Tchaikovsky whom the ballerina has already tried (Disastrous! "Women were not his glass of tea."), he and Watson have similar tendencies. It is an irreverent but amusing scene, disappointing only in that Holmes has everything translated to him by the ballerina's manager. Holmes surely would have spoken Russian.

The remainder of the film (the major part) is much more in character and centres on a glamorous Belgian woman (Genevieve Page) who, after escaping from drowning in the Thames, is dumped by a cabby one night on the steps of 221B. The curious case that follows involves some Trappist monks, six midgets, thirty budgerygahs, the Loch Ness monster, and, in the last event, Queen Victoria. It is almost as good a story as a Doyle original, and in its final scene, when Holmes learns of the death of the woman (in reality a German spy) and takes refuge in cocaine, desperately moving. This story implies that the woman spy has almost as strong an emotional effect on Holmes as the mysterious Irene Adler in A Scandal in Bohemia.

Wilder admires Holmes. "To me he is wildly romantic," he says, "elegant, all that Baker Street setting, great sharpness, precision and imagination. One of the great minds of the twentieth century."

During the months that he spent writing the screenplay and shooting the film in England, Wilder concentrated on exploring Holmes's character and personal life and filling in some of the gaps in the Doyle stories. One of the questions that intrigued him most was: "Why was Holmes such a cold-blooded thinking machine and so indifferent to women?"

This practically unknown side of the detective's life is investigated in some detail in the final film, and Wilder succeeds in humanising Holmes without omitting any of his well known characteristics and eccentricities.

The most intriguing question to arise out of The Private Life of Sherlock Holmes is "Where is the rest of it?" At one time it was anticipated that the film would run for three hours and would concentrate on three unpublished cases. Three?

Co-writer Diamond, when interviewed in British Photoplay magazine, said: "We show Holmes at Oxford in love with a girl. It's all very disappointing, and he comes to the conclusion that if the emotions get involved the judgment becomes warped."

But nowhere in the film is Holmes shown at Oxford, and the film begins instead with the ballerina episode. A well known British film magazine has carried photographs that do not appear in the final picture. One, for instance, is of Holmes rowing (obviously at Oxford); a second shows Holmes and Watson with the redoubtable Inspector Lestrade (played by George Benson, but nowhere to be seen in the final film); and a third shows the same trio investigating the case of the "upside-down room."

By using Holmes's own methods of deduction, one would believe that the film was originally intended to be made up of three—or possibly four—stories, all linked together by Holmes's relations with women. The Oxford episode and the case of the "upside-down room" were probably intended to open the picture, and the ballerina episode and the Scottish adventure were meant to take up the middle and final sections.

Good as it is (and the film is good)—the sets of Baker Street and the interiors of 221B are superb; Wilder's direction, the ballerina sequence apart, is romantic and respectful; and the playing of Robert Stephens and Colin Blakely is immaculate—The Private Life of Sherlock Holmes seems to be only half or at best two-thirds of a film. Whether movie-goers will ever get the chance to view the complete, uncut version remains to be seen. Perhaps Billy Wilder will one day run a complete version at a retrospective of his work or especially for Sherlock Holmes fanatics.

ROBERT STEPHENS, in The Private Life of Sherlock Holmes

Editor's note: Some additional papers on Sherlock Holmes in films that have been noted in this Journal:

"Sherlock Holmes on the Screen," by Edward Connor, in Films in Review (31 Union Square, New York, N.Y. 10003), August-September 1961. (See BSJ Inventory, 11:249, December 1961.)

"Always Holmes," by Ray Cabana, Jr., in Kaleidoscope (95 Dearborn St., East Longmeadow, Mass. 01208), Vol. 2, No. 1, 1965. Discusses Rathbone's Sherlock Holmes films.

The Universal Holmes, The Twelve Sherlock Holmes Films Made by Basil Rathbone. . . . A Portfolio of Poster Art, Compliments of The Priory Scholars (c/o P. Christian Steinbrunner, 62-52 82nd St., Middle Village, N.Y. 11379), Christmas, 1966.

"'The Adventures of Sherlock Holmes,'" by Thomas Hammond, BSJ 17:199-201, (December) 1967.

HERE ARE YOUR WAGES

by Norman M. Davis

Sherlock Holmes handed each of the original Baker Street Irregulars a shilling and said, "Here are your wages." As you know, today's Irregulars have as a symbol the Victorian shilling.

This, more than any other, is the coin we associate with Holmes. Though the Canon mentions other British (and a few foreign) coins, the shilling is the one we immediately bring to mind.

A Study in Scarlet introduced "the Baker Street division of the detective police force." It also provided the famed "wages" quote. In The Sign of Four, the Master once more called on the Irregulars, at their usual shilling-per-day wage, in seeking the steam launch that Jonathan Small and Tonga meant to use as a getaway vehicle.

Usually we gloss over the shilling. We accept it as part of the cases' Victorian background. But let us for once take a second look.

The coin is the size of our own quarter-dollar. It was worth just about as much during the 1880's. The edge is reeded, like the edges of U.S. dimes, quarters, and half-dollars of today. Modern shillings (and coins worth five new pence, which replace them) are cupronickel, but the shillings issued while the Master was active were silver.

Queen Victoria's "Young Head" type shillings were issued with only minor portrait changes from 1838 (the year after her reign began) through 1887. On the obverse of the typical shilling used by Sherlock Holmes we find the young queen's left-facing portrait, wearing a double hair-ribbon at the front of her head and with most of her hair gathered at the back in a loose bun or small pony-tail. This portrait was drawn by William Wyon, one of England's great coin-designers.

Around the obverse ("heads") rim, just inside the beaded outer rim, is: "Victoria Dei Gratia Britanniar· Reg· F· D·" This Latin inscription is the last vestige of the old "divine right of kings," for it is translated "Victoria, by the Grace of God Queen of All the Britains, Defender of the Faith."

The reverse was drawn by J. B. Merlen for the shillings of William IV. It simply was continued on Victorian shillings. This has a wreath around the rim; a small open space at the wreath's top is filled by an ornate imperial crown. "One" is above "Shilling" in the centre. At bottom, below the wreath, is the date in tiny numerals.

Some Victorian shillings, especially those issued in

the 1864-1879 period, have an additional number above the date. This is a die identification, and it appears on some other denominations, too.

Collectors are used to finding one feature that I've omitted from this description: national identification. It isn't on the coin at all.

Rule Britannia! England was England, and the world was expected to be able to recognise coins issued by that land on whose domains the sun never set.

In 1887, a new design appeared; this is the "Jubilee Head" type, issued only 1887-1892. It shows an older portrait wearing a small crown; the portrait was enlarged in 1889. The old reverse gave way to a new coat-of-arms design by Sir J. Boehm.

The "Old Head," more often called the "Veiled Head," shows a heavy, aged portrait in a low crown from whose top a veil descends to cover the queen's hair and part of her neck and shoulders. The design is by Sir Thomas Brock. A new reverse drawn by Sir Edward Paynter features three shields within the Garter.

Many shillings remained in use for many years, so we may safely deduce that most of the shillings handled, paid out, or received in daily life by the Master were "Young Head" type coins.

The shilling is absent from the narratives of most cases, but it reappears in The Hound of the Baskervilles. You will recall that the boy who searched through the waste paper of 21 hotels for the newspaper from which Beryl "Stapleton" cut her warning message paid his way with shillings.

Those who have earned the honour already own one of these coins—but can non-Investitured Irregulars do so? They not only can, but probably do—if they happen to be numismatists. Almost every coin collector who owns British coins has a shilling among them.

For non-collectors, there are two easy ways to obtain one of these Sherlockian coins. One is to visit the nearest coin store; the other is to read advertisements in one of the hobby's papers or magazines, find a dealer whose ad offers British shillings, and order one by mail.

Despite their age, Victorian shillings cost very little. Demand for Young Head ones remained low for a long time; dates with mintage of four million or more cost only about $1 in Good condition and $3 to $4 in Fine. I would recommend that you buy the highest condition you can, so as to see as much detail as possible.

Many Victorian shillings are rare, of course. In the early years, mintage often dropped below one million. The rarest date is 1851, with just 470,071 minted; 1872 is the top-minted date, with 8,897,781 struck. All of these coins were struck at the Royal Mint, in London.

In addition to the major design changes, there are a large number of sub-types created by minor design revision done to improve the coin's appearance or to show the queen's advancing age.

But all the coins have three points in common:

1. They are well designed and beautiful.
2. They feature the portrait of an August Lady.
3. And they form a part of the heritage of every coin collector—and every follower of the Master.

[Most of this material appeared in the author's syndicated column, "The Coin Box."]

Under date of 20 May 1964, Dr. Douglas Guthrie, of Edinburgh ("The Field Bazaar"), wrote to this editor:

You may be interested to know that the shilling affixed to my Certificate of Investiture, bearing the head of Queen Victoria as a young woman, has now become rare and is prized by coin collectors. The other silver coins of that period are not as rare. My banker tells me that the silver coins of that time were withdrawn from circulation some years ago (1920 or so) and returned to the Bank of England to be melted down, and the silver content of such coins is now much less than it was.

*   *   *   *   *

What a beautiful coin the shilling is which bears the famous Wyon head! J. C. Horsley, RA—victim of Whistler's savagely contemptuous "Horsley soit qui mal y pense!" —did a sketch of the 19-year old Queen, and William Wyon engraved the head for a medal struck to commemorate the Queen's first visit to the Mansion House. HM liked the Wyon head so much that it was adopted for both the coins and the first postage stamp—the Penny Black. Not until the Golden Jubilee (1887) was the Queen represented as older than eighteen or nineteen.

—Michael Harrison, BSJ 15:195, December 1965, p. 195

A COMING PLAGUE

by W. E. Dudley

Author's note: I am sure that many of us have been concerned and perhaps upset by the coming of Decimalisation.
It strikes me as being one of the most idiotic things
since the United States tried Prohibition. Surely a lot
of tourists have had difficulties with British money, but
most of them have mastered them, and have probably come
to enjoy the daily tussles with pounds, shillings, and
pence. Now it seems that we are going to lose even those
wonderful but elusive guineas. They were the "gaseous
vertebrates" of the financial kingdom. We are not liable
to appreciate all those little peculiarities of the British coinage until we lose them forever. Just because we
love America does not mean that we want the whole world
to imitate her in every detail. I trust the Canon will
survive the change to decimals, and I hope that no one
will ever add a footnote to The Blue Carbuncle helpfully
explaining that 7s. 6d. means 37.50 in the new British
currency—or is it .3750? I don't think that we really
want to know.

*   *   *   *   *

The horrors of Decimalisation, now that it is upon us,
do remind one of H. G. Wells's "generation by generation
the danger came closer," or of the words of the great
Winston Churchill, "the Battle of France is ended, and
the Battle of Britain has begun"—in other words, "it is
upon us."

But why should we be concerned about Decimalisation?
Why man, because of the Irregular Shilling, of course.
In the future will it be the Irregular 5¢? Surely not!
We cannot go on under such conditions.

What would the Master say if he were here? Look at
all the damage that will result. Can we imagine that
dirty crew, the original Baker Street irregulars, being
presented with five cents, the twentieth part of a new
British dollar? God forbid! The whole change to coinage
based on the metric system is part of a diabolic plot,
and one may well suspect that Professor Moriarty is behind it. By Jove, it does sound like the Binomial Theorem
at that.

Why has Britain decided to abandon that treasured and
distinctive money that was so long its own? Because of
the Communists, that's why, and, of course, Moriarty was
one of the first Communists. That is not surprising, for
Karl Marx used to study at the British Museum. We all
know the story, how the Father of Communism sat there,

day after day, while the water dripped down on his shoulders from the faulty sky-light above, and somehow wrote the words that were to set the world in flames. There he must have met Moriarty and infected him with his grandiose dreams of a world in chains and totally subservient to the whims of Marx—and Moriarty. Or were they the same man? This we shall leave for other scholars to decide.

What does Decimalisation mean? Oh, just the end of the world, that's all. You know how it used to be in Britain. After a short visit you could be an expert—on British money, that is.

How delightful it was in 1943! Holding the high rank of private, one could absolutely mystify the newcomers. It went like this: "That will be two quid and three bob." Hearing that, the newly arrived American soldier thought that he might be on Mars. He had no knowledge of these terms, and not the foggiest idea as to their meaning. All that is over now, and no more will we be able to confuse matters by saying, "The price of that is only three guineas." That was enough to send tourists skimming through their phrase books. Now we can only say, "That is 1.05 pounds." How hideous! The Master would be appalled at that kind of nonsense.

Decimalisation is typical of the madness of these declining years of the twentieth century. The London and the Britain of the Master are being destroyed from all sides. Soon it will be like this: "Watson, give these underprivileged lads of Baker Street a full dollar for their information, with the understanding that it is subject to the Miranda decision, and that no information may be used against a mass-murderer unless he understands and signifies by nodding that he is aware that any information which he may give can be used against him in a court of law—subject, of course, to review by higher authority." This sort of thing is highly repulsive, and not only would the Master object strongly to it, but, we suspect, Professor Moriarty would not like it either. No one wants to be the Napoleon of Crime in such a sterile society.

The old British system of pounds, shillings, and pence was part and parcel of the Canon. We cannot go along with people who buy the Pink 'Un for 10¢. Somehow that seems vulgar and possibly obscene.

Look, for instance, at the Gloria Scott, a sturdy ship of 500 tons. Shall we now translate that into kilos? It is not the same. The Master dealt with tons, and a ton is a solid thing; it was part of the Victorian age. Somehow the kilo is mixed up with decay, with the loss of the Empire, and the coming to power of long-haired creeps from Liverpool. No, we will not have it! If the Master were here, he would be disgusted by what is happening.

Anyway, in the story of the Gloria Scott, we are told that the distressed sailors were about five hundred miles from the Cape Verdes, and the African coast was about seven hundred miles to the east. How definite that, and how British. Now are we to say so many kilometres from here to there? The Canon must be preserved inviolate!

Or let us turn briefly to The Musgrave Ritual. In how many lads has that delightful tale first aroused an interest in mathematics? One would not be surprised to learn that one of our astronauts first decided to follow a career in science after reading how our Master unravelled the Ritual. There we learn of that patriarch among oaks with a girth of twenty-three feet. I suppose that one could give that in metres, but who would want to? It would be like giving the dimensions of the ark in feet. We like to read these things as they were in the original.

The Musgrave Ritual is rich in mathematical data, and it stirs even those with no particular interest in figures: an old elm sixty-four feet in height, and (we are told) "the calculation was now a simple one. If a rod of six feet threw a shadow of nine, a tree of sixty-four would throw one of ninety-six . . . ." None of us wants that in the metric system. To do that would be like putting the national anthem into rock and roll. We will not have it. And later in the same chronicle: "A small chamber about seven feet deep and four feet square lay open to us." Would that be helped by conversion to metrics?

What about The Speckled Band: "Nothing was left save a few acres of ground . . ."? Do we want to put that into United Nations gobbledegook?

In A Scandal in Bohemia we have plenty of nice Victorian numerals: "There are three hundred pounds in gold and seven hundred in notes"; "The Church of St. Monica, . . . and half a sovereign if you reach it in twenty minutes." To change these amounts into decimal currency would simply destroy the story. The Canon is sustained by all these little authentic details. The Master cannot be made into a member of the Jet Set.

Again, take a look at the rich detail in The Man with the Twisted Lip: "Near Lee, in Kent. We have a seven-mile drive before us. . . . Here's half a crown. . . . I may add that his whole debts at the present moment . . . amount to £88 10s., while he has £220 standing to his credit in the Capital and Counties Bank. . . . Every pocket stuffed with pennies and half-pennies—421 pennies and 270 half-pennies." Decimalisation would rip the heart out of that part of the Canon. Don't think it can't happen. The Bible has already been put into basic English—and also the speeches of Sir Winston Churchill.

What would happen to A Case of Identity? There the dear lady (Victorian style again) earns two pence a sheet for typing. Now they will want to put that into the decimal system. For you see that those who opt for decimalisation are humourless men, and, furthermore, they have not had the benefit of learning from the Canon.

In A Case of Identity we are also told that the despicable (was he?) Hosmer Angel was about five feet seven inches in height. Would anyone be truly interested in giving us that in metres? Only an outsider would tamper with the Canon in such an outrageous way.

All through the Canon we find these references to the fine old solid British currency: "Four pounds per week" (The Red-Headed League); "How many half-crowns?" (The Dying Detective); and "December 22d. Twenty-four geese at 7s. 6d." (The Blue Carbuncle). Where is the man who would change a word of it?

A footnote from Time, 29 December 1961:

The [English] currency really got unmanageable around 770, when Offa, King of Mercia, decided to issue pennies weighing the equivalent of "32 wheat corns in the midst of the ear." Since the pound sterling was based on a pound of silver, this later came out to 240 pence to the pound.

*   *   *   *   *

EARLY DECIMALISATION (?)
The five-shilling dollar of George III

-83-

THE "SMALL, BUT VERY EFFICIENT, ORGANIZATION"
and Other Small Problems

by Glenn S. Holland

During the twenty-three years that Sherlock Holmes was in practice he often found a confederate helpful. Watson served in this capacity for seventeen years, but sometimes the good doctor's assistance was not enough. As a result Holmes built around himself a group of friends and confidants who served him in various ways. Little is known of this organization, except for an occasional mention by Watson of someone to whom "Holmes often turned for assistance." A definite analysis of Sherlockian assistants is needed, and an attempt to supply this need is made below.

I. The Early Years with the Younger Set: 1881-1889

Soon after settling down in Baker Street, Holmes gained several young allies who were responsive to his every command. When the Master was still relatively unknown, he may have found children more cooperative than adult informants. We may also assume that Holmes took a fatherly attitude toward his protégés.[1]

a. "The irregulars are useful, sometimes, you know."[2] This group of young people was the Master's greatest source of necessary information in the early years. At the price of a shilling Holmes could have a man traced or a launch located. The exact nature of the group is lost in its very irregularity. One problem in particular presents itself to us. According to most chronologists A Study in Scarlet took place in 1881 and The Sign of Four in 1888. These two cases contain the only appearances of the Baker Street irregulars, and they occur more than seven years apart. What were the irregulars doing during that time? There are two possibilities. First, that the irregulars were a constant force, kept up by Holmes and provided with enough material by him to keep them busy in the interim. This is doubtful, since they would in that case appear more often in the writings. It is possible that they were engaged in the unchronicled adventures, but the small number of these which took place in London would hardly keep the lads occupied. The second, and far more likely possibility is that Wiggins (along perhaps with Simpson) was the only true irregular, and he would lay his hands on the other boys (any friends who were available) only when Holmes needed them. He himself probably helped Holmes more than we know, as a single boy is more handy than a dozen. Wiggins, in fact, was probably the boy in buttons of A Case of Identity and Billy of The Valley of Fear in 1888, having been given a position for convenience and gratitude. Billy Wiggins could merely change from his uniform to his street clothes to drum up some irregulars when they were needed.[3] That the irregulars formed a transient organization can be demonstrated by the fact that in both Study and Sign Holmes had to tell the boys that only Wiggins should report.

It is certain that soon after the denouement of The Sign of Four Wiggins was forced to retire from Holmes's service in order to get a job, as befitted a boy of his age. We may be assured that Holmes used his influence to get him started and that he led a successful life after his illustrious beginning.

After Wiggins's departure, Simpson must have taken over as captain, as he is the boy who shadows Henry Wood in The Crooked Man. This boy must have been quite young, since Holmes congratulated him by patting him on the head. The irregulars, as such, were probably permanently disbanded by Dr. Watson after Holmes's disappearance in Switzerland in 1891. It would have been difficult to reorganize them after three years, if indeed Holmes had wanted to do so.

b. Cartwright (of The Hound of the Baskervilles) was "a lad of fourteen, with a bright, keen face." Employed by the district messenger office, he had shown some ability during Holmes's investigation of the manager's little case. This diligent lad, in lieu of Wiggins, searched twenty-three hotels for a single page of The Times. He was also Holmes's source of food and maintained Holmes's contact with London while he was living in Neolithic man's hut on the moor. We may be sure that Holmes often relied on Cartwright from 1888 to 1891 (and perhaps later), and in 1900, when the lad was twenty-six, the Master must have been glad to have him as part of his organization.

c. An older, but invaluable, ally was old Sherman, the bird-stuffer, and the only person besides Mycroft to call the master by his Christian name—i.e., "Mister Sherlock." Baring-Gould[4] took this to mean that Holmes had lived part of his boyhood in the South of London and had come to know and respect old Sherman. It was probably from him that the Master picked up most of his zoological knowledge, although it is doubtful that Sherman was involved in the later "agency."

d. Toby, the half spaniel and half lurcher, would fol-

low "that scent [of creosote] to the world's end." "I
would rather have Toby's help than that of the whole detective force of London."[5] High praise, indeed! We may
be sure that Holmes used Toby many times in his investigations and that the dog was a faithful member of the
Agency as long as he lived.

e. Apart from old Sherman, Fred Porlock would seem to
be the only adult contact of Holmes before the Great
Hiatus. The name was ". . . a nom-de-plume, a mere identification mark, but beneath it lies a shifty and evasive
personality . . . important, not for himself, but for the
great man with whom he is in touch . . . a link in the
chain some little way from its great attachment."[6] For
an occasional ten-pound note Holmes could gain information from the very heart of Moriarty's web. Monsignor
Knox put forth the conjecture that Porlock was the Master's brother, Mycroft.[7] Ruth Douglass said, on the
evidence of "irrepressible" Greek "e's," that Porlock
was none other than Mrs. Cecil Forrester of The Sign of
Four. Lord Donegall, I believe, has cast a vote for
Col. Sebastian Moran. After Moriarty's destruction, all
of his gang were captured, with some very important ex-
ceptions, notably Col. Moran. If Holmes found out who
Porlock was, he surely would have seen that he also went
free, so that after the Master's return (Holmes, of
course, did not anticipate Reichenbach Falls) he would
have a ready contact in the underworld. It is our belief that Porlock was a member of the Agency in the early
1900's.

II. The Transition: 1891-1896

During the first three years of this period Holmes was
presumed dead, and consequently Mycroft was his only
ally. Indeed, for some time after the return, Holmes
went his own way, having only Mycroft and Watson as his
confederates. Perhaps he found that in his absence his
other colleagues had vanished or that, with Professor
Moriarty out of the way, he could handle his cases sans
amis. Whatever his thoughts, by 1896 he had started to
build his formal organization, and it grew steadily from
that time on.

III. The Later Years of the Formal Organization: 1896-1903

The evidence shows that Holmes's organization began
as early as November 1896. It is found in The Sussex
Vampire, where Holmes twice refers to "this Agency," and
Watson notes it is spelled with a capital "A." Since
this is the only time he mentions the Agency as such, we
can assume that this was when the idea for the organization first struck him. It did not come to its zenith un-

til the early years of this century, when Holmes relied on it heavily.

  a. Mercer "is since your [Watson's] time.[9] He is my general utility man who looks up routine business."[10] Not a bright star in our firmament, surely, but a good man, for he freed Holmes for more important work.

  b. "Langdale Pike was his human book of reference upon all matters of social scandal. . . . Holmes discreetly helped Langdale to knowledge, and on occasion was helped in turn."[11] Pike spent his waking hours in his St. James's Street club soaking up information about the indiscretions of the upper classes. He also, apart from earning a four-figure income from the paragraphs he contributed to the garbage papers, was a good friend of both Holmes and Watson, for Watson refers to him as "Langdale." This leads us to believe that Pike first came into Holmes's ken shortly after the return. Baring-Gould[4] disclosed that Langdale Pike was the stage name of the scion of one of England's oldest families and that it was he who first introduced Holmes to the theatre. The Langdale Pikes are two hills in Westmorland overlooking Wordsworth's Gramere. Pike is featured only in The Three Gables, although he undoubtedly helped Holmes in similar circumstances many times.

  c. Shinwell (Porky) Johnson ". . . made his name first as a very dangerous criminal and served two terms at Parkhurst. Finally he repented and allied himself to Holmes, acting as his agent in the huge criminal underworld of London and obtaining information which often proved to be of vital importance."[12] Johnson was undoubtedly Holmes's best agent in the later years. He had greater freedom to operate than a "copper's nark," since Holmes's view of the British law was, as we know, lenient. How might Holmes have come to know Johnson? If the Master had been the one who sent him to Parkhurst, Porky surely wouldn't have been eager to join him as soon as he got out. But how might he have met Holmes or come to know about him? It is doubtful that the Master would have gone to a very dangerous criminal in search of an ally. Instead, it is likely that "the very cunning mind" of Shinwell was once under the influence of Professor Moriarty. Johnson was one of the agents who was caught, and money was found for his bail or his defense. But to Parkhurst he went, harbouring some resentment against the Professor for reasons we may never fathom. When released, circa 1899, he decided against his former life and chose to work for the man who had eliminated his former employer. It is possible that Johnson was

Fred Porlock, but Watson's description of him and his actions seems at odds with Porlock's braggadocio.

Shinwell Johnson's cunning mind joined that of Holmes in 1900 or early 1901,[13] and it may have been partly this assistance that led Holmes to retire for want of a decent challenge.

d. The later Billy of Thor Bridge and The Mazarin Stone was a great help to Holmes and helped fill the gap that Watson's second (or third) marriage made in the detective's life. His deep admiration was sometimes a source of embarrassment to Holmes, but the "wise and very tactful page" was as much a part of the Agency as was Shinwell Johnson.[14]

e. Pompey, "the pride of the local draghounds, . . . a staunch hound on a scent," the dog "between a beagle and a foxhound," was Toby's successor and a great fan of aniseed. Holmes used his services in The Missing Three-Quarter and in many other cases, as yet unchronicled, when his own speed and tracking powers were not up to the demands made upon them.

IV. Some Other Members, Postulated at Best

The following worthy gentlemen were helpful to Holmes in one case at least, and their unique positions were of a nature that would make them invaluable allies. This has led us to believe that they may have been members of the Agency.

a. Mycroft Holmes, albeit not specifically mentioned in this capacity, was undoubtedly part of his brother's organization. The fact that he often was the British Government led him to use his brother as a confidant, and Mycroft was used in the same capacity by Sherlock. What many rôles Mycroft may have played in his brother's career we may never know, for "we also have our diplomatic secrets."

b. Lomax, of the London Library, gave Watson some helpful information on Chinese pottery in The Illustrious Client. A man with such a source of specialised knowledge and with Dr. Watson as a friend may have ended up helping the detective himself in some matters not covered by the information crammed into the crowded stockroom of his mind. We may file Lomax under "Information Source" in the roster of the Agency.

c. Wilson Hargreave[15] of the New York Police Bureau often drew on Holmes's knowledge of criminal London and at least once served the Master in turn. He may have been an official "informer" for the Holmes organization, a member in absentia.

d. Merivale of the Yard[16] is referred to by Holmes as "my friend" in what appears to be a sincere manner. The growth of Holmes's reputation may have mellowed Scotland Yard's attitude towards him to the point that he had this man Merivale as a referral and information source.[17]

V. Conclusion

We have now discovered fourteen members of the "small, but very efficient, organization." The question which now arises is why the Agency was necessary. Watson has given us the answer in The Solitary Cyclist: "From the years 1894 to 1901 inclusive, Mr. Sherlock Holmes was a very busy man. It is safe to say that there was no public case of any difficulty in which he was not consulted during those eight years, and there were hundreds of private cases . . . ." When Holmes's talent was required by so many, he had to find a way to conserve his energy, to be in several places at once. A group of loyal assistants would naturally suggest itself. He had found the irregulars useful in his early career. Why not an expanded organization with underworld contacts, special information sources, and a few general utility men? Being a man of action, he went to work in late 1895. His intense interest and labour are suggested by the fact that late 1895 to late 1896 is known as "The Missing Year." Undoubtedly, Holmes handled cases in that year, but his main energies were used in establishing and testing his confidants. By November 1896, Mycroft, Langdale Pike, Cartwright, Fred Porlock, and Wilson Hargreave were all in action for Holmes. By 1900, Mercer, Johnson, Billy (the latter), Pompey, Lomax, and Merivale had added their talents. Thus, in his busiest years, Sherlock Holmes was still "free to devote his life to examining those interesting little problems which the complex life of London so plentifully presents."

---

1. It has never been speculated on, but there may well have been a group of Montague Street irregulars in the early years whose members might have included some of the Baker Street boys.
2. The Retired Colourman.
3. He probably kept his position a secret so as not to lose his "street-boy" status.
4. In Sherlock Holmes of Baker Street.
5. The Sign of Four.   6. The Valley of Fear.
7. In "The Mystery of Mycroft," in Baker Street Studies.
8. In "The Camberwell Poisoner," Ellery Queen's Mystery

(Continued on page 96)

SOME NOTES ON THE NAME OF THE BROTHERS MORIARTY

by David Skene Melvin

Part I—The References

For years Sherlockians have been puzzled as to why
Watson gave both, if not all three, brothers Moriarty
the same first name. One or another of the brothers Mor-
iarty is mentioned in five of the cases in the Canon:
There are the Professor, the Colonel, and the station-
master. The Professor appears or is referred to in The
Valley of Fear, His Last Bow, The Missing Three-Quarter,
The Final Problem, and The Empty House; the Colonel in
The Final Problem; and the station-master in The Valley
of Fear.

The Professor is spoken of in The Valley of Fear as
"Professor Moriarty," or simply as "Moriarty" or the
"Professor." Holmes says, "You have heard me speak of
Professor Moriarty?" and Watson replies, "The famous
scientific criminal, as famous among crooks as . . . he
is unknown to the public."[1] It is obvious from the
tenor of the conversation in this instance that Holmes
knows that Watson is cognisant of the Professor and that
therefore that individual can be referred to in an informal and familiar manner. It is not as if Holmes were
introducing the subject of the Professor to Watson for
the first time; it is important to realise this. In His
Last Bow, Holmes reminisces familiarly about Professor
Moriarty, more to himself than for the benefit of Von
Bork, and in The Missing Three-Quarter he casually mentions Moriarty in a way that leaves no doubt that he has
no fears that Watson will misunderstand. Bear in mind
the circumstances in both cases in which the Professor
is mentioned.

In The Final Problem, Holmes introduces Watson to the
existence of the Professor and speaks of him as "Professor Moriarty," "the Professor," or "Moriarty." When
Holmes is visited by the Professor he speaks sarcastical-
ly to that person as "Mr. Moriarty." Note that in all
these instances two old friends are conversing familiarly together. (I allow myself license to so describe the
exchange between the Professor and the Master.) In The
Empty House, Holmes and Watson refer to him between themselves as "Moriarty" and "Professor Moriarty." It is
only towards the end of this tale that for the only time
in the Canon the Professor is referred to as "Professor
James Moriarty." Note that the man's title is included
and that he is not referred to solely as "James Moriarty."
It is necessary to examine carefully the circumstances

be known, however, professionally, as Mme. Norman-Neruda."[9]
Note the use of the hyphen in Grove's. Park's entry is
in error, but we cannot blame him too much for taking
"Norman Neruda" as a given and a last name in that order,
for other Sherlockians have been making a similar mistake in
another Canonical instance for a great many years.

My attention was drawn to Park's error for two reasons:
One, I was familiar with the violinist and knew the proper
form of her name, and two, my own surname is a compound
name with two words and no hyphen, "Skene Melvin," and I
have become inured to the vagaries of usage to which
such a compound name can be subjected. This started me
on my present train of thought. I reread the Canon and
checked other entries in Park, not in an effort to find
fault with his encyclopædia, but rather to use it as an
example of American usage in the indexing of compound
names.

Having a compound name myself, and being a professional librarian, I am familiar with the correct modes of
address regarding such surnames, either with or without
a hyphen, and the vagaries of indexing and cataloguing
entries regarding such names. It must be realised that
all compound surnames do not have, nor need to have, a
hyphen. See the entry for Professor George Kitson Clark,
the British historian, in Who's Who. Further, compound
names that are hyphenated do not always have the hyphen
included, nor are they invariably listed under the first
part of the compound name. Indeed, to someone who does
not know personally the bearer of an unhyphenated compound name, it is not unusual for him (or her) to assume
that only the last part is the surname. I had a personal
experience with this via the Library of Congress in connection with the added entry that institution made for me
as co-compiler of a particular work. Its cataloguers
made the erroneous assumption I have just mentioned.

There are two varieties of compound names, British
and European. To take the latter first, the operative
part of a Continental European compound name is the first
part, the second part being adjectival. For example,
General Tadeo Bor-Komarowski, the Polish underground
leader who led the Warsaw uprising against the Germans
in 1944, is commonly referred to simply as General Bor.
British usage, on the other hand, is exactly the opposite. The important and operative part of a British compound name is the last part. There is in British formal
etiquette a formula for the use of compound names. When
one is speaking to a person with a compound name or about
that person in a familiar manner to others acquainted
with him (or her), one uses only the last part of the

name; contrariwise, when one is speaking of a person
with a compound name to others unfamiliar with the person, one uses both parts; in short, last part only in
direct address, both parts in indirect address.

Now, Holmes's clients came by and large from the
aristocracy. Here a definition is in order, and once
again Continental European and British terminology and
usage differ. On the Continent, the aristocracy is synonymous with the nobility and includes only that class.
All descendants of a titleholder also hold his title.
For example, the sons of a Baron Wolfgang Prerau would
all likewise be styled Baron, as his daughters would be
Baroness, and his sons' sons would each be entitled to
be styled Baron. In the United Kingdom, however, the
term "aristocracy" encompasses two classes—the nobility
and the gentry. The nobility are the peerage, those heads
of a family bearing a title. Only the actual titleholder
is noble, while all his brothers, sisters, sons, daughters, etc., are legally commoners. For example, let us
take plain John Smith, Esq. For services to the state
he is elevated to be the Earl Wookey of Mendip. His
brother Hugh remains plain Hugh Smith, Esq. John has
two sons, Michael and George, and a daughter Felicity.
Since his father is an Earl, Michael is by courtesy known
as a Baron, let us say styled "Baron Overton." Note that
this is a courtesy title only and has no legal status.
The second son and the daughter are respectively the Hon.
George Smith and the Hon. Felicity Smith. When George
marries and has a son Frederick, that lad will be simply
Frederick Smith, Esq. The death of Frederick's grandfather would not change this, and he would remain Frederick Smith, Esq., while his uncle Michael was a peer of
the realm.

To return to matters Holmesian, the Master's clients
came largely from the aristocracy—the nobility and gentry, i.e., the upper classes. In the milieu of Victorian
Britain, compound names were not uncommon. It was the
practice to perpetuate the family names of heiresses by
linking their names with those of their husbands, sometimes with, and sometimes without, a hyphen. It should
be noted that the literary agent himself had a compound
name. Sir Arthur Conan Doyle is properly "Conan Doyle,
Sir Arthur," not "Doyle, Sir Arthur Conan." Compound
names are quite common in the Canon, but such being relatively uncommon, not to say rare, in the United States,
I am not surprised that they have not been recognised as
such, even when it is obvious. In Wisteria Lodge, there
is Mr. John Scott Eccles, whose surname is quite obviously,
from the way and manner in which it is used, the compound
name of Scott Eccles, even though he is referred to as

both "Mr. Scott Eccles" and "Mr. Eccles." Even more obvious is the compound surname of Arthur Cadogan West in The Bruce-Partington Plans. That unfortunate young man is referred to as "Arthur Cadogan West," "young West," and mostly as "Cadogan West." Park in his encyclopædia assumed, as would most Americans, that that junior clerk's surname was West, with Arthur and Cadogan as his given names, and that he preferred to use his second given name rather than his first. This hypothesis, however, is proven wrong by Sherlock Holmes's own words upon announcing that he and Watson are leaving to visit the boy's parents. "Now we shall turn to the Cadogan Wests,"[10] he says. If Arthur's second given name was Cadogan, and his surname merely West, no one would refer to his family as the "Cadogan Wests." The only given name of the clerk that we are cognisant of is Arthur, and his surname is Cadogan West. Q. E. D. Thus we can readily see that compound names are taken for granted in the Canon and appear regularly.

What is my point in all this? In The Final Problem, Holmes describes the Professor as "a man of good birth and excellent education."[11] He is obviously upper middle class in the context of the times. I submit that the Colonel and the Professor did not have the same first name of James, but that all three brothers Moriarty did have the compound surname of James Moriarty. Both James and Moriarty are well known Irish surnames,[12] and the combination of James Moriarty is both a probable and a possible Irish family compound surname. Recalling the Master's dictum to the effect that when you have excluded the impossible, whatever remains, no matter how improbable, must be true, I can see no objection to my hypothesis. Henceforth, the Colonel, the Professor, and the station-master shall always be to me the brothers James Moriarty, given names unknown.

1. The Valley of Fear, in The Complete Sherlock Holmes Long Stories, London: John Murray [1962], p. 409.
2. The Empty House, in The Complete Sherlock Holmes Short Stories, London, John Murray [1961], p. 579-580.
3. Ibid., p. 580.
4. The Sussex Vampire, in The Complete Sherlock Holmes Short Stories, pp. 1178-1179.
5. The Valley of Fear, op. cit., p. 420.
6. The Final Problem, in The Complete Sherlock Holmes Short Stories, p. 536.
7. A Study in Scarlet, in The Complete Sherlock Holmes Long Stories, p. 37.
8. Park, Orlando: Sherlock Holmes, Esq. and John H.

Watson, M.D.: An Encyclopædia of Their Affairs,
[Evanston, Ill.:] Northwestern University Press, 1962,
pp. 127-128.
9. Grove's Dictionary of Music and Musicians, 5th ed.,
London: Macmillan, 1954-1961, Vol. 6, pp. 50-51.
10. The Bruce-Partington Plans, in The Complete Sherlock
Holmes Short Stories, p. 982.
11. The Final Problem, op. cit., p. 539.
12. MacLysaght, Edward: Irish Families: Their Names, Arms,
and Origins, Dublin: Hodges Figgis, 1957.
———: More Irish Families, Galway: O'Gorman, 1960.

———: Supplement to Irish Families, Baltimore: Gene-
alogical Book Co., 1964.

THE "SMALL, BUT VERY EFFICIENT, ORGANIZATION"

(Continued from page 89)

Magazine, February 1947.
9. Circa January 1903, although possibly much earlier
without Watson's knowledge.
10. The Creeping Man.   11. The Three Gables.
12. The Illustrious Client.
13. "During the first years of the century he became a
valuable assistant" (The Illustrious Client).
14. It was suggested by Bruce Dettman ("In the Master's
Footsteps," The Pontine Dossier, Vol. 1, No. 2,
December 1967) that Billy fared better than we previously knew and became Solar Pons. I offer no comment.
15. The Dancing Men.   16. Shoscombe Old Place.
17. I am somewhat hesitant in my judgment. Although
Gregson (in The Red Circle) and Lestrade (in Lady
Frances Carfax and The Three Garridebs) are more respectful to Holmes than they were in A Study in
Scarlet and subsequent cases, the official Yard delay in Lady Frances Carfax nearly cost said lady her
life.
        *   *   *   *   *

I owe much in this article to Appointment in Baker Street,
by the late Edgar W. Smith, and to the late William S.
Baring-Gould.

JOHN CLAY AND LEBANON, PENNSYLVANIA, U.S.A.

by Richard W. Foster

It is stated unequivocally by Peter Jones, the official police agent: "John Clay, the murderer, thief,
smasher, and forger. He's a young man, . . . but he is at
the head of his profession."

Jabez Wilson describes John Clay as "Small, stout-built,
very quick in his ways, no hair on his face, though he's
not short of thirty."

What does Jones mean by "He's a young man," and what
does Wilson mean by "not short of thirty?" I would guess
32. After all, Clay had been to Eton and Oxford, and I
presume he finished at Eton in order to matriculate at
Oxford. If he had been at Oxford, as Jones says, it does
not mean he received a degree, but he could scarcely
have started his career of murderer, thief, smasher, and
forger while at Eton, although he may have begun it at
Oxford (forgery, anyway). Let us assume he was 20, bored
with Oxford, when he took up thievery and murder and became a forger and smasher. (Incidentally, a smasher is
one who passes counterfeit money.)

So we see this grandson of a royal duke embarked on a
life of remarkable crime. And he achieves all this in
about ten years. And yet Jones states: "I've been on his
track for years and have never set eyes on him yet."

There is only one explanation for this. He was one of
Professor Moriarty's boys, and well protected. No ordinary criminal he, grandson of a royal duke (my guess is
the Duke of Cambridge) and one who was obviously a trifle
over-educated. Could it be possible that one so gifted in
crime could escape the notice of the Professor, especially if he escaped the eye of Jones? Jones also says: "His
brain is as cunning as his fingers, and though we meet
signs of him at every turn, we never know where to find
the man himself." This latter phrase seems an understatement. Jones goes on: "He'll crack a crib in Scotland
one week, and be raising money to build an orphanage in
Cornwall the next." Why want to arrest such a man in the
dead of night in a bank vault? Why not simply ascertain
when he is in Jabez Wilson's shop and seize him? This,
of course, is due to the Sherlockian propensity for melodrama.

But the essence of the whole adventure is to understand that Moriarty was badly deceived by this young man.
In the attempt to steal money on such a grandiose scale
one may detect great flights of imagination, but in the
execution we perceive only the most juvenile understand-

ing of human intelligence and credulity.

Therefore it is obvious that Clay, unstable, childish, full of vanity, had, somehow or other, learned of a way to rob a bank by burrowing underground. Just as the military had plans for a possible invasion of the Kingdom of Scandinavia, so must Professor Moriarty have pored over plans and ideas of his own. I see John Clay, after a Moriarty staff meeting, saying to himself, "Now that's an idea—dig a hole and rob a bank." But it is one thing to crack a crib in Scotland one week and raise money in Cornwall the next under the tutelage, guidance, and discipline of Moriarty, and another to organise your own crime.

Consider that remarkable fact, the dissolving of the Red-Headed League before, as Baring-Gould points out, it had accomplished its purpose. One reason is, of course, the contempt of John Clay for Jabez Wilson, which was unbounded. For who could not feel contempt for this numskull so readily taken in by the hoax of the Red-Headed League? Perhaps Clay's money ran out and he was forced to give up the room at 7 Pope's Court. But this seems hardly likely. I think he merely could not bear to pay one more shilling to Jabez Wilson. It was arrogance and vanity which led to his downfall. Moriarty would never have permitted anything so gauche.

But here one must consider the greatest enigma of the adventure—Lebanon, Pennsylvania, U.S.A.

The invention of a Red-Headed League shows a touch of genius; the premature dissolving of it shows merely petulance and impatience. But what does the invention of Ezekiah Hopkins reveal? And, above all, the reference to Lebanon, Pennsylvania? How could John Clay, forger, smasher, murderer, and thief, of Eton and Oxford, ever hear of Lebanon? This serious question must somehow be resolved. In order to do so, a visit to Lebanon seemed in order. It is a small city today, but in 1850 the population was 2178; in 1860, 5438; 1870, 6727; in 1880, 8787. In those days a certain amount of small manufacturing took place. Just how an Englishman ("This American had started from London when he was young . . .") could make a fortune in Lebanon seems beyond comprehension. In addition, why he should settle there if he made his fortune elsewhere is also difficult to understand. A visit to Lebanon will reveal to you a typical southeastern Pennsylvania town: much red brick, no architecture worth seeing, but some pleasant, shaded streets. A call at the public library of Lebanon was significant. The librarian is a native who assured me that Hopkins is a name seldom if ever met with in that part of the world. In addition, I have perused Dr. Egle's **History of Lebanon County**, published in 1883, and can find no Hopkins of any kind among the lists of directors of stone, lumber, and feed companies, nor among Civil War names.

How then did John Clay's imagination create this philanthropist from Lebanon? Baltimore, Boston, New York, Philadelphia—they are places which could have produced philanthropists—but John Clay must pick Lebanon, Pennsylvania. Again, the only proper explanation is Clay's temperament. His invention of the league was outré, a faraway place of no importance is in order; the choice is due to contempt and disdain.

I have searched guide-books, Pennsylvania genealogies, and local histories, and in none of them can I find anything out of the ordinary about Lebanon. There is one possible answer: Lebanon is possibly not more than 25 miles from Vermissa Valley. It is not in the coal region, but south of it. And yet it is close enough to have supplied a Scowrer or two.

If we accept Baring-Gould's chronology, The Valley of Fear occurred in January 1888, and The Red-Headed League in October 1887, only three months previously. You will recall Holmes's remarks to Barker at the end of The Valley of Fear: "Having an English job to do, they took into partnership, as any foreign criminal could do, this great consultant [Moriarty] in crime. From that moment their man was doomed. At first he would content himself by using his machinery in order to find their victim. Then he would indicate how the matter might be treated." All this, no doubt, took time, particularly the finding of Birdy Edwards, alias Douglas, at Birlstone. And what did Ted Baldwin do while Moriarty's men searched? He waited and made friends with those of his own ilk. Surely, Ted Baldwin and John Clay hit it off immediately— by temperament, desire, and calling, they shared much. And during one of their talks, Baldwin mentions his boyhood town, Lebanon, Pennsylvania. And so, as John Clay invents Ezekiah Hopkins, he places him, sardonically, as from Lebanon, Pennsylvania, U.S.A.

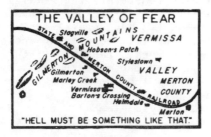

THE VALLEY OF FEAR

"HELL MUST BE SOMETHING LIKE THAT."

APROPOS OF CONAN DOYLE

by Maurice Leblanc
Translated by Dr. Kai-Ho Mah

If an author of detective stories agreed to take this wonderful device of deductions and observations from which he resolves all problems, and turn it against one of his novels, I think that from a strictly detective point of view there wouldn't be much left of the novel. Let Sherlock Holmes take his best magnifying glass and coldly examine the path which my friend Conan Doyle, by means of marvelous reasoning, has made him travel to reach the truth, and he will see, not without amazement, that this path would never have led him to the truth. The lines of reasoning which guided him were usually falsified by an imperceptible error, or cut off by an obstacle, or linked together by the most arbitrary connections.

How different is reality! A crime is committed. The police, immediately in action, are forced to go from the unknown to the known, and from an impenetrable shadow towards a clear region. The novelist acts in the reverse order. He sets out from the point of arrival, which he himself has chosen, in full light, and he retraces his steps, setting traps along the way, blurring the tracks, and accumulating darkness. Having arrived at the point of departure, he places the reader in the expert hands of a Sherlock Holmes, who has to do no more to succeed than to turn up some clues left about in good places, than to pick up some cigarette butts, than to ferret, analyse, deduce, go through some dictionaries, and hunt in some old newspapers for some articles prepared by Conan Doyle. If he is perplexed, he lights his pipe and discerns the answer to the riddle in the blue curls of smoke.

Such is the process. The detective novel, or to speak more precisely, the novel of mysterious adventures, is a construction in air. It is a problem that one concocts oneself, that one complicates to the farthest limit, and that one resolves before the reading public, saying to it constantly, "Is it strange enough? How ingenious my detective must be to unravel such a plot!"

So then, one will object, here is an author known all over the world, whose work, translated into every language, has been relished for more than thirty years by the elite as well as by the crowd. And this work is really nothing but illusion!

The fame of Conan Doyle, I shall reply, does not come from his qualities as a detective and his conspicuous

SILVER BLAZE

Some Identifications with Respect to Dartmoor

A Paper Delivered to The Five Orange Pips

by Evan M. Wilson

Gentlemen, this evening I want to take you on a journey to a part of England that is a setting for two of the Sherlock Holmes stories—Dartmoor. I refer, of course, to The Hound of the Baskervilles and to Silver Blaze, and we are going to undertake this journey in full awareness of the ominous warning received by Sir Henry Baskerville:

as You value your life or your reason keep away from the moor

I will be talking mostly about Silver Blaze, but also a bit about The Hound of the Baskervilles, and I will end up by indulging in one of my old hobbies, nineteenth-century British railways.

As in the famous case where Holmes's attention was first attracted by the depth to which the parsley had sunk into the butter on a warm day, so was my eye caught by certain geographical discrepancies with respect to Silver Blaze when I was recently rereading this adventure in preparation for a meeting of our Washington Scion Society, The Red Circle, at which it was to be the "adventure of the evening." As I read along, I noticed that in the train going down from Paddington to Exeter Holmes says that the incident occurred in "the north of Dartmoor," while we are told that "the little town of Tavistock . . . lies, like the boss of a shield, in the middle of the huge circle of Dartmoor." We are also told, when the locations of the two training stables, Colonel Ross's King's Pyland and Lord Backwater's Capleton, are pinpointed, that Capleton lies to the westward of King's Pyland. Now it happens that I have some personal familiarity with this area, and on reflection I recalled that Tavistock does not lie in the centre of the moor, but on its western edge. Nor could the region where the adventure takes place be described as the northern part of Dartmoor. I also concluded that the events recounted in the story would make much more sense if Capleton could be regarded as east, not west, of King's Pyland. In other words, as far as these points are concerned, I am tempted to use Holmes's words as he pulled Watson out of a railway carriage at a suburban station when they were returning to London from Abbey Grange: "It's wrong—it's all wrong—I'll swear that it's wrong."

I should explain that while I was at Oxford I played cricket, and every spring our eleven, known as the New College Nomads, made a tour of Devon and Cornwall, using Tavistock as a headquarters. These experiences of village cricket, incidentally, have given me every reason to

agree with Holmes's characterisation, in The Missing
Three-Quarter, of amateur sport as "the best and soundest
thing in England." I was therefore prompted to get out
my atlas and my books of reference and attempt a more
precise identification of some of the localities mentioned in Silver Blaze, particularly King's Pyland, the
racing stable of Colonel Ross, "the well-known sportsman,"
and the home of Silver Blaze. I have put down the results
of my research on a rough map which I have here.   In

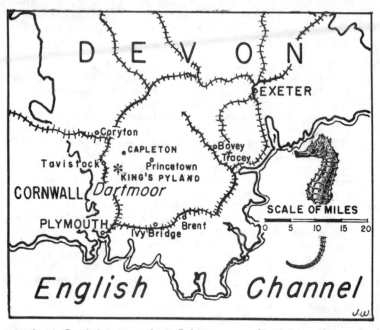

passing, I might say that I have consulted a number of
dictionaries and encyclopædias but have drawn a complete
blank as to the meaning of the word "Pyland" in King's
Pyland. Perhaps some of you can enlighten us.
    I have also consulted a number of commentaries on the
Canon in an effort to ascertain how the experts have
identified King's Pyland in the past. I find that Michael
Harrison in his book, In the Footsteps of Sherlock Holmes,
makes the statement, for which he does not adduce any
proof whatsoever, that King's Pyland "can be identified
as Princetown." This statement is repeated, without comment, by William Baring-Gould in his monumental work,
The Annotated Sherlock Holmes. Speaking of Baring-Gould,
I think it is of interest that the basic work of reference on Dartmoor, titled A Book of Dartmoor and published
by Methuen in the year 1900, should have been written by
the Reverend Sabine Baring-Gould, a nineteenth-century
exponent of "muscular Christianity" and known to us all

as the author of the hymn, "Onward Christian Soldiers." No doubt they are related. [Yes; grandfather and grandson.—Ed.]

At all events, my researches have convinced me that King's Pyland cannot possibly be identified with Princetown. The latter is described in one book on Dartmoor as "the one substantial settlement on the open moor," while my encyclopædia calls it a "thriving town." My guidebook says that it contains three hotels, so it is evidently a place of some size. It is, of course, as all readers of The Hound of the Baskervilles know, the site of a famous prison, originally built to house French and American prisoners during the Napoleonic wars and the War of 1812, and designed to hold 9,000 men. It was from this prison that Seldon, the Notting Hill murderer, had escaped shortly before Dr. Watson and Sir Henry Baskerville arrived on the moor.

I do not see how this place could correspond to the location described in Silver Blaze. I will take the liberty of reading to you the two passages in which the setting of the adventure is given:

"The country round is very lonely, but about half a mile to the north there is a small cluster of villas which have been built by a Tavistock contractor for the use of invalids and others who may wish to enjoy the pure Dartmoor air. Tavistock itself lies about two miles to the west, while across the moor, also about two miles distant, is the larger training establishment of Capleton, which belongs to Lord Backwater, and is managed by Silas Brown. In every other direction the moor is a complete wilderness, inhabited only by a few roaming gipsies."

And again:

". . . our driver pulled up at a neat little red-brick villa with overhanging eaves, which stood by the road. Some distance off, across a paddock, lay a long grey-tiled outbuilding. In every other direction the low curves of the moor, bronze-coloured from the fading ferns, stretched away to the skyline, broken only by the steeples of Tavistock and by a cluster of houses away to the westward, which marked the Capleton stables."

I think it highly significant that in neither of these passages is there any mention of the famous prison, described by observers as "vast" or "grim," and as dominating the landscape for miles around Princetown. In fact, the prison is not mentioned anywhere in the adventure. It seems to me that the whole effect of the words I have quoted is to create an impression of isolation, of a place far removed from any other habitation. Moreover, according to the map, Princetown is a good eight or nine miles, not two miles, from Tavistock—and we must bear in mind that Watson speaks of being able to see the steeples of Tavistock from King's Pyland. The use of the word "steeples" is accurate, by the way, for my Baedeker confirms my recollection that Tavistock contains a tenth-century abbey, a Unitarian chapel, and a parish church.

So, I would submit that King's Pyland is not identical with Princetown, but should be located in an isolated location in the open country, some two miles east of Tavistock, as indeed the text states it to be. I have marked this approximate location with an asterisk on my map. I would also suggest that it would seem more logical to place Capleton to the east of King's Pyland. If it were two miles to the west, as we are asked to believe, its location would coincide with that of Tavistock.

So much for geography. I would now like to invite your attention to the fact that the main line of the Great Western Railway, now the Western Region of British Railways, does not pass through Tavistock, which, as I have indicated on my map, is on a branch line. This would mean that Holmes and Watson would have had to change trains at Exeter or Plymouth and would account for Watson's statement that it was evening before they arrived at Tavistock. It would also suggest that it is highly unlikely that they would have been able to take the "night train" back to London that same evening.

Plymouth, I may add, is the principal town of this entire area, and so it would be quite natural for Holmes to ask Mrs. Straker if he had not met her at a garden-party there, or for Sir Henry to bring in decorators and furnishers from there to refurbish Baskerville Hall. A couple of further points occur to me with reference to The Hound of the Baskervilles. If the "small wayside station" at which Watson and Sir Henry alighted on their way to the Hall is taken to be either Ivy Bridge or Brent, as mentioned in Baring-Gould's book, these points are on the main line of the Great Western Railway, to the south of the moor. If, however, we accept Baring-Gould's own preference for Coryton, to the north and west of the moor, it is located on the branch line through Tavistock, and again a change of trains would be required. I cannot, in any event, agree with Baring-Gould's identification of the Coombe Tracey of The Hound with Bovey Tracey, since it also is located on a branch line, and it is difficult to see how it could be there that "the London express came roaring into the station," and Lestrade sprang from a first-class carriage, to be greeted by Holmes and Watson. Finally, reverting once more to Silver Blaze, I entirely concur in Baring-Gould's comment that Holmes, Watson, and Colonel Ross could hardly have been returning to Victoria Station in London from the races at Winchester. The station for Winchester, plainly, is Waterloo.

In concluding these few superficial comments, I would like to emphasise once again that there still exist many lapses in the Canon which deserve to be subjected to the strong light of scholarly research.

DEVONSHIRE AGAIN

by Bartlett Dale Simms

For some time I have wanted to share some views and questions with other Sherlockians, and although the site and locale of the story of The Hound has been exhaustively investigated by expert researchers, nevertheless I want to pose some questions to all who are interested, and please remember that I have been reluctant to write about this subject.

One can hardly uncover more than William S. Baring-Gould did with his article[1] in which he says that Widdicombe of Fair fame is Coombe Tracey, and Lew House, or Hall, is Baskerville Hall, or Dr. Julian Wolff in his pinpointing the actual locale of The Hound of the Baskervilles.[2]

I think that Baring-Gould might have been disappointed that the scene of The Hound was not laid in Yorkshire rather than in Devon. Rev. Sabine Baring-Gould was a Yorkshire historical writer, and I am certain that William Baring-Gould was as familiar with Yorkshire's North Riding as he was with Devonshire. His evident love of Yorkshire and his statement that Sherlock Holmes was born in the North Riding of Yorkshire[3] would seem to indicate that perhaps he would have liked to see the site of The Hound in that area because of the austere atmosphere and the lofty fells and the small hamlet-type villages. Also, "The Surgeon of Gaster Fell," by Sir Arthur Conan Doyle, would suppose some knowledge and love of the Yorkshire moors.

Robert Holmes (was he a forbear of Sherlock Holmes?) was a Yorkshire writer and the author of Farquhar Frankheart; or Incidents in the Introduction of Methodism into Yorkshire, a Tale (Ward, 1860). This might account for Sherlock's reluctance to take part in any formal religious practice. ("Art in the blood is liable to take the strangest forms.") Sir Arthur Conan Doyle must have visited the North Riding when he was a student at Edinburgh.

In the Spring 1967 issue of The Sherlock Holmes Journal, Roger Lancelyn Green identifies Lustleigh as Baskerville Hall. Lustleigh is approximately three miles north of Bovey Tracey and has a good claim. It is also about 14 miles from Merrymeet and near Hay Tor and Hound Tor and Grimspound. This house was used as Baskerville Hall in the first talkie of The Hound in 1932.

Now then, I ask this: Has Newton Tracey been considered as a possibility for the locale of The Hound? It is a parish and village about twenty miles north of Bratton Covelly. Could some of the booming sounds that Stapleton said were possibly bitterns—could these have come from the south of Oakehampton near Yes Tor? This is the artillery practice range on my map.[4]

Then there is this to consider: Milverton in Devonshire—did this inspire another Canonical tale? Also, Black Dog, a village off A373, could this have suggested the subject for The Hound? Also, Holcombe Rogus, not far from Templeton and Templeton Bridge, again near A373 on my map.

True, Newton Tracey and Bovey Tracey are on a railway. Did Sir Henry Baskerville and Watson arrive at the railway station and take the Baskerville coach to the Hall? If so, how could they have been near Princetown? Of course, the wardens were possibly searching the area from Bittern Hill on the north to Butterdon Hill in the south, and Tavistock on the west to Totnes on the east, with a high concentration around Yes Tor and Lynch Tor. There are on my map hut circles—this must be the site where Sherlock sequestered himself until Watson found him.

Then possibly the area could be bounded as follows: north by Yes Tor, west by Cox Tor, east by Corndon Tor, and south by Stall Moor and Ford Moor. The village of Themar Coombe—and near this the village of Merrymeet—could these be Coombe Tracey and Merripit House? The elevation would seem to be against this, as there is scarcely any area above 600 feet.

I should like to quote from Down Devon Lanes, by Herbert Carey, May 1929: "I had always thought of a moor as a wide, gently undulating land clothed in heather and gorse. Nothing like it. Dartmoor is a great granite bulge, torn into wrinkles of valleys by the storms of centuries. The roads run along the hilltops when they can. A man wandering in the hollows is lost before he knows it. The turns are so infinite that the prospects are all alike. Sooner or later, he finds the mire. They do not seem dangerous at first, these Dartmoor bogs. Brilliant, rug-like patches of neat grass, on which those who have an abiding faith in Providence may progress by bounding. Not frightening at all at first. One idly tosses a bit of flat stone on the green mat. Nothing happens for a time. Then a shiver passes over the surface. The stone sinks. One ventures to thrust a stick into the mire. It is drawn down as if a hand were pulling from below. What chance has a man wandering blindly through a Dartmoor fog? There are places on the moor that dogs will not go near, so reputable men have said. Ghost or no ghost, I know how the dogs feel. Reason pointed out that herds of the Dartmoor ponies capered about the hills—although the pony is no longer an economic proposition and so is gradually disappearing—and that a pony is presumably as susceptible to the presence of wandering demons as is a dog. No matter. We fear the moor. Not even the beery mutterings of the drinkers in the Three Crowns Inn at Chagford reassured us" [italics mine].

He makes some reference to Princetown: "We shuddered through Princetown where the convict settlement is, and were afraid. Lest someone suspect me of undue sentiment I offer in self-defense that I have been familiar as a visitor and reporter with more than one penitentiary; but this Dartmoor prison is cold and bare. Drivers are directed not to stop their cars in the vicinity and holiday-makers may not use their cameras. We met a group of wardens in Princetown's streets. They seemed cold, precise, muscular men. As they tramped past they seemed steel and bone and muscle husks of men. A squad of convicts hurried past—clunk, clunk, clunk—almost at the double, with the regularity of an iron-shod machine. Their faces were gray and bleak and hideously alike."

Chagford, population 1715, near Moreton Hampstead—is this also in the Grimpen area? Almost ten miles to the west are the hut circles. Twenty miles by A30 is Bratton Clovelly. Note the proximity of Chagford to the area described. I submit that Sir Arthur Conan Doyle went there on holiday—since it is a tourist town and there would have been side trips to all of these little hamlets and areas—after hearing tales of the supernatural at the Three Crowns Inn.

Sir Arthur Conan Doyle used Sir Richard Cabell, Lord of the Manor Brooke, Parish of Buckfastleigh, as the inspiration for Sir Hugo Baskerville, the inspiration of the original tale. His place is about ten or fifteen miles northwest of Totnes, which is about the eastern limit of the area. At Sir Richard Cabell's death, black hounds were reported breathing fire and smoke over Dartmoor, howling around the manor house.

To all the experts on The Hound of the Baskervilles, to paraphrase Dr. James Mortimer: "I trust, sirs, that I have not inadvertently . . . ."

---

1. "'Dr. Watson Has Gone to Widecombe,'" BSJ (NS) 15:8-14, (March) 1965.
2. The Sherlockian Atlas, 1952, Plate X.
3. Sherlock Holmes of Baker Street.
4. Newnes Motorists' Touring Maps & Gazetteer, Maps No. 84, 85, 86, and 89.

THE IMMORTALITY OF SHERLOCK HOLMES

by D. F. Rauber

While many call Sherlock Holmes immortal, few pursue the implications of the statement. But if we take the designation seriously, as all true Holmesians must, simple logic forces the conclusion that Holmes existed before his local manifestation in nineteenth-century England, and that he exists today. The latter has been recognised, although in a mocking, non-believing way, by Edmund Wilson in his essay, "Why Do People Read Detective Stories?" (conveniently available in the collection, Classics and Commercials). Wilson notes the close similarities between Holmes and Nero Wolfe; indeed, he considers Wolfe only "a dim and distant copy of an original." This curiously Platonic phrase suggests an archetypal phenomenom, and that is exactly what I think exists. My contention is that Wolfe is Holmes; is the contemporary manifestation or appearance of a literally immortal figure, the archtype Holmes. Holmes has undergone a series of metempsychoses, but he has never been absent from the human scene.

My particular interest here, however, is not the present, but the past, the investigation of earlier incarnations of Holmes, especially very ancient ones. I do not pretend to be exhaustive; I wish merely to lay the foundations and to prepare the way. My hope is that some thoroughgoing scholar will accept the challenge and compile what we so desperately lack at present, a massive and systematic tabulation of all the appearances of Holmes throughout history. It goes without saying that this will be no easy task.

I am convinced, for example, that Holmes is to be found in the Bible, or at least in the Apocrypha, in the persona of the Daniel of "The Story of Susanna" and "Bel and the Dragon." When Daniel refuses to accept the slanders of the elders against Susanna, objecting "Are ye such fools . . . that without examination or knowledge of the truth ye have condemned a daughter of Israel?" he exhibits the invariable gallantry of Holmes and his passion for definite and exact knowledge. Even more apropos is the way in which Daniel convinces Cyrus of Persia that the priests of Bel are arrant rascals. After offerings have been placed, Daniel has ashes "strewed throughout the temple." Next day the offerings have disappeared, but the ashes clearly reveal the footprints of the priests, their wives, and their children. "Then laughed Daniel." (This open laughter is admittedly not what we would expect from Sherlock, who is more in the habit of smiling or at most chuckling. But this is a minor variant, merely the difference between North European and Mediterranean modes of expression. The basic impulse, delight in having sprung the trap, is identical.) [Editor's note: For more about Sherlock as Daniel, see Ruth Berman's "Daniel Retold, or: Sherlock Holmes Slightly Misquoted," BSJ (NS) 8:87-89, (April) 1958.]

However, what gives this incident its theoretical importance is that, as devotees of Holmes have doubtless noticed, Sherlock Holmes employs precisely the same technique in clearing up the murder of Mr. Willoughby Smith in The Golden Pince-Nez.

So exact is the parallel that it is not distorting the evidence to suggest that Sherlock remembered this technique from his earlier Daniel incarnation. One of the strengths of this theory of reincarnation and its concomitant, the unconscious persistence of memory, is that it permits the solution of many of the most troublesome problems in Holmesian scholarship. I refer, of course, to the well known discrepancies. My claim is not that all the cruxes can be disposed of in this manner. For example, whether the Jezail bullet struck Watson's shoulder or his leg remains a difficulty, and can only be explained in terms of the general fuzziness of the good doctor's mind. (Holmes was perfectly right when, in The Dying Detective, he told Watson, "But facts are facts, Watson, and after all, you are only a general practitioner with very limited experience and mediocre qualifications. It is painful to have to say these things, but you leave me no choice.") Leaving this painful subject, one can observe that other troublesome problems may rather neatly be disposed of. For instance, the contradiction between Watson's positive declaration in A Study in Scarlet that Holmes had no knowledge of literature and the fact that Holmes refers to many literary figures—Petrarch and Hafiz come immediately to mind—this contradiction, I say, simply disappears. Holmes, from time to time, remembers these things from previous epiphanies, while remaining ignorant of literature most of the time. This seems to me a much more persuasive interpretation than the theory of multiple authorship of the stories proposed by Ronald Knox in "Studies in the Literature of Sherlock Holmes" (reprinted in Essays in Satire).

To return, however, to the main point, the pièce de résistance of this note: I believe that I have located the first appearance of Holmes in history. Unfortunately, precise (or even imprecise) dating is impossible, but that is not unusual when dealing with ancient materials.

It is also impossible to present the material in direct
translation from the original, but this also is common
in comparable situations. Consequently, I shall have to
quote from an English translation of a French version
based upon an Arabic rendition which—through heaven
knows how many intermediate stages—goes back ultimately
to an original in ancient Chaldean. I refer to the story
of Zadig, best known through Voltaire's French version.
Zadig, who turns out to be Holmes, lived in Babylon "in
the time of King Moabdar." This king is not included in
any of the king lists known to us, the natural supposi-
tion being that he antedates them, which would make the
material exceedingly ancient.

That Zadig is really Holmes can be seen clearly in
Chapter 3 of the tale. One day when Zadig was out walking "he saw one of the queen's eunuchs running to meet
him, followed by several officers, who appeared to be in
the greatest uneasiness, running hither and yon
like men bewildered, searching for some most precious
object which they had lost." Is this not precisely
the basic Sherlock Holmes situation? Lestrade and Gregson, also be it noted servants of the queen, always
appear "in the greatest uneasiness," always run "hither
and yon like men bewildered" until Holmes sets them
straight. The story continues:

"Young man," said the chief eunuch to Zadig, "have
you seen the queen's dog?"
Zadig modestly replied: "It is a bitch, not a dog."
"You are right," said the eunuch.
"It is a very small spaniel," added Zadig; "it is not
long since she has had a litter of puppies; she is lame in
the left front foot, and her ears are very long."
"You have seen her, then?" said the chief eunuch,
quite out of breath.
"No," answered Zadig. "I have never seen her, and
never knew that the queen had a bitch."

Every detail in the foregoing could be supported by quotations from the Canon, but that is unnecessary. No
Holmesian would deny that this is perfect Holmes technique and tone, down to his well known habit of concluding a series of observations with a remark intended
to surprise and confound his listeners.

Later, Zadig explains his chain of reasoning, quite
in the manner of one of Sherlock's familiar explica-
tions to Watson:

I saw on the sand the footprints of an animal, and
easily decided that they were those of a little dog.
Long and faintly marked furrows, imprinted where
the sand was slightly raised between the footprints,

told me that it was a bitch whose dugs were hanging
down, and that consequently she must have given birth
only a few days before. Other marks of a different
character, showing that the surface of the sand had
been constantly grazed on either side of the front
paws, informed me that she had very long ears; and,
as I observed that the sand was always less deeply
indented by one paw than by the other three, I gathered that the bitch belonging to our august queen was
a little lame, if I may venture to say so.

gain, no citations from Sherlock Holmes stories are re-
ired, for once more we find an exact replica of the
mous detective, even in such points of detail as his
verence for the sovereign and his habit of affecting
desty after an amazing performance. Zadig gives us, in
ort, the typical Holmesian virtuoso display. We are
mpted to burst out, as old Mr. Trevor did in The Gloria
ott, with "What an eye you have!" So marvelous, indeed,
e such powers that they appear almost magical. We are
t, therefore, surprised to find that Zadig was later
rested as a consequence of this logical demonstration
that the magi "were of the opinion that he ought to
burned as a wizard." Sherlock, living in the solidity
ich was Victoria's England, suffered no such conse-
ences, but that he was aware of the possibility can be
en from Watson's paraphrase of Holmes's essay, "The
ok of Life," in A Study in Scarlet: "So startling
uld his results appear to the unitiated that until they
arned the processes by which he had arrived at them
ey might well consider him as a necromancer."

This, then, is the argument, and it appears sound to
. Holmes has always existed, but he has gone through
ny metamorphoses, the tracing out of which should be a
imary task of Holmesian scholarship. I have proposed
e theory and given a terminus a quo in Zadig and a
rminus ad quem in Nero Wolfe, as well as an intermedi-
e example in Daniel. It remains for others to pick up
e torch and pursue the quest. I will rest content in
ving begun the work, convinced that, as Tacitus has
: "Suum cuique decus posteritas rependit."

itor's note: See Morris Rosenblum's "Anticipating
erlock Holmes, or A Grecian Irene Adler and the Fire
ick," BSJ (NS) 2:135, (April) 1952, for what may have
en still another previous reincarnation of Holmes.

THE IDENTITY OF THE KING OF BOHEMIA

by Julian Blackburn

A number of suggestions have been made as to the identity of the King of Bohemia and of Irene Adler, but none so far has been satisfactory or convincing. It has been suggested that the king was the Prince of Wales (later King Edward VII) and that Irene Adler was Lily Langtry. But the prince was born in 1841, and he would have been too old ("I am but thirty now") at the time of the Scandal, whether it occurred in 1887, 1888, or 1889. Furthermore, by then Lily Langtry had lost her place in the primary affections of the prince to Lady Warwick. Crown Prince Wilhelm von Hohenzollern and the Archduke Franz Ferdinand would have been too young, and, apart from this, the Crown Prince married in 1881, while Franz Ferdinand contracted a morganatic marriage with a lady in waiting in 1900. The Grand Duke Rudolf of Austria is the only one of the suggestions so far made who would have been of the right age, but he married in 1881, and it is unlikely that Irene Adler can be identified with his mistress, Baroness Mary Vetsera. They both died in the tragedy of Mayerling in 1889.

The problem of the identity of the King of Bohemia can now be solved. He was in fact Prince Alexander of Battenberg (1857-1893), monarch of Bulgaria, uncle of Lord Louis Mountbatten (Lord Mountbatten of Burma), and great-uncle of Prince Philip, Duke of Edinburgh. Notice that both Bulgaria and Bohemia begin with the same letter, and that Bohemia had no monarch of its own whereas Bulgaria had. It is true that Alexander abdicated on 8 September 1886. Thereafter there developed a struggle over his future among Germany, Russia, Austria-Hungary, France, and Britain, with the Crown Princess of Germany determined that her daughter, Victoria, should marry him. If one places the date of A Scandal in Bohemia in 1887 (as does Baring-Gould), the international intrigues could not have been very far advanced, and there would have been an extremely strong incentive for Alexander to recover the compromising photograph which would have become a heaven-sent excuse to those who were manoeuvering to exclude him from any further important part in the international game of high politics.

That the Scandal took place in 1887 is likely for two other reasons. In the first place it is consistent with Alexander's statement, "I am but thirty now." This is very strong evidence for Baring-Gould's date of 20-22 May 1887. Alexander was born on 5 April 1857. Entering a new decade is always a turning point in a person's life, and the fact that Alexander was just thirty must have been uppermost in his mind. In the second place it allows a sufficient period of time to elapse between the marriage of Godfrey Norton to Irene Adler and its complete and irrevocable collapse two years later. This is not surprising, in view of the indecent haste with which the marriage was conducted in the first place. It is hardly likely that a marriage of this sort would be happy and enduring.

Furthermore, it is reasonable to assume that Irene and Alexander were still in love with each other. In spite of Irene's "I love and am loved by a better man than he," she not only left a photograph of herself for Alexander, but kept the compromising one.

In the account given by Watson the "compromising" nature of the photograph was that both Alexander and Irene were in it together. In fact, the photograph was even more compromising than this. It was a photograph of Alexander accompanied by the following charming and delightful note in Alexander's own hand: "You were recently kind enough to ask for my picture, and I am therefore giving myself the pleasure of presenting it to you personally with the modest hope that it may remind you of your most sincere admirer. So that my picture may have a companion, and as proof that I thought of you, I have brought for you from Nice a picture of the most beautiful singer I know, and it would make me very happy if you will look at her lovely and enchanting features as often as possible." Attached to the picture of the prince was a charming little mirror. No wonder Irene determined that nothing would make her part with this enchanting gift. And in spite of what she said about retaining it in order to protect herself, she really kept it as a sentimental memento because she couldn't bear to part with it. As to Alexander, there can be no doubt about his continuing infatuation for Irene. "What a woman— a, what a woman! . . . Would she not have made an admirable queen? Is it not a pity that she was not on my level?"

By 1889 Alexander had been cold-shouldered by the great powers, and the proposed marriage to Princess Victoria had been broken off. He was living in reduced circumstances, and Irene, freed from her disastrous marriage, might well appear to him now to be closer to his own level. Hence in 1889 Prince Alexander of Battenberg, by permission of the Grand Duke of Hesse, laid aside the name of Battenberg and took the title of Count von Hartenau and thereupon married an opera singer whose name is

(Continued on page 116)

THE MARQUIS OF DONEGALL, Editor of <u>The Sherlock Holmes Journal</u>, has received the highest honour of The Baker Street Irregulars, the Two-Shilling Award.

The Irregular Shilling has been awarded to:

MATTHEW FAIRLIE of The Hounds of the Baskerville (<u>sic</u>), with the Investiture of "Barrymore."

HENRY C. POTTER of The Five Orange Pips, with the Investiture of "The Final Problem."

EVAN M. WILSON of The Five Orange Pips, with the Investiture of "Right Honourable Trelawney Hope."

THE IDENTITY OF THE KING OF BOHEMIA
(Continued from page 115)

given in the reference books as Johanna Loisinger. It is not known if Johanna Loisinger was Irene Adler's stage name or if Irene Adler was the pseudonym used by Watson to conceal the identity of Johanna Loisinger.

The marriage, while it lasted, was a blissfully happy one, and Johanna was heartbroken when it ended with Alexander's untimely death in 1893. There were two children of the marriage; first a boy who was given the name of Assen, the name of the old Bulgarian czars, and, two years later, a daughter, Zvetana.

J wonder what contribution could be made to the solution of these problems if the family archives were thrown open?

*　　　　*　　　　*　　　　*　　　　*

Author's Notes:

1. The style of the note that Alexander sent to Irene differs very considerably from that of the letter to Holmes announcing his intended visit. The reason is, of course, that the letter to Holmes was written in English with which the prince was not completely familiar. The note to Irene, however, was written in German, and the above is a translation into English of the prince's excellent style.

2. The reason Watson refers to Irene as "the late Irene Adler" is, of course, that by then she had ceased to be Irene Adler and had become, successively, Mrs. Norton and the Gräfin von Hartenau.

The Scion Societies

THE NON-CANONICAL CALABASHES
of Los Angeles

Correspondence: Stephen Verebelyi, Secretary,
4559 Lexington Ave., Los Angeles, Calif. 90029.

The celebration of Mr. Holmes's birthday took place on 8 January at the Los Angeles Stockyard Steak-House. We started by being sworn in by John Ball ("The Oxford Flyer"), our president. Then the Canonical toasts were drunk. Chairman Sean Wright read Vincent Starrett's poem, "221B," and excerpts from Basil Rathbone's accounts of his meetings with Holmes and Dr. Watson, as presented in The Baker Street Journal.

After dinner, Mr. Ball showed slides of his visits to areas of Sherlockian interest (including the Reichenbach Falls and Tibet) and to the Dalai Lama as a prelude to his talk, which received a standing ovation. Dr. Ronald Lawrence rounded out our bill by relating (through courtesy of Lancet) an entertaining theory of how Dr. Watson's war wounds were received.

The meeting concluded with the presentation of awards to those who were in attendance at the first gathering on 10 September 1970. It was a great meeting, attended by 72.

*　　　　　*　　　　　*　　　　　*

HUGO'S COMPANIONS
of Chicago

Correspondence: Robert W. Hahn,
938 Clarence Ave., Oak Park, Ill. 60304.

The annual birthday party was held in the Baker Street Pub on 6 January. More than 150 were on hand for the festivities, which were covered by the Chicago newspapers and television networks. Bob Hahn presided, and Vincent Starrett proposed the toast to Sherlock Holmes. After the main event, a scene involving Holmes and Moriarty, Bob Mangler announced that Hahn had been voted the Sherlockian of the year. The birthday cake with 117 candles was brought out for the finale.

Thirty were in attendance at the meeting on 18 February. Among the announcements made by Hahn was that of a pending Holmesian exhibit in the Royal London Wax Museum. The display will be unveiled in our Baker Street Pub before being set up in the museum. The quiz, based on The Beryl Coronet, was won by Charles Stahl.

Twenty-nine were on hand for the carousal on 25 March. After the quiz there was the featured speech by FBI Agent Berard Huelskamp which, together with the discussion and questions, occupied all the rest of the meeting.

*　　　　　*　　　　　*　　　　　*

THE MUSGRAVE RITUALISTS BETA

Correspondence: William J. Walsh,
6 Ernst Drive, Suffern, N.Y. 10901.

Nine Sherlockians attended the meeting on 23 January at the home of Head Game-Keeper Tregellis Jenkins in Suffern. It was an informal gathering, with parliamentary law discarded in favour of much scholarly discussion of such topics as Billy Wilder's film, Scion Societies, and Scion publications. There were two quizzes, but no discusssion of serious business.

*　　　　　*　　　　　*　　　　　*

THE SIX NAPOLEONS
of Baltimore

Correspondence: Steve Clarkson, Harker,
          69 Straw Hat Rd., Apt. I-D, Owings Mills, Md. 21117.

Twenty-five Napoleons gathered at the Baltimore Bar Association Club on 28 January to toast the woman and to discuss The
Veiled Lodger. The conclave was highlighted by George Tullis's
record of Julie Andrews singing "Don't Go in the Lion's Cage
Tonight" and by an amazing report of an actual murder case
by Assistant State's Attorney Barry S. Frame. The evening's
quiz, which concluded the meeting, was won by Phil Sherman.

Thirty Napoleons were present at the meeting on 25 March, and
they explored the mystery surrounding Lady Beatrice Falder's
strange behaviour in Shoscombe Old Place. Guests were introduced after the reading of interim correspondence. Following
the quiz (won by John Carroll) the meeting disbanded.

     *   *   *   *

THE TIDEWAITERS
of San Francisco Bay

Correspondence: William A. Berner, Recorder,
          47-12 17th St., San Francisco, Calif. 94117.

This is a newly organised group of hard-core Scowrers who
are devoted to serious study. Seven members attended the first
meeting on February 5 at Mechanics Institute Library. It was
decided that a particular Canonical subject would be discussed
at each meeting, and that The Valley of Fear would be the subject for the next meeting. Our publication, The Morning Letter,
will be appearing shortly.

     *   *   *   *

THE PRIORY SCHOOL
of New York

Correspondence: Andrew Page, Saltire,
          3130 Irwin Ave., Bronx, N.Y. 10463.

This active Scion met on 20 February and planned the final
stages of their publication, The Holmesian Observer. Chronology of A Study in Scarlet was discussed, and a short quiz was
given.

On 13 March a large group of Students met at the Saltire's
house and put together the first issue of the publication.
Two papers were read—one on philosophy in the Canon and the
other a pastiche of The Hound. There was a quiz on The Sussex
Vampire, after which the members viewed a showing of The Voice
of Terror, starring Basil Rathbone and Nigel Bruce. The meeting
was topped off by a recording of the 1964 BSI dinner-meeting.

There was another meeting on 27 March at which the format of
our publication was altered, and the next issue planned. The
main section of the discussion centered on Sherlockian films,
past, present, and—hopefully—future.

We are anxious to recruit as many junior Sherlockians as
possible. They are all warmly urged to join up.

     *   *   *   *

THE GREEK INTERPRETERS
of East Lansing

Correspondence: Dr. Donald A. Yates, Melas,
          537 Wells Hall, MSU, E. Lansing, Michigan 48823.

The Interpreters reconvened on 11 March at Brauer's 1861 House, their numbers being augmented by five newcomers. The group was perplexed by a challenging quiz devised by Steve Clarkson, and it ended in a tie. The <u>Melas</u> spoke on <u>The Valley of Fear</u>, and, after a long supper, Robert Vincent presented a tape on which were captured the voices of several noted actors and Sir Arthur Conan Doyle. So long were the discussions that a scheduled paper had to be put off until the May meeting.

*   *   *   *

THE BROTHERS THREE
from Moriarty

Correspondence: John Bennett Shaw,
1917 Fort Union Drive, Santa Fe, N.M. 87501.

The first meeting was held at the home of John Bennett Shaw on 14 March (Einstein's birthday), and 16 attended from Sante Fe and Los Alamos. Among events planned are a dinner-meeting for the visit of Peter Blau; another at the State Pen at which a noted penal official will talk on "Crime Does Pay"; a birthday meeting on Moriarty's 125th birthday anniversary in Moriarty, N.M., at which it is hoped the chief of police will speak. Name badges will be provided for all members, and all will be identical—"James"—including those for the two ladies admitted to membership. It is hoped to include some members from Albuquerque —any reading this are asked to write John Bennett Shaw.

*   *   *   *

THE SUB-LIBRARIANS SCION of the BSI in the American Library Association will have their 5th annual meeting in Dallas, Texas, on Monday, 21 June, at noon, during the annual ALA conference. It will be the usual champagne luncheon, and will be held at The Lancer's Club in downtown Dallas; cost $9, including champagne. All librarians and interested Sherlockians are invited. Write John Bennett Shaw, 1917 Fort Union Drive, Santa Fe, N.M. 87501.

This will be a joint meeting with the Dallas-Ft. Worth Scion, the Crew of the Barque <u>Lone Star</u>, and Miss Francine Morris who is in both Scions will see that this will be a stellar event.

*   *   *   *

THE SILVER BLAZERS is a new Scion Society in Louisville, Ky., founded by William E. Solt (7513 Greenlawn Road, Louisville Ky., 40222; telephone 502-426-1618). All those interested in joining are asked to communicate with him.

*   *   *   *

The first running of the SILVER BLAZE (Southern Division) was held at Bowie Race Course in Maryland on 10 April and was attended by more than 45 Sherlockians and their guests. Tommy Lee rode North Flight, the favourite, to an easy victory, and Margaret F. Morris presented the traditional trophy on behalf of the Red Circle of Washington and The Six Napoleons of Baltimore. All those wishing to attend next year's event are invited to communicate with the sponsoring Scions.

*   *   *   *

<u>Re</u> SILVER BLAZES

The 12th annual Chicago Silver Blaze will be held on Friday, 8 July. Write R. W. Hahn (address above) for information.

The 20th New York Silver Blaze will be run on 17 September. Write Thomas L. Stix, Jr. (34 Pierson Avenue, Norwood, N.J. 07648) for all details.

Henry Lauritzen, who <u>is</u> the Danish Silver Blaze (founder, ranger, handicapper, <u>etc.</u>), announces that the 9th running will take place on 19 June. (A horse named Silver Blaze is entered.)

-119-

Letters To Baker Street

From Stanton O. Berg, firearms examiner, 6025 Gardenia Lane, N.E., Minneapolis, Minn. 55421:

Thank you for your kind comments concerning my article, "Sherlock Holmes: Father of Scientific Crime Detection," as set out in the Inventory section of the March Journal [on page 58]. I have been very pleased with the reception my article has received and have been told tha it is to be reprinted in The Criminologist, a profession al and technical journal published in London. The editor of The Armchair Detective, Allen J. Hubin, has also indicated an intention to reprint it. I have received a large number of requests for copies from Journal readers as a result of your notice and have been more than happy to provide the copies. I have also received a number of follow-up comments from the recipients of the copies, and I am sure that there are no more enthusiastic, responsive and kindly people than the Sherlockians. There are a few reprints remaining.

* * * * *

From Walter N. Trenerry, alias Otis Hearn, a famous St. Paul attorney—not Minneapolis, as stated on page 54 of the March issue:

Thanks for your kudos in the last issue, but you are risking having the whole St. Paul Chamber of Commerce on your neck. Minneapolis, indeed! Not that I really care, but officially there is a great rivalry between the two cities, and much claptrap comes forth, like between Fort Worth and Dallas, etc.

If anyone cares about the nom de plume Otis Hearn, any cryptanalyst should recognise it—an anagram of ETOANIRSH, the frequency table of single letters in the English language which everyone refers to in breaking down simple ciphers.

Your issues keep up to standard. In the midst of all the flying fluff these days there are still some oases of bemused scepticism and leisurely thought.

* * * * *

From Robert A. W. Lowndes, of Hoboken, magazine editor and member of The Scandalous Bohemians:

Dear me—I must take exception to Mr. Levy's suggestion that had Holmes turned to crime, he would have been caught in no time at all, simply because there were no clues—and who else in those days could have done it so well? [See "On the Morality of One Mr. Sherlock Holmes," in the March BSJ.] What our good Sherlockian has overlooked is the elementary matter of the first requirement for a perfect crime: that no one so much as suspects that a crime has been committed at all!

Editor's note: This quote from Agatha Christie's "The Dream" may serve as an epilogue to Mr. Levy's paper:

"'Motive and opportunity are not enough,' said Poirot. 'There must also be the criminal temperament!'

"'I wonder if you'll ever commit a crime, Poirot?' said Stillingfleet. 'I bet you could get away with it all right. As a matter of fact, it would be <u>too</u> easy for you—I mean the thing would be off as definitely too un-sporting.'"

*   *   *   *   *

From George Fletcher ("The Cardboard Box"):

In reading Lamb's essay, "Amicus Redivivus," the other evening, I came across the following comments: "He pass-eth by the name of Doctor. . . . His remedy . . . is a sim-le tumbler, or more, of the purest Cognac, with water, made as hot as the convalescent can bear it. Where he findeth . . . a squeamish subject, he condescendeth to be the taster; and showeth, by his own example, the innocu-us nature of the prescription. Nothing can be more kind or encouraging than this procedure. It addeth confidence to the patient, to see his medical adviser go hand in hand with himself in the remedy. When the doctor swallow-th his own draught, what peevish invalid can refuse to ledge him in the potion?" What harbinger of Watson is not this?

*   *   *   *   *

From Anne Marie Giardina, of Lansdale, Pa.:

I received my Baker Street Journal on March 10, and I m very pleased with it. It was more than I had ever oped. I showed it to my English teacher friend, and she s going to see if they can use it in the English Depart-ent. Isn't that fantastic! I really hope she can use it. am also very glad that there is a picture of Basil athbone.

*   *   *   *   *

From William J. Walsh, of The Musgrave Ritualists Beta:

I received the latest copy of the Journal on March 2nd, and I take this opportunity to compliment the Edi-or, as well as the contributing Irregulars, for an ex-ellent presentation. Especially good (as usual) was the nnual poem by Ezra Wolff, and John Ball is to be com-ended for "The Path of the Master," an excellent piece. hilip Schreffler's "The Dark Dynasty" appears to have een the result of demonic possession. Warlocks and itches indeed! Black magic is stronger than white magic, nd a good black magician would not be caught either by mortal or another magician unless the other magician as a practitioner of black magic of a more powerful ort. Did the Master practice black magic?

COOK, DORIS E.
  Sherlock Holmes and Much More
      [Hartford:] The Connecticut Historical Society,
      1970.
      This is the life story of William Gillette (with
      much about his play, Sherlock Holmes, of course),
      well written, competently researched and docu-
      mented, and nicely illustrated. The author's inter-
      est in Gillette dates back to the 1950's when she
      began cataloguing part of his library. Since it is
      of great value to all aficionados of Holmes and
      Gillette, this work is highly recommended to our
      readers. Obtainable from the publisher at 1 Eliza-
      beth St., Hartford, Conn. 06105 for $3.50 plus 25¢
      postage (and 18¢ tax for Connecticut residents).

LAUTERBACH, CHARLES E.
  Baker Street Ballads
      [Culver City, Calif.: Luther Norris, c.1971.]
      An excellent collection of the late Dr. Lauter-
      bach's delightful poems—and Henry Lauritzen's
      superb illustrations are a joy also. Obtainable for
      $3 from the publisher, 3844 Watseka Ave., Culver
      City, Calif. 90230.

SIMPSON, A. CARSON
  Simpson's Sherlockian Studies, Volume 9, 1961.
      [Philadelphia, 1971.]
      This last scholarly Study of the late, great mem-
      ber of The Copper Beeches, previously unpublished,
      has been privately reproduced and made available to
      Sherlockians by William R. Smith. The subject of
      this monograph is "Canonical Philately," and, as to
      be expected, it is a work of great erudition.

*   *   *   *   *

It is indeed pleasant to announce that Ron De Waal's
long-awaited World Bibliography on Sherlock Holmes and Dr.
Watson has been accepted for publication by the New York
Graphic Society, of Greenwich, Conn. The projected date of
publication is the spring of 1972. The book will consist
of approximately 1000 pages and will be illustrated.

Ruth Berman writes that April Fantasy and Science Fiction is a Poul Anderson special, with his picture on the
cover and much about him inside. (Ruth issues No which
appears three times a year, and No 7 contains an extensive review of The Private Life of Sherlock Holmes by
Dean Dickensheet.)

The Mystery Writer's Art, edited by Francis M. Nevins,
Jr. (Bowling Green University Press; cloth $8.95, paper
$3.50), contains contributions by Journal subscribers J.
R. Christopher and Robert A. W. Lowndes. (In Startling
Mystery Stories for March 1971, Bob Lowndes, who was then
the editor, has an excellent article on Nero Wolfe.)

"Doctors Afield, Doctors Criminal and Criminous," by Jacques Barzun, appeared in The New England Journal of Medicine for 1 April 1971. Of course Sherlockian Barzun mentions Holmes's reference to Drs. Palmer and Pritchard.

Judging from my correspondence, many readers have seen the advertisement of the Radiola Co. (Box H, Croton on Hudson, New York 10520) for records of old radio programmes. Crime Series #1 includes The Bruce-Partington Plans, starring Basil Rathbone and Nigel Bruce, "exactly as heard on NBC on November 6, 1939." The price is $5.95 plus 30¢ postage (and plus sales tax in New York state).

An excellent reprint of a very desirable item, Dr. Watson, by S. C. Roberts, has been published by The Three Students Plus and is available for $1, postpaid, from Bruce Kennedy, 80 Roaring Brook Road, Chappaqua, N.Y. 10514.

Paul Clarkson ("The Red Leech") is Curator of Rare Books and Special Collections, Goddard Library, Clark University, Worcester, Mass., and also Editor of that library's publication, The Goddard Biblio Log. This is a most interesting publication for bibliophiles. The main article in Vol. 1, No. 1, deals with the Nuremberg Chronicle and is illustrated with the cut of "Pope Joan."

*   *   *   *   *

PERIODICALS RECEIVED

THE DEVON COUNTY CHRONICLE, Vol. 7, No. 1, November 1970. Published by the Chicago BSI and edited by R. W. Hahn, 938 Clarence Avenue, Oak Park, Ill. 60304

THE HOLMESIAN OBSERVER, Vol. 1, Nos. 1, 2, & 3, March, April, and May 1971. Published by The Priory School, of New York, and edited by Andrew Page, 3130 Irwin Avenue, Bronx, N.Y. 10463. A monthly publication distributed free of charge to those who send 4 self-addressed (4 1/8" by 9½", or larger) stamped envelopes.

THE SCANDAL SHEET, Vol. 1, No. 1, January 1971. Published Irregularly by The Scandalous Bohemians, of New Jersey, and edited by Robert A. W. Lowndes, 717 Willow Avenue, Hoboken, N.J. 07030. Subscription: $2 per volume.

SHADES OF SHERLOCK, Vol. 5, No. 1, 6 January 1971. Published twice a year by The Three Students Plus and edited by Bruce Kennedy, 80 Roaring Brook Road, Chappaqua, N.Y. 10514. Subscription: 40¢ a year.

THE SHERLOCK HOLMES JOURNAL, Vol. 10, No. 1, Winter 1970. Published by The Sherlock Holmes Society of London (The Studio, 39 Clabon Mews, London S.W.1, England) and edited by the Marquis of Donegall.

SHERLOCKIANA, Nr. 1, 1971. The publication of Sherlock Holmes Klubben i Danmark, now edited by Henry Lauritzen.

THE VERMISSA HERALD, Vol. 5, No. 1, January 1971. The official publication of the Scowrers and Molly Maguires, edited by William A. Berner, 4712 17th Street, San Francisco, Calif. 94117.

WANTS AND OFFERS

William A. Berner (4712 17th St., San Francisco, Calif. 94117) offers LaCour & Mogensen: The Murder Book (see page 186, September 1970 BSJ), English translation, for $8.95; Barzun & Taylor: A Catalogue of Crime (see p. 44, March 1971 BSJ) for $18.95. Also, interested Sherlockians may receive his current list and an announcement about the American appearance of the Sherlockian records mentioned on page 59 of the March Journal by sending him a stamped and addressed envelope.

Walter Klinefelter (R. D. 1, Dallastown, Pa. 17313) invites offers for The Baker Street Journal, Original Series complete; New Series, Vol. 1, nos. 1-4 (reprint issue), to Vol. 20, no. 4, as issued.

Herman R. Jacks (172 Freihage Drive N.E., Sierra Vista, Arizona 85635) wants The Exploits of Sherlock Holmes, by A. C. Doyle & J. D. Carr; Ellery Queen's The Misadventures of Sherlock Holmes; The Incunabular Holmes, edited by Edgar W. Smith.

Nathan Bengis (658 W. 188th St., New York, N.Y. 10040) is selling his extensive Sherlockian collection—only to private collectors, not to dealers. Preference will be given to purchasers who can come to his home by appointment. Due to the size of the collection there is no list, but he will try to take care of those who are unable to call if they send lists of their special wants.

Sandy Harbin (7433 Quartz Ave., Canoga Park, Calif. 91306) has arranged with Doubleday for Scion Societies to obtain discounts on volume orders for The Complete Sherlock Holmes. (The one-volume edition is listed at $7.95, and the two-volume set at $12.50.) Discounts to be given:

25 to 49 copies, 10%; 50 to 99, 25%; 100 to 249, 33 1/3%; 250 to 499, 35%; 500 to 999, 40%; 1000 plus, 41%.

All orders (no remittances as yet) should be sent to Sandy Harbin, and Doubleday will send the books to each Scion Society.

Norman S. Nolan (68 Crest Road, Middleton, N.J. 07748) is preparing a photo of the 1971 dinner with a key identifying those present. He is generously offering it to interested Sherlockians without charge.

Anne Marie Giardina (1536 Garden Road, Lansdale, Pa. 19446) wants a copy of Basil Rathbone's autobiography, pictures of him, and his records.

Bruce Kennedy (80 Roaring Brook Road, Chappaqua, N.Y. 10514) announces that the second printing of Four Wheels to Baker Street is available from him for $1.

In late June The Priory School will offer a small 15-page pamphlet, The Priory Papers: A Study in Exams, for 75¢. Inquiries and orders, but no money as yet, should be sent to Andrew Page, 3130 Irwin Ave., Bronx, N.Y. 10463.

Andrew Fusco (643 Trovato Drive, Morgantown, W.Va.

26505) wants Doyle's <u>Memories and Adventures</u>, Christ's <u>Irregular Guide to Sherlock Holmes</u>, and Roberts's <u>Doctor Watson</u>.

Daniel J. Morrow (105 East Court, Blackwood, N.J. 08012) has some Sherlock Holmes broadcasts starring Basil Rathbone that he would like to exchange for other Sherlock Holmes programmes on tape.

Andrew Jay Peck (2968 Perry Avenue, Bronx, N.Y. 10458) wants Zeisler's <u>Chronology</u>; <u>Baker Street Pages</u>, nos. 1-25; <u>Sherlock Holmes Journal</u>, Vols. 1 & 2; any material, including reviews and ads, on "The Private Life of Sherlock Holmes"; and other Sherlockiana of interest.

J. David Reno (169 Beacon St., Basement Rear, Boston, Mass. 02116) is seeking information about the type of caped coat worn by the Master. Any information as to type, style, or where one similar to it could be purchased in the Boston area would be greatly appreciated.

Marcello Truzzi (1239 Wines Drive, Ann Arbor, Michigan 48103) has a number of tape recordings of old radio shows dealing with the Canon, and he would like to trade them for other Sherlockian items. A list is available.

Gerald Parker (540 E. Portage Trail, Cuyahoga Falls, Ohio 44221) wants Doyle's <u>Memories and Adventures</u>. Also, he would like to hear from Sherlockians in the Akron-Cleveland area.

I am informed that a very few copies of <u>Leaves from the Copper Beeches</u> (called by Edgar W. Smith one of the finest productions of the Scion Societies) are still available. To take advantage of this opportunity, rush $5 to James G. Jewell, 145 Stockton Road, Bryn Mawr, Pennsylvania 19010.

Robert Saal (115B Idaho Drive, Grand Forks AFB, N.D. 58201) offers: The Baker Street Journal, Old Series, Vol. 3, Nos. 2 & 4, $6 each; 1960 Christmas Annual, $4. All those ordering are asked to enclose a stamp to facilitate return of duplicate orders. Also, he invites bids for copies of the BSI reprint of <u>Beeton's Christmas Annual</u>.

Robert Haney (422 Amsterdam Avenue, Apt. 3C, New York, N.Y. 10024; telephone 799-1144) offers a run of bound volumes of <u>The Times</u> (London). The late nineteenth century is practically complete. The volumes will be sold in one lot or individually. Also, he offers for $175 <u>The Works of A. Conan Doyle</u>, text of the author's edition (New York: Appeltom Co., 1902), 13 volumes, 3/4 leather binding (slightly rubbed), text in mint condition.

Albert Silverstein (32 Helme Road, Kingston, R.I. 02881) distributed a questionnaire at our January dinner asking Irregulars about their 12 favourite novels of detection, Canonical and otherwise. The results have been trickling in at a very slow rate, and he would appreciate it if those who have not already replied would do so as soon as they conveniently can.

-125-

From the Editor's Commonplace Book

The newspaper items that have aroused the greatest interest on the part of our readers are those concerning the proposed sale of the assets of the Sir Arthur Conan Doyle Estate, and the follow-ups telling about the consequent legal complications—which will be very involved, I am quite sure. Under the circumstances, the suggestion received from several Sherlockians that we ought to all get together and purchase those assets (mainly copyrights) is not practicable, especially since "people in Geneva are talking of 'several million pounds' as the value," accord- to a cutting from The Financial Times of 8 April, supplied by Alan H. Foster.

        *   *   *   *

That new movie, They Might Be Giants, has also been mentioned in my correspondence. It concerns a brilliant lawyer (played by George C. Scott) who suffers a nervous breakdown and believes he is Sherlock Holmes. His female psychiatrist is named Watson.

        *   *   *   *

Many reviews of The Private Life of Sherlock Holmes are still being received. Worthy of notice are: one from The Observer Review of 6 December 1970 which quotes Billy Wilder as saying that he made the 128th film about Holmes "because I love him and I wanted to"; one in Hebrew, from the Israeli newspaper, Haaretz, supplied by Matthew Simon; and one in French, from Paris Match of 2 January, supplied by Ruth Berman.

        *   *   *   *

Miss Mary McMahon, Head of the Literature Section at Metropolitan Toronto Central Library, has produced "Sherlock Holmes Is Alive and Well at the Central Library," an interesting article about the goings-on at the library's month-long exhibition of its great Sherlockian collection. Miss McMahon reports on the great success of the exhibit and adds, "We are particularly pleased by the enthusiasm of the teen-agers."

        *   *   *   *

Evan Wilson, of Washington, D.C., has forwarded an ad for Baker Street Scotch Whisky. I earnestly hope that it is better than Watson's Scotch Whisky (produced by James Watson & Co.) or that imitation of Duggan's Dew of Kirkintilloch, the favourite of Mr. Colin Glencannon whose exploits (malfeasances?) were described in the Saturday Evening Post by the late Guy Gilpatric years ago.

        *   *   *   *

Howard Haycraft ("The Devil's Foot"), an Old Irregular who has received many deserved honours, recently earned another. He was awarded Honorary Membership in the Catholic Library Association, and this is the first time that this honour has been bestowed upon a non-Catholic.

*   *   *   *

Arthur Ihsen's letter (on page 55 of the March issue) in which he says that the type used for part of the Journal is too small has evoked some discussion, and several suggestions have been received. As a result, we shall avoid using the smallest type-size—and we may have to discourage articles that are longer than usual.

*   *   *   *

Through the thoughtfulness of Hal Dewar, of San Antonio, Texas, we have an interesting announcement from the Bohemian Club. Headed "Everything You've Always Wanted to Know about Sherlock Holmes but Were Afraid to Ask," it describes an evening honouring the Master, complete with a show including a replica of 221B as well as a display of mementos from Holmes's greatest cases.

*   *   *   *

Several readers, headed by Paul Clarkson, have sent copies of a letter that appeared in <u>Antiquarian Bookman</u>, 15 March 1971. It is from W. H. Bond, <u>Librarian of the</u> Houghton Library at Harvard; reveals that the manuscript of <u>The Adventure of the Three Students</u> disappeared from the Reading Room on 5 February, and concludes "Needless to say we will be grateful for information concerning its whereabouts and assistance in its recovery."

*   *   *   *

I had always believed it to be general knowledge that the best-known actor who ever appeared in a Sherlockian dramatisation was Charlie Chaplin, whose name is listed in the cast of <u>Sherlock Holmes</u>. (See the back cover of the March issue.) But apparently some readers are not sure that this was <u>the</u> Charlie Chaplin. It was.

*   *   *   *

Stewart Lauterbach, the son of Edward Lauterbach and the grandson of the late Dr. Charles Lauterbach, is a real third-generation Sherlockian. Since art in the blood is liable to take the nicest forms, it is not surprising that he turned in this poem as an English assignment:

> There was a detective named Holmes
> Who answers could feel in his bones.
> To catch Moriarty
> He had to be smarty,
> That sly, slippery sleuth, Sherlock Holmes.

(Stewart is eleven years old and is in the sixth grade.)

*   *   *   *

It is indeed sad to record that two great figures in the field of detective-story literature, both of whom attended our dinners years ago, have dropped from the ranks since this Journal last appeared. We have lost Clayton Rawson, author and editor, and Manfred Lee, one-half of the illustrious Ellery Queen team. I am sure that all of us appreciate the valuable contributions that these truly talented men made to our enjoyment of their favourite subject.

WH☺DUNIT

BARBARA HODAN, twenty-two years old, attended the University
    Illinois, where she concentrated on the geological science
    and where she is currently employed. Besides her scientifi
    interests, she enjoys Victorian literature, Irish folk mus
    and book hunting. 3645 S. Euclid Ave., Berwyn, Ill. 60402.

ROY PICKARD, 33 years of age, is an Editor with Lutterworth
    Press in London. He has been in the publishing business fo
    12 years and has been writing for three years. He has thre
    books on the films to his credit, including the forthcomi
    An Index to American Film Directors (Museum of Modern Art,
    New York). 51, Ringwood Ave., Redhill, Surrey, England.

NORMAN M. DAVIS, a numismatist, writes a syndicated column,
    "The Coin Box," and is the author of The Complete Book of
    United States Coin Collecting. He previously appeared her
    in June 1969. 4915 Chevy Chase Blvd, Chevy Chase, Md. 20015.

W. E. DUDLEY, a long-time student of the Master, has done so
    writing over the years and recently had some articles in
    dustrial Security. Box 2020, Las Vegas, Nevada 89101.

GLENN S. HOLLAND, one of our younger Sherlockians, has been
    writing about Holmes for some years, and this is his thir
    appearance in the Journal.
    10469 Lindbrook Drive, Los Angeles, Calif. 90024.

DAVID SKENE MELVIN, Chairman of the Sub-Librarians Scion in
    the Canadian Library Association, is Assistant Director/
    Secretary-Treasurer of the Lake Erie Regional Library Sys
    tem and has written for various professional journals. Ou
    side of the Canon he is interested in military history an
    speleology. 253 Huron St., London 11, Ontario, Canada.

RICHARD W. FOSTER, after working for a medical book publish
    founded Rittenhouse Book Distributors, dealers in medical
    books. His earliest recollection is having his elder brot
    (a devoted Sherlockian) read the Sacred Text to him.
    205 Strafford Avenue, Wayne, Pa. 19087.

EVAN M. WILSON, a member of The Five Orange Pips, is a trul
    great Sherlockian scholar who previously appeared here in
    June 1970. 3145 O Street N.W., Washington, D.C. 20007.

BARTLETT DALE SIMMS, D.C., a graduate of Logan College of
    Chiropractic, is a member of The Noble Bachelors and The
    Sherlock Holmes Society of London. His hobbies are the
    Sacred Writings, Dr. Thorndyke, music, and fishing.
    5815 Nottingham Avenue, St. Louis, Mo. 63109.

JULIAN BLACKBURN, B.Sc., Ph.D. (Cambridge), Associate Dean
    Arts and Science at Trent University, Peterborough, Ontar
    is an outstanding educator who has held many important po
    tions in England and this country, as well as in Canada, a
    has served on many committees having to do with social
    sciences. He writes that he is also interested in cooking
    and bird-watching. R.R. 3, Lakefield, Ontario, Canada.

D. F. RAUBER, Ph.D., who has had much teaching experience, i
    Associate Professor of English, San Diego College. His ma
    interests are 17th-century literature, Renaissance studie
    and classical and biblical literature. He claims no exper
    tise in Sherlockian scholarship—only a deep and abiding
    love for the stories.
    English Dep't, San Diego State College, San Diego, Calif. 921

W. CORTI

Practical Boot & Shoe Maker.

BY SPECIAL APPOINTMENT TO

H.R.H. THE PRINCESS OF WALES,

AND OTHER MEMBERS OF THE ROYAL FAMILY.

HUNTING, SHOOTING, FISHING, MILITARY & WALKING BOOTS

OF EVERY KIND AND MATERIAL.

Special Department for Ladies' Boots and Shoes.

318   REGENT STREET, W.   318

(NEAR THE LANGHAM HOTEL.)

Volume 21, Number 3
(New Series)

September 1971

An Irregular Quarterly of Sherlockiana

Editor: JULIAN WOLFF, M.D.

THE BAKER STREET IRREGULARS
NEW YORK, N.Y.

Volume 21, Number 3
(New Series)

September 1971

THE
BAKER STREET
JOURNAL

Founded by **EDGAR W. SMITH**, Esq.

"Si monumentum quaeris, circumspice"

Subscription $4 a year

All communications and remittances should be sent to the Editor
Julian Wolff, M.D.
33 Riverside Drive, New York, N. Y. 10023

CONTENTS

HOLMES AT HURLSTONE
or
The Royal Diadem Recovered
by Dr. Joseph E. Merriam, Jr.

In sixteen forty-nine,
King Charles's head asunder,
His crown was snatched away
And Hurlstone hidden under.
    —"And so under."—

Its presence then forgot,
It lay in mould and rust,
The gold begrimed beneath
Two centuries of dust.
    —(A lot of dust.)—

Until the butler read
The Musgrave Ritual
And tore its secret out,
But lost his life as well.
    —Yes, his life as well.—

In eighteen seventy-eight
Holmes spent some time and pains
And solved the mystery:
No substitute for brains.
    —No, not for brains.—

The crown is found at last,
Can see it if you look
At Hurlstone—or at least
It says so in my book.
    —It's in my book.—

So let us all give thanks
And celebrate in poems
The genius of this man.
Three cheers, I say, for Holmes!
    —Three cheers for Holmes!—

THE CASE OF THE MISSING CALENDAR
by Edward A. Merrill

The literary style of Doctor Watson has generated many of the Writings about the Writings. Some debatable interpretations have inspired volumes; others, no less controversial, have received less attention, among them the month when Sherlock Holmes travelled to Hurlstone to investigate the disappearance of Reginald Musgrave's butler. Not that this case has been ignored, but research has not yet been carried to the point where there is consensus. As is shown in Mr. Peck's new and invaluable Compendium of Chronological Data,[1] the Seven Chronologists divide into 3 nearly equal camps: Bell, Baring-Gould and Zeisler favour autumn; Christ and Folsom pick summer; and Blakeney and Brend remain neutral. It appears to this writer, however, that an analysis of the incompatibilities, if any, between the conditions imposed by the seasons of the year and the reports of events at the Manor House as described by Holmes may eliminate the impossible and determine what is the truth, however improbable.

In this paper we examine only evidence leading to the selection of the season, summer or autumn. Once that is established we will leave to abler researchers the specific date in a specific year, as may be determined by the phases of the moon, the weather reports, post office schedules, and the working habits of the late 19th century.

To state the problem we can do no better than to quote the masters of Sherlockian scholarship as reported in Mr. Baring-Gould's The Annotated Sherlock Holmes.[2] Referring to the lines in The Musgrave Ritual, "What was the Month? The sixth from the First," Mr. H. W. Bell wrote: ". . . the chief problem in the dating of this case is to determine the season in which it happened. In the Ritual of the Musgraves itself there is a fundamental ambiguity: the month specified . . . might have been reckoned either from March 25th, the legal beginning of the year in England from the fourteenth century until 1752, or from January 1st, as was common among historians during the period of the Stuarts."

To this, Dr. Ernest B. Zeisler adds:[3] "If January is counted as the first month, the sixth from this is . . . July, and if one reckons from March 25th then the sixth month from the first is the month from September 25th to October 24th. . . . But the Ritual was not written later than 1660. In 1752 the Gregorian Calendar was adopted in England, and this entailed skipping eleven days, so that we must add 11 days to the above dates. Hence the intervals under consideration are July 12th to August 11th and October 6th to November 4th." Then, by considering the implications of Brunton's appeal for a fortnight's reprieve, Dr. Zeisler advances the initial day of each period to July 5th and and September 29th, respectively.

Let us start our analysis with some premises based on statements in Holmes's narrative which are not ambiguous, and information in the public domain.

1. The treasure was located by pacing 20 steps north,

10 steps east, 4 steps south, then 2 steps west through the old door into a passage from which a stair led down under to the vault in which it had been concealed. Let us call it "The Traverse."

2. This stepped traverse started from a point (let us call it the "Point of Departure") 96 feet from the stump of an elm tree, on a straight line extended through that stump from the trunk of an oak tree, which was right in front of the house. The stump was nearly midway between the oak and the house.

3. The time was afternoon, on a day when the shadow of the topmost branch of the oak fell on the stump of the elm; the axis of that shadow, therefore, coincided with the line through the stump to the "Point of Departure." The hour was that at which the elevation of the sun above the horizon was measured by a slope of 2 vertical to 3 horizontal. This is an angle of 33.7 degrees. Let us call it the "Critical Angle."

4. The initial leg of the traverse, as it moved north, was close to, and parallel with, the west wall of the old wing.

5. The old wing formed the shorter leg of an L-shaped building, a newer wing forming the longer leg. The old wing had enormously thick walls and tiny windows; a portion of it, dated 1607, had been added to a much older nucleus.

6. The Ritual was written after the execution of Charles I (1649), and before the restoration of Charles II (1660).

7. At the time Holmes passed through the old door, the sun shone full on the passage floor, inside.

8. The 51st parallel of north latitude passes through West Sussex.

From these premises, and from the related statements in the narrative, we may draw some corollaries. There may be some differences of opinion about details, but not to a degree, I believe, which will invalidate conclusions to be reached as to the season of the year.

From Premise No. 1: The length of the steps would be normal for an active, adult male—3 feet, give or take a few inches. The lengths of the legs of the traverse were approximately 60 feet N, 30 feet E, 12 feet S, and 6 feet W. The traverse passed around, and close to, the north end of the old wing.

From Premise No. 4: The old wing was aligned north and south.

From Premise No. 6 (and from records of observations which indicate no significant variation—or declination, or deviation—of the magnetic compass in the 1650's[4]): "North" means true north.

From Premises Nos. 1, 3 and 7: In the afternoon, the sunlight on the floor of the passage could not have come through the old door. We may deduce an opening in the west wall.

It is apparent that two, and only two, of the conditions imposed by the season of the year must be considered in our analysis of the events at the site: (1) the hour at which the sun descends to the "Critical Angle"; (2) its direction at that hour. How do these related variables affect the premises? On Plates I and II are plotted, for the

opening and closing days of the two periods defined by Dr.
Zeisler, the approximate[5] positions of the sun, and the
corresponding positions of the two trees, their shadows,
the "Point of Departure," The Traverse," and the two wings
of the Manor House, at the hours in the afternoon (there
would be a different set of conditions in the morning)
when the sun reaches the "Critical Angle." Let us examine
their effects on the events.

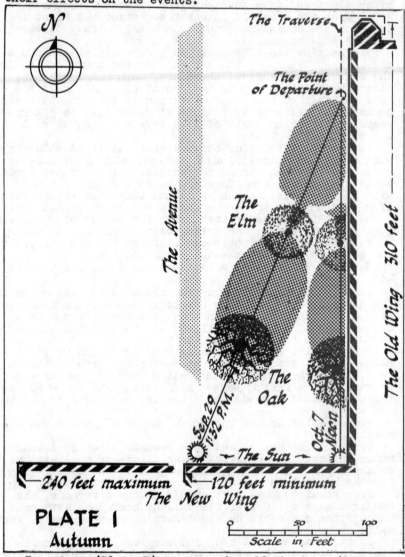

PLATE I
Autumn

In autumn (Plate I) on September 29 the hour (let us
call it "H-Hour") is 1:32 P.M. and the direction 67.9 degrees south of west; on October 7 the hour is noon, the
direction due south. We may disregard the remaining days

in Dr. Zeisler's autumn period; at latitude 51 the sun
never rises as high as 33.7 degrees on October 8 or thereafter.
In summer (Plate II) on July 5 "H-Hour" is 5:17 P.M.

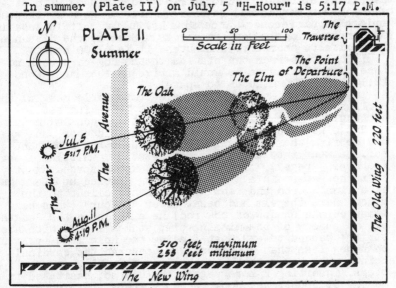

and the direction 10.8 degrees south of west. What clues
present themselves?

1st Clue: When did Holmes arrive at the Manor House?
After noon and about an hour before "H-Hour." He observed
the oak as the two men drove along the avenue. Before entering the house they walked over to the oak and then to
the scar on the lawn where the elm had been. After discussing the height of the elm Holmes looked up at the sun,
low in the heavens and calculated that in less than an
hour it would lie just above the topmost branches of the
oak. The dog-cart must have pulled up at about H-minus-1.

This further restricts the autumn period. "H-Hour" cannot be earlier than 1:00 P.M. or Holmes must arrive before
noon, but it is 12:56 P.M. on October 4. October 3 is the
last day we must consider.[6] Even on September 29, the most
favourable day, Holmes must travel to Hurlstone Manor House
by 12:32 P.M. Is that possible?

Let us reconstruct his morning. Musgrave walked into
Holmes's rooms some time after breakfast. Holmes was an
early riser, but the aristocrat would hardly have break-
fasted and driven over to call, unannounced, before 9 A.M.

The opening introduction, reminiscences of college days,
recital of the events of the past four years, a statement of
the problem and discussion of the details, examination of
the Ritual and speculation on its significance; then the
decision to travel to the scene—at least an hour; it is
10:00 A.M.

I recall no instance when Holmes had to wait for a train
in London, but he must change his dressing gown for his
cape and deerstalker, pack, scribble a note to his landlady, call a cab, and drive to Victoria; including paying

off the cabbie, buying tickets, and finding a first-class
carriage: 30 minutes. It is 10:30 A.M.

Having no access to a Bradshaw of the period, I can only
estimate the time for the rail trip by comparing it with others
where time is mentioned. It took two hours to go to Winchester
and the Copper Beeches. Accepting Dr. Julian Wolff's location
of Hurlstone on the western border of Sussex, the distance
is about 25% shorter: 90 minutes. It is 12:00 noon.

If the ride from the station in the dog-cart took no
more than 30 minutes he would arrive at the Manor House at
12:30 P.M. Two minutes to spare!

In summer he would have a more comfortable margin; the
earliest H-minus-1 is 3:19 P.M. But this clue settles
nothing; either season is possible, but the odds favour summer.

2nd Clue: When did Holmes reach the old door, and what
did he find there? The time before "H-Hour" is accounted
for. He went into the house to the study, whittled a peg
(perhaps 3 pegs?), tied at least 33 knots spaced exactly
36 inches apart in a piece of string, picked up 2 lengths
of a fishing rod and went back with his client to the
place where the elm had been. After "H-Hour" (when he
measured the shadow of the rod) he calculated the length
of the shadow of the missing elm; staked it out with his
string; paused to exult at finding the hole left by Brunton's peg less than 2 inches away; checked the cardinal
points with his pocket compass; and carefully paced off 32
steps, inserting 2 more pegs as he did so; hesitated in a
moment of doubt; and took two more steps. 30 minutes? Certainly no more; perhaps less. He finds the sun shining
full on the passage floor.

The sun has advanced half an hour from the positions
shown on the two plates. On September 29 (2:02 P.M.) it
is west, 60.4 degrees south; on August 11 (4:49 P.M.) it
is west, 17.7 degrees south; and on July 5 (5:47 P.M.) it
is west, 3.3 degrees south. In each case its elevation
is a few degrees lower.

So what? Let us consider a point raised by Mr. Bell,
again as reported by Mr. Baring-Gould:[7] ". . . we are told
that this old wing of the house had 'enormously thick
walls and tiny windows'; therefore, unless the . . . sun had
been shining straight through such a tiny window in the
west wall, its light could not possibly have reached the
pavement. We have seen that the house faced the cardinal
points; hence the sun must have been setting due west and
the season, consequently, was late September. . . . In June,
when the sun sets in the north-west, the light would have
been lost in the deep window-embrasure, or would, at the
farthest, have illuminated a small portion of the south
wall of the passage." Mr. Baring-Gould concurs.

But I believe that both these respected authorities
have overlooked two important facts: (1) The sun was not
only shining in, it was shining on the floor, and (2) windows in fortified strongholds, from the Crusades to the
American Indian Wars, appear to be narrow slits, true, but
only to the attacker on the outside, to expose a small
target. Inside, their embrasures are splayed to permit a
wide angle of fire by defenders. Furthermore, their sills
are breast high to furnish body-protection and a rest for

the weapon. See Plate III.

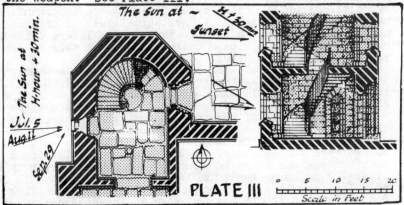

The Sun at ~ H+30min. Sunset

The Sun at H-hour + 30 min.

Jul. 5
Aug. 11

Sep. 29

PLATE III

Scale in Feet

On September 29 the sun in the early afternoon is too far south for its rays to enter a room through such a window; in the late afternoon it is so low on the horizon that its near-horizontal rays would not reach the floor. There is no such problem during the period July 5 to August 11; both direction and elevation are within the limits imposed by the window. Of course, if one is a strict constructionist and insists that the sun does not set until its disk touches the horizon, it would then be too low (though not too far north) for its rays to reach the floor. But, when it is convenient to do so, we can agree with Mr. Baring-Gould and his suggestion[8] that "setting sun" should be modified to "settling sun" and choose an earlier hour.

This clue, then, appears to prove the case for summer beyond a reasonable doubt. But tarry a little; there is something else. We cannot be certain that this particular opening was indeed the type we have described; it was not in the ancient nucleus but in the addition dated 1607. While architects, then and now, are prone to copy older details, there were, even in the 16th and 17th centuries, independent souls who refused to be guided by anything which had been done before. In this Jacobean period, architects across the channel were developing, at Fontainebleau, windows which became so popular in later centuries that to this day we call them "French doors." Even in autumn their generous width and slender jambs would have been open to the sun in early afternoon; their low sills would have admitted its rays almost until sunset. In this latter case, however, we must assume that Holmes, hot upon the scent, would have dallied along for $4\frac{1}{2}$ hours to finish a task which we have shown could have been performed in 30 minutes. Highly improbable? Yes. Impossible? No. He himself paid little attention to meal times when on a case, but he was with a client. If we are to consider the autumn dates we must realise that Reginald Musgrave had either had no lunch at all by 1:32 P.M. or, at best, an unappetising snack at the station—an intolerable situation. Holmes had measured the shadow and determined the direction; he no longer needed the sun—if indeed he ever did.[9] Later in his career Holmes would have rejected the suggestion of a

luncheon break with asperity; at this period he was a young
practitioner on his third case. Clients were important. If
he had yielded he would not have been likely to disclose
such a temporary weakness to Watson, years later. While the
odds for summer now appear overwhelming, the case is not
yet closed. But we have:

The Final Clue: the conformation of the Manor House.
Note its outline if autumn conditions prevail (Plate I).
The length of the old wing encompassing, as it does, the
20 paces, north, of "The Traverse," the north-south compo-
nent of the length of the two shadows, and a reasonable
clearance between the oak and the house, scales 310 feet—
and this is the shorter wing! We have fewer data on which
to estimate the length of the new wing, but we are told
that the oak was right in front of the house. Taking this
literally as being at its midpoint, the new wing would be
only 160 feet long. But, since the place was a rambling
one, "right in front" may not mean its precise centre. A
reasonable interpretation would, however, place the oak
somewhere opposite its middle third, which would make the
wing as long as 240 feet (not longer) or as short as 120
feet.

If summer conditions prevail (Plate II), the situation
is reversed. The old wing scales but 220 feet, the distance
to the oak, 170 feet. If the oak is centred, the new wing is
340 feet long; on the middle-third principle it is anywhere between 255 and 510 feet long, truly the longer, as
Holmes said it was. We rest our case for summer.

If there be those who protest that dimensions of this
magnitude make Hurlstone Manor House a most formidable
residence—we agree. A paper, for which the world may now
be prepared, will demonstrate that such an appellation is
not incompatible with its history.

We must not, however, ignore such rebuttal as has not
already been demolished. Dr. Zeisler writes:[10] "The Ritual
. . . was written in the time of Charles II by one of his
staunch adherents, who would probably date things not in
the manner of the historians but in the usual legal manner
of the time, so that there is, perhaps, a small probabilit'
in favor of the autumn date over the summer date, but too
slight to be of much use." Even from that pale shadow of
a doubt we must dissent. The Stuarts were most concerned
for their place in history. Charles I's fatal obstinacy
was due, in part, to his reluctance to go down in the annals of the English kings as one who had permitted the
royal prerogatives to be weakened. Watson asks: "These
relics have a history, then?" Holmes replies: "So much so
that they are history." We can be sure that Sir Ralph Musgrave, the Cavalier, the right-hand man of Charles II in
his wanderings, would have recognised their significance.
He would have chosen the Historian's Calendar.

1. Peck, Andrew Jay, The Date Being—? N.p. [1970.]
2. Vol. I, p. 132, Note 22.
3. Ibid.
4. For a discussion of the use of the magnetic compass
   see: Merrill, Edward A., "Holmes and Brunton, Civil

Engineers," BSJ (NS) 20:39-47, (March) 1970, p. 40.

5. I have used modern tables of Sun Declinations and Sunset Times, a simplified trigonometric method for calculating the sun's declination at hours other than noon, and slide-rule computations. Distances are scaled, angles plotted with a protractor. Time is quoted to the nearest minute, and angles to the nearest tenth of a degree. These approximations may affect times by five or ten minutes, but while the errors so introduced would be unacceptable to the astronomer predicting an eclipse, or a space pilot plotting his course, they are not of a magnitude, I believe, which would invalidate conclusions regarding the choice between two seasons nearly three months apart.

6. Apparently this entirely eliminates Dr. Zeisler's basic month, October 6 to November 4, referred to in the passage quoted above. We might claim a decision for summer right here—but allow us to continue with the research which had already been developed before this fact was noticed by the present writer.

7. Op. <u>cit</u>., Vol. I, p. 136, Note 31.

8. <u>Ibid</u>.

9. This writer has submitted the theory that the Ritual could have been solved at any hour of any day in the year, including cloudy ones (<u>op</u>. <u>cit</u>.).

10. See note 2.

> Whose was it?
> His who is gone.
> Who shall have it?
> He who will come.
> What was the month?
> The sixth from the first.
> Where was the sun?
> Over the oak.
> Where was the shadow?
> Under the elm.
> How was it stepped?
> North by ten and by ten,
> East by five and by five,
> South by two and by two,
> West by one and by one,
> and so under.
> What shall we give for it?
> All that is ours.
> Why should we give it?
> For the sake of the trust.

HURLSTONE AND THE RITUAL

by Nicholas Utechin

> "'That must have been difficult, Holmes.'"
> —The Musgrave Ritual

The emplacement of Hurlstone, the ancient hall of the Musgraves, and its exact position in relation to the cardinal points of the compass have long been subjects for discussion. The difficulty is to produce a solution which agrees with both the internal evidence of the story and with the pacings and directions of the Ritual. Let me straightaway put before you all the relevant data:

"'. . . it is built in the shape of an L, the long arm being the more modern portion, and the shorter the ancient nucleus . . . .'"

"'Over the . . . door, in the centre of this old part . . . .'"

"'Right in front of the house, upon the left-hand side of the drive, there stood a patriarch among oaks.'"

"'. . . the scar . . . where the elm had stood . . . was nearly midway between the oak and the house.'"

"'I measured out the distance [of 96 feet], which brought me almost to the wall of the house . . . .'"

"'Ten steps with each foot took me along parallel with the wall of the house.'"

The Ritual runs as follows: "North by ten and by ten, east by five and by five, south by two and by two, west by one and by one, and so under." Now let us see if there is any one emplacement which would fit all these facts.

The sun was "setting," or, as the late William Baring-Gould says, more likely "settling," since it was only 4:30 P.M. Therefore it was in the west; and therefore the sun, the oak, and the indentation where the elm had stood were all in a straight line running west to east, a line continued for 96 feet "almost to the wall of the house." The question is, which wall?

There are eight possible positions for the L-shaped house:

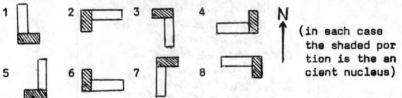

(in each case the shaded portion is the ancient nucleus)

Let us narrow down these possibilities. Fig. 1 is clearly impossible: for the Ritual to work, one must be able to turn left (north) on meeting the initial wall at the end of the shadow, right (east) and right again (south) and end up at the centre of one of the walls of the <u>old</u> wing. This one cannot do with Fig. 1. At first sight, Fig. 3 seems a possibility, but on further examination falls short of the requirements; the oak could only be in line with the edge of the south wall of the nucleus, thus: ●－－－▭ . So the north-south wall would have to be fifty feet (linear distances throughout are in accordance with Baring-Gould's equivalents given in <u>The Annotated Sherlock Holmes</u>). A right turn and ten paces (25 feet) should then bring us to the centre of the wall. In the case of Fig. 3, this would mean a box of 50′ x 50′ (50′ north-south walls and 2 x 25′ east-west walls) as the original building, which is rather unlikely—while 50 feet is acceptable as the <u>width</u> of a manor, such a measurement cannot be accepted as the <u>length</u> of a building which housed one of the oldest families in the kingdom. This last point also rules out Fig. 7 (which would give a length of 50 feet).

Thus far, Figs. 1, 3, and 7 have shown themselves impossible. I cannot hold either with Fig. 8—it does not fit a single piece of the data. Fig. 5 is equally unfeasible; even vaguely to fit the required data, the oak would have to be in a straight line with the east-west wall at the south, and by no stretch of the imagination could it be called "right in front of the house" in such a position.

Therefore we are left with Figs. 2, 4, and 6. Fig. 2 does fit the facts, but I think it is unlikely to be the true emplacement, for that would mean that the old, lintelled door would be in the middle of the east-west wall at the north end, which was continued by the wall of the newer wing, <u>i.e.</u> ⌐‖－－－┐ Door . Surely Holmes would have commented upon this. There is nothing in the evidence to go against Fig. 2, but aesthetically it is not pleasing. Also, if this were the true emplacement, there would be the minor complication of the driveway twisting and turning. The drive comes in at the house from the west (one assumes, since they passed the oak). If Fig. 2 were the case, the drive would have to run either thus:

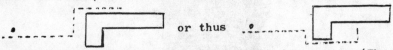

or thus

depending on where the main door of the house was. (The drive would, of course, lead up to the main door in the modern portion.)

Fig. 4 is the same as that chosen by Baring-Gould in the _Annotated_. In passing, it might be mentioned, his sketch illustrating this choice is either very badly drawn or atrociously reproduced (in the British edition, at least). The elm scar was approximately 96 feet from the wall of the house, and the oak was the same distance from the elm (". . . the scar . . . was nearly midway between the oak and the house."). In the _Annotated_ reproduction of the sketch the scale goes completely berserk. It must be admitted that Fig. 4 is quite plausible—I don't even have any aesthetic objections. Although there is nothing Sherlockian on which to fault it, it still doesn't seem right, with the modern wing looming hugely alongside the path of the shadow. However, you will see here that I have left the realm of hard facts and am now expressing personal preference.

So five of the eight emplacements can be dismissed on the evidence, one other is unlikely, and a further one is possible. The last is Fig. 6, which I submit as the true emplacement of Hurlstone. It fits all the data given in the story; there is ample room for the oak to be "right in front of the house"; the driveway need not twist too much; and, most important, it fits the wording of the Ritual, as shown below. Shoot me down in flames, if you can!

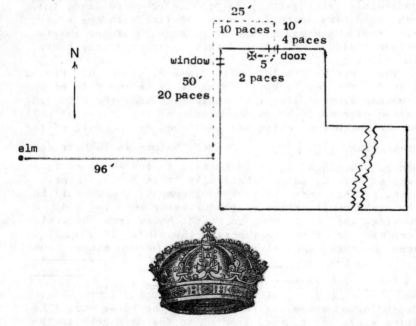

SHERLOCK HOLMES'S HONEYMOON
by Benjamin Grosbayne

It will no doubt come as a major though pleasurable
shock to the countless admirers of Sherlock Holmes to
learn at long last that the most famous consulting detective of his age was not the stranger to the grand passion
that he was made out to be; that he married and left a son
to carry on his own contribution to the world; and, most
intriguing of all, that he became a distinguished operatic
conductor and toured the musical centres of the world with
his wife, the famous contralto, Irene Adler.

How all this came about and how and why the story was
not permitted to reach the public will soon be understandable. In revealing the main facts of this seemingly fantastic yet wholly factual story which has been suppressed
until this moment, the present writer feels as did Dr.
Watson when he felt compelled to write (in FINA): "I am
satisfied that the time has come when no good purpose is
to be served by suppression. . . . I have no choice but to
lay the facts before the public as they occurred."

Those who have read Dr. Watson's chronicles of his
friend's incomparable deductions will recall to what extreme lengths the good doctor went to present the Baker
Street sleuth as so wrapped up in the detection of crime
and the apprehension of malefactors that he had neither
the time nor the inclination for the gentler and more
poetic activities of man. To effect the deception the
better and to mislead the reader the more, Watson repeatedly pictured the Master as cold, incisive, steely, objective, cynical, and as a mere thinking machine. Thus (in
SIGN) he quotes Holmes as saying: "But love is an emotional
thing, and whatever is emotional is opposed to that true
cold reason which I place above all things. I should never
marry myself, lest I should bias my judgment." In the same
tale we find Watson exclaiming: "What a very attractive
woman!" Whereupon Holmes replied languidly: "Is she? I did
not observe." Watson cried in return: "You really are an
automaton—a calculating machine. There is something posi-
tively inhuman in you at times." At this, Holmes gently
smiled and replied: "It is of first importance not to allow
your judgment to be biased by personal qualities. A client
is to me a mere unit, a factor in a problem. The emotional
qualities are antagonistic to clear reasoning. I assure you
that the most winning woman I ever knew was hanged for
poisoning her small children for the insurance money."

We realise, of course, that all this was part of Dr.
Watson's game to lead the reader astray, to shield his
famous friend from the curious gaze of the world. Watson
had good cause to know Holmes's passion for privacy. He
tells us (in GREE) how little he knew about the personal
affairs of the man with whom he shared lodgings and whom
he had known so long; of the man who was his closest
friend: "During my long and intimate acquaintance with Mr.
Sherlock Holmes, I had never heard him refer to his relations, and hardly ever to his own early life. This reti-
cence on his part had increased the somewhat inhuman

effect which he produced upon me, until sometimes I found myself regarding him as an isolated phenomenon, a brain without a heart, as deficient in human sympathy as he was eminent in intelligence. His aversion to women and his disinclination to form new friendships were both typical of his own unemotional character, but no more so than his complete suppression of every reference to his own people. I had come to believe that he was an orphan with no relatives living, but one day, to my great surprise, he began to talk to me about his brother. . . . 'My brother possesses [my powers] in a larger degree than I do. . . . When I say . . . that Mycroft has better powers of observation than I, you may take it that I am speaking the exact and literal truth.'"

If Holmes would wait so long before even mentioning his brother to Watson, we begin to understand somewhat his feelings about divulging to the world his one great romance, that with Irene Adler. Watson's determination to keep the facts secret is simply evidence of his loyalty to his best friend and is wholly understandable. We now know that he was aided and abetted in this deception by Mycroft, by Scotland Yard, and by relatives of Irene Adler.

It is quite easy at this late date to see through Watson's naïve attempts to lead the reader astray. Grim official vaults have yielded the tender love letters, the press cuttings, and numerous other documents which reveal the greatest romance of our grandparents' times. Indeed, Holmes himself, with all his care, gives himself away on more than one occasion: when he lets his true soul speak through the yearning and melancholy music of his violin, when he lets his fingers wave dreamily to romantic music. Do we have to be told in so many words that here is a poetic soul searching for a woman's love and understanding?

We begin to see through Watson's false picture if only because Holmes protests too much. The impact made upon Holmes by Irene Adler is cataclysmic. In SCAN Watson tells us: "To Sherlock Holmes she is always the woman. . . . It is not that he felt any emotion akin to love for Irene Adler. All emotions, and that one particularly, were abhorrent to his cold, precise but admirably balanced mind. . . . Grit in a sensitive instrument, or a crack in one of his own high-powered lenses would not be more disturbing than a strong emotion in a nature such as his. And yet there was but one woman to him, and that woman was the late Irene Adler, of dubious and questionable memory."

Dr. Watson, however unselfish his motives, is guilty of questionable taste in more ways than one. In the first place, he is simply fibbing when he speaks of the late Irene Adler. She was at that time very much alive—very much alive indeed. In the second place, to describe a great actress and singer as "of dubious and questionable memory" simply because she refused to be threatened into parting with a photograph taken with a King who broke his word to her, and which she needed for self-protection, is, to put it euphemistically, unchivalrous, ungallant, and ungenerous. Dr. Watson must be pardoned on the grounds that he was frantically trying to hide his hero's romance from the world. Perhaps a contemporary psychiatrist might explain this lapse in an English gentleman by saying that Watson hated to share Holmes with anyone, especially a wife, since that eventually might lead to the end of the partnership. What Holmes thought of Miss Adler is easily seen from the facts that he refused to take the hand proffered to him by his royal visitor (in SCAN); that he disdained any honorarium; and that he amazed the King by asking only for Irene's photograph. Watson's own words point this up: "He used to make merry over the cleverness of women, but I have not heard him do it of late. And when he speaks of Irene Adler, or when he refers to her photograph, it is always under the honourable title of the woman."

Nobody today is at all deceived by Watson's feeble attempts to cover up the true feelings between the greatest singer and the greatest sleuth of their epoch. It is now easy enough to see through Watson's childish subterfuge. He had been around a lot in his time and could hardly have lived so long without being able to read something of his friend's mind. After all, Watson was a physician, with years of practice in and outside of the army, and, even without the benefit of the art of psychoanalysis as we know it today, he must have learned much about the workings of the human mind as well as the body. Perhaps, as a last thought in this connection, the guess may be hazarded that Watson was merely playing naïve, not only to hide his friend's secret, but also to point up Holmes's brilliance.

The protagonists that walked and talked and loved and hated in those far-off days in Baker Street have long left this earthly scene. The silence may now be broken. The letters between the great pair, their diaries, the press clips, the official documents—everything may now be consulted. At last we can follow, at least in outline, the marriage and the honeymoon, their operatic tour and artistic collaboration, the birth of their son, the singer's tragic death. For the proper telling of this tender story we must of course await more competent hands than the present writer's.

It will be recalled that Holmes's activities between the spring of 1891 and the spring of 1894 have never been revealed definitely. It was in the spring of 1891 that he fell to what everyone thought was certain death at the Reichenbach Falls, locked in a death grasp with Professor Moriarty, his arch-enemy. When he returned to London in the spring of 1894, he made vague references to Lhassa and two years in Tibet, to the Khalifa at Khartoum, to Montpellier in France. Patently a man of Holmes's temperament could never have spent so long a time in what amounts to inconsequential sight-seeing. Those who have thus far withheld the true story may now wrestle with their consciences. Here is the true story at last.

When Holmes scrambled up the pathway leading to safety, after baritsu had enabled him to elude Moriarty's fiendish grasp, the latter had also saved himself by grasping a rock half-way down the Fall. Here he clung for hours, hidden by the descending torrents of water. Later he was hoisted back to safety by the same false messenger who had summoned Watson back to the hotel. Although Holmes did not know of Moriarty's escape at the time, he was soon to learn of it from Mycroft.

It will be recalled that Irene Adler had married Godfrey Norton—not the first time, nor the last, that a lady has married the wrong man in pique to punish the man she really loved. What would have happened to the romance between the singer and the detective if Mr. Norton had not been fatally injured a few weeks after the marriage while riding horseback is beyond our province. Here only the actual happenings need concern us.

It did not take long for Holmes to learn of Moriarty's escape and Norton's death. It was then that he decided at once upon two plans of action: one, to go underground and to disguise himself, the better to trap his arch enemy; and two, to bring Irene over to the continent and make her his wife. She, too, was to travel incognito, for the henchmen of Wilhelm had never ceased to search for that photograph.

The details of Sherlock and Irene's meeting in Paris; his hasty wooing; their almost immediate marriage; and their hurried preparations for their combined trip of a honeymoon and artistic collaboration need not detain us at this time. What concerns us is the condition that Miss Adler placed upon Holmes: that she be allowed to resume her operatic career. Holmes was to prepare himself to conduct the operas in which she was to appear. They were both, from that moment on, to appear to the world only in disguise and under assumed names.

For Holmes, who was a consummate actor, and for Irene, who was a professional singing actress, all this was a simple matter, but it took considerable wangling to get bookings under their new names. For Holmes to assume another rôle, that of operatic conductor—an ambition which he had had secretly for a long time and which he had concealed even from Watson and Mycroft—was not as difficult as would appear at first glance. We must remember that, in addition to being a violinist of no ordinary calibre, he was a musical scholar who had even written a monograph on the polyphonic motets of Lassus. Also, he had been an opera-goer for years. We are reminded (in LAST) that he knew his Wagner enough to jump in at any point. "By the way," he exclaims to Watson, "it is not yet eight o'clock, and a Wagner night at Covent Garden. If we hurry, we might be in time for the second act." Scholars will some day ascertain where he studied his musical theory and instrumentation and under what masters, for such abilities are not achieved without long and arduous apprenticeship. The world lost a great actor when he decided to dedicate himself to criminal investigation. Fortunately, the world did not also lose a gifted orchestra conductor, though this has not been generally known.

The first place the honeymooners betook themselves for the start of their honeymoon and to prepare their operatic repertory was the tiny town of Brigue in Switzerland, known even today to few tourists. They rented a doll-like chalet with the only piano in town and had to send to Montreux for a competent tuner.

The story of their first evening together is of special charm. Mrs. Holmes, like so many opera singers, was passionately fond of cooking and prepared the Forellen (local trout) with her own hands. During the evening she sang to her own accompaniment and to Holmes's improvised violin obligato variations of Schubert's exquisite lyric, "Die Forellen." Those who have unjustly pictured Holmes as a mere thinking machine should have seen the real Holmes that night as he spent the first evening of his honeymoon playing operatic airs and folk-songs with his wife. Here he was a tender husband and an unaffected musician.

This idyllic existence continued for some weeks to allow the two artists to prepare for their public performances. While she reviewed the rôles which had made her famous, he, in his new rôle of conductor, pored over his scores. Their life at this time, as shown by their diaries, is one of the most beautiful episodes in the history of great romances of all time. With that of the Brownings it is a complete refutation of the oft-repeated charge that two professional artists cannot live together harmoniously as husband and wife.

The ideal arrangement of having Holmes in the orchestra pit while his wife was only a few feet away on the stage can be understood. He was in a position to come to her aid almost at once in any emergency, for both the King's emissaries and Moriarty's henchmen, Holmes was sure, would not hesitate to get at him through the person he most loved.

It is not difficult to trace the main points of their itinerary during parts of the years 1891 and 1892 from this time on. We find frequent accounts in almost every operatic centre on the continent of the pair who soon became famous all over again. The daily newspapers and periodicals were full of the triumphs of the mysterious new couple who were always seen together, she singing and he conducting. The mystery was heightened by their arriving at the last possible moment and leaving directly after the final curtain. The fact that their musical antecedents were wholly unknown aroused a tremendous amount of gossip and speculation. So well did they guard their real identities, however, that the names of Irene Adler and Sherlock Holmes, known all over the world in their original characters, were never once linked to their new personalities.

Engagements filled every available date. The tour was an unprecedented success for each artist. They appeared in every important city in Europe; everywhere the critical reactions were the same. Thus, in Paris, where the operatic fare was Bizet's Carmen, superlatives and adjectives lost most of their original meanings. Carmen has long been the supreme test for a contralto's art on the French lyric stage. To appear in it in Paris is a doubly difficult test, for the French feel that only their own singers understand the part. Yet the critic of Beaux Arts, after devoting two columns of rhapsody to the singer, ended by writing:

"That a previously unknown singer could interpret the rôle as did this singer, so faultlessly from every point of view! First, she is not French nor Spanish nor even Latin; secondly, she is unknown! From the beginning of the work, every note, to the impassioned defiance in the face of certain death at the end profoundly moved this veteran reviewer. This artiste was Carmen; there was no illusion; it was not opera; it was life." The final sentence of the review was significant: "No little credit goes to the conductor who was so perfectly en rapport with the singer; they were indeed as one artistically."

The Chronique Musicale described the frenzy of the hearers for both the singer and the conductor: "Who is this chef d'orchestre of whom we have hitherto heard nothing?" In Vienna, where the bill was Gluck's immortal tale, Orpheus and Eurydice, the critic of the leading Tageblatt asked again: "Who is this unknown singer, and who is this unknown conductor who can so tenderly project to us again a work of ageless nobility?"

It was the same story elsewhere. In Rome, in Florence, in Prague, even in Scandinavia, where the music-lovers accept no second-hand critiques but insist on forming their own judgments and are notoriously hard on newcomers, the receptions were merely variations of the main theme. The papers of Helsinki, Budapest, Zurich, Turin, and a score of other leading dailies were in accord for once. In some of the theatres it was difficult to prevail upon the audience to leave.

In Berlin, where the pair presented Samson and Delilah, the German critics wrote abstruse essays on the psychological, physiological, vocal, mental, æsthetic, musical, and histrionic facets of the singer's and conductor's arts. One asked rhetorically: "Have we really heard this work before? It is a serious question in this writer's mind."

It must not be assumed that Irene and Sherlock ceased for even a single moment in their constant vigil against the agents of Moriarty and of the Bohemian King. They were only too well aware that the slightest slip would inevitably reveal their identities to their enemies and that they might pay with their lives.

It was in the spring of 1892 that it happened. Holmes had tried again and again to convince his wife that she ought to stop singing. But the phenomenal success of each evening had caused her to postpone her retirement. Holmes, who had known for some months that he was about to become a father, finally put his foot down and named the Carmen performance at La Scala in Milan as the last public appearance in which he would permit his wife to sing. Their baby was due in a few months, and it was only after much pleading and tears that, against his better judgment, he was at last prevailed upon to permit this final performance.

For some days Holmes had experienced an indefinite sensation, an old occult faculty harking back to the Baker Street days, that they were being shadowed. He knew that certain members of the hotel staff and of the opera company were watching their every move. He did not have to be told this; he knew and felt it with the famous instinct which had carried him so brilliantly through so many tough battles. But this time, fighting for the safety of the only woman he had ever loved, he was perhaps not at his best. Like a surgeon, he should not have been concerned with a

case so close to his heart. Perhaps he should have called
in his colleagues of the efficient Italian Secret Service
with whom he had collaborated on more than one international cause célèbre. Or perhaps he felt that this was not
a matter for officialdom and unconsciously he felt that he
had to stand alone. If he had foreseen the outcome he
might not have decided to carry his burden alone as he had
always done. He had reason to regret his decision for the
rest of his life. After all, he reasoned in cold logic, he
had only furtive and stealthy glances to base his case on.
He must bide his time and never let his wife out of sight.
He redoubled his watchfulness, saw no strangers, and
guarded their disguises with renewed vigilance.

Mrs. Holmes had been dispirited and listless for the
days preceding the performance in Milan. Their hotel faced
the Teatro alla Scala, which simplified their problem.
Holmes again attempted to dissuade his wife from appearing,
but after the first rehearsal, when the papers printed the
accounts of the orchestra's and choristers' frenzied reactions, there seemed to be nothing left to do but to go on
as scheduled. He was determined, in any event, that this
was to be the final performance for all time.

From the moment that the famous contralto walked onto
the stage it was painfully evident to seasoned theatre-
goers that all was not well with her. Although she maintained a reasonable level of competence, it was obvious
that she was under great strain. It did not take a musician to sense that she was employing every device to save
her voice and strength. She was singing sotto voce and
moving about as little as possible. Those in the first
rows could not escape a feeling of something sinister in
the air, and the effect was considerably heightened by the
noticeable lack of apprehension on the singer's face whenever the Don José of the evening was on the stage with her.

Holmes, his whole instinct warning him of impending
danger, had desperately endeavoured to dissuade his wife
from going on for the last act. This she flatly refused to
agree to. She, who had never missed a performance in her
whole career, would simply not end her career so. Just before the denouement, when Carmen's companions, Mercedes
and Frasquita, warn her that Don José means to kill her,
she uttered her words of defiance with such vehemence and
passion that the whole auditorium became electrified. All
had an uncanny feeling that this was not merely theatre,
but that something terrible was in the offing.

When the singer faced the infuriated Don José in the
final scene and was given the choice of love with him or
death, she was seen to stagger and turn chalky white. She
recovered quickly, however, and threw his ring at him
viciously as she screamed: "Here is the ring!" At that moment, Don José, who had been more realistic throughout the
evening than even the most realistic stage business could
possibly demand, dealt her a tremendous blow directly under
the heart instead of the traditional make-believe stabbing.
She managed to give a stifled sob and then sank in a dis-
ordered heap on the stage.

Holmes, who had been watching the stage action with intensity, had dropped the baton in a fraction of a second and was racing under the stage and bounding up the steps four at a time. The concertmaster, who made a feeble attempt to lead the orchestra through the last few measures of the music, gave up when the players and the members of the audience rose in frantic excitement and began shouting for a doctor, for it was apparent to all that the singer was gravely hurt. By this time Holmes was at his wife's side, but not soon enought to prevent the escape of the singer's assailant, who was never seen again.

When the curtain was lowered and the audience repeatedly assured that the singer was merely indisposed and would soon sing again, a physician, hastily summoned, had her removed to her dressing room. One glance revealed to his trained eyes that the shock had brought on the premature birth of the baby and that the mother was in the gravest condition possible. Within a few hours, despite his own and a consultant's heroic efforts, Mrs. Holmes was dead, leaving behind her a baby boy.

Of the father's thoughts at this moment, of his ultimate revenge on the Moriarty gang that had perpetrated this evil deed, it is not the present writer's intent to dwell. This painful task he leaves to the literary executors, who have the relevant documents. It is upon their shoulders that this ordeal must devolve.

This writer, however, is happy to reassure his readers that Sherlock Holmes did bring the malefactors to justice, however unorthodox that justice may appear to traditional law-enforcement officials. Of Harold Holmes, the new scion of the Holmes clan, we must await a more opportune time than the present to speak. In the not too distant future no doubt many of the secret documents in the official British Government files will be made accessible to all.

It is enough for the countless admirers of the greatest consulting detective of his generation to know that Sherlock Holmes was not merely just a combination of reflexes, as he has hitherto been pictured, but was in addition a tender lover, a devoted husband, the kindest of fathers, and a gifted operatic conductor. Surely that is enough for any man.

AN ENQUIRY INTO THE IDENTITY
OF THE BRUCE-PARTINGTON SUBMARINE

by J. S. Callaway, U.S.N.

Sherlockian scholarship has long accepted as one of its primary responsibilities the unravelling of the tangled skein in which Dr. Watson has so diligently entwined the true rôle of Sherlock Holmes in the international affairs of the late Victorian era. Nowhere is this policy of artful deception more in evidence than in The Adventure of the Bruce-Partington Plans. Watson's care in handling so delicate an affair of state is readily appreciated, but it is regretted that a more accurate account was not entrusted to the keeping of Cox & Co. for the benefit of historians.

Nonetheless, an attempt must be made to reach the truth, and an excellent example has been set by the late Fletcher Pratt, respected naval historian and Sherlockian. Mr. Pratt has written:

> The date was 1895; and not for a decade and a half thereafter was a submarine produced which made the operations of surface ships dangerous, to say nothing of impossible. As a matter of fact England herself built no submarines of any kind until 1905... from the designs of John Holland.[1]

Based on the date 1895, Mr. Pratt goes on to speculate that the Bruce-Partington plans were used to build the French submarine Morse of 1896, which he unfairly branded a failure.

What, then, does Mr. Pratt's research do to the statement of Mycroft Holmes to his brother Sherlock that "naval warfare becomes impossible within the radius of a Bruce-Partington's operation"? Two conclusions are clearly justified: (1) The Bruce-Partington submarine was not a British invention; (2) a working model existed at the date of the adventure, and it had given convincing demonstrations of its fighting ability.

It must now be pointed out that Mr. Pratt has been incorrect in dating the invention of the Bruce-Partington submarine in 1895, for Mycroft clearly states: "Two years ago a very large sum was smuggled through the Estimates and was expended in acquiring a monopoly of the invention." Thus, the Morse may be dismissed as the Bruce-Partington submarine on the grounds that it had not been designed or built in time to fit the required dates.

But what, it must be asked, has been gained by fixing the date of the origin of the Bruce-Partington plans in

1893? What has been gained, it must be said, is nothing less than the solution to the problem.

In 1893 the French navy completed work on a submarine of 270 tons displacement designed by the great naval architect, Dupuy de Lome. This electrically propelled vessel, the *Gustare Zede*, had an operational radius of 175 miles and a submerged speed of five knots. With the ability to remain submerged for up to eight hours, the *Zede* could attack surface ships with three 18-inch Whitehead torpedoes. The British were greatly impressed by this submarine's performance in manoeuvres and surely recognised the danger of squadrons of such craft operating in narrow seas such as the English Channel or the Straits of Gibraltar.[2]

When all other possibilities are eliminated that which remains must be the truth. Thus the evidence points to the French *Gustare Zede* as the true Bruce-Partington submarine.[3] But the matter cannot be allowed to rest here, for other questions come quickly to the surface: (1) How did plans for a French submarine come to be in the British army arsenal at Woolwich? (2) Why was the loss of another nation's secret considered such a blow to the security of Great Britain? (3) Why were British submarines never built from the plans? (4) Who was Bruce-Partington, if he was not an inventor? (5) Why has the Bruce-Partington affair remained a secret for so long?

Consider the following hypothesis: In 1893 the British government was given an opportunity to obtain for "a very large sum" the plans for a new French submarine which it had reason to believe would be highly successful. At that time only army funds could be obtained for the clandestine purchase, so the "Bruce-Partington" plans became the responsibility of the British army, and the agent dropped back into obscurity.

In buying the plans the British never intended to build submarines of their own; rather they hoped to prevent a third naval power from obtaining the weapon and also to use the plans in devising defenses against submarine attacks on their surface ships. As the *Gustare Zede* demonstrated its effectiveness, and defensive measures proved elusive, concern at the Admiralty deepened.

Happily, the possibility of war with France lessened as Germany became an increasing threat to both nations. Then, in November 1895, seven pages of the Bruce-Partington plans were found on the body of a murdered government clerk, while three vital pages were missing. The British government was confronted with a grave crisis, for it faced the possibility of war with the United

States over the Venezuela boundary dispute and with Germany over the Kruger telegram. Either nation might obtain the plans and use them with telling effect.

Disaster was averted, however, when Sherlock Holmes recovered the missing pages and captured the conspirators. In the wake of the Bruce-Partington crisis, the importance of the plans decreased as *Zede*-type submarines became obsolete, so that when England decided to acquire submarines of her own, she turned to the Holland design. Nevertheless, the true nature of the Bruce-Partington plans had to remain secret lest the Anglo-French Entente be jeopardised, a policy that has remained in force up to the present day.

1. Quoted from William S. Baring-Gould, The Annotated Sherlock Holmes, Vol. II.
2. Philip Cowburn, The Warship in History, New York: The Macmillan Company, 1965, pp. 249 and 255; Donald Macintyre and Basil W. Bathe, Man-of-War, New York: McGraw-Hill, 1969, pp. 167 and 169.
3. Those who wish to seek other possibilities than the *Gustave Zede* will find Robert W. Jones's article, "The Garrett-Nordenfeld Submarines," appearing in the Winter 1968 issue of Warships International, most interesting. Also, an interesting comment on submarines in Sherlockian days will be found on page 134 of the Spring 1969 issue of WI.

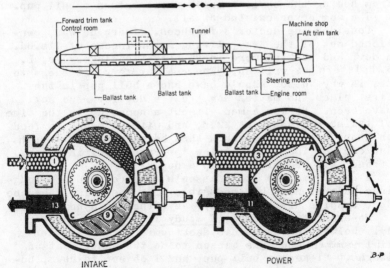

INTAKE POWER *B-P*

DOUBLE VALVES WITH AUTOMATIC SELF-ADJUSTING SLOTS

A LOT OF BULL PUP

by Jack Tracy

"I keep a bull pup," Watson said to Holmes when asked to confess his shortcomings that memorable day in the chemical laboratory of St. Bartholomew's Hospital. As we know, it is never heard of again. The bull pup, I mean.

The question of what became of Watson's bull pup has been debated for years. The dog froze onto Holmes's ankle, recalling Victor Trevor's terrier, and Holmes ordered it out. Mrs. Hudson refused to have the pup in the house. The puppy was accidentally killed, or Holmes sacrificed it on the altar of science. The dog, "unable to stand the Baker Street ménage," ran away. Watson's pup and Mrs. Hudson's "poor little devil of a terrier" were one and the same animal. And so on.

Yet, as the Master himself was careful to point out, an active, imaginative mind is often apt to seek a complicated explanation where a simpler explanation is more obvious and more logical. There can be no doubt that Sherlockian scholars are blessed with active, imaginative minds, and it is often their trademark to seek complex, obscure, and even outlandish solutions for quite simple problems. It is my opinion that just such a handicap has prevented commentators on the Canon from seeing the obvious truth about Watson's bull pup.

The dog never existed at all.

Consider the doctor's finances. There he was, pensioned out of the Army, living on an income of 11s.6d. a day, and seeking more inexpensive lodgings. Mr. L. S. Holstein has written, "The real mystery, it seems to me, is why Watson should have had a bull pup in the first place, no matter how great a dog-lover he may have been. He was a man without a home, up to the time of taking residence at 221B, and without means to feed an extra mouth even though that be only a dog's mouth. And can you imagine that the 'private hotel in the Strand' allowed him to keep a dog?"[1]

I can't imagine it. Watson's finances and his lodgings made it all but impossible. He most likely had no dog, despite his statement. Why, then, did he make it?

Re-examine the scene (A Study in Scarlet, Chapter 1). Holmes confesses his shortcomings to his potential roommate and asks Watson to do the same. Watson laughs. "I keep a bull pup, and I object to rows, because my nerves are shaken, and I get up at all sorts

of ungodly hours, and I am extremely lazy. I have
another set of vices when I'm well, but those are the
principal ones at present."

I believe the context allows us to read the truth.
Watson is detailing his habits—his propensities—and
the fact that he mentions the non-existent bull pup first
indicates the depth of his loneliness. "I keep a bull
pup," he says—meaning that, whenever circumstances allow, he likes to have a puppy around. A man may say,
"I raise vegetable marrows," even though he hasn't got
around to planting them yet—or, "I smoke 'ship's,'"
even though he has Arcadia mixture in his pocket at the
moment. Watson meant to buy a bull pup at the first
opportunity, once he was established at 221B. It was
probably a practice begun in childhood—in Australia
or Hampshire or wherever—and continued whenever and
wherever possible.

Then why did he not do so? Partly, perhaps, due to
Mrs. Hudson's objections when he mentioned the matter
to her—if he did. She had an aging terrier of her own,
which she did not want excited by an enthusiastically
playful puppy. And partly due to Watson's own condition. "I object to rows," of which puppies are the consistent epitome, and he explains, "My health forbade
me from venturing out unless the weather was exception-
ally genial"—making the care of a pet taxing to his
constitution.

With the death of their landlady's terrier and the
return of his health, Watson might have made good his
threat to purchase a dog—but by then he was involved
in Holmes's cases and had little time or interest for
pets. Although the Canon does not mention it, I am
sure that during his married years the good doctor
kept a succession of bull pups—though their care no
doubt fell for the most part to the Mrs. Watsons, considering how often Watson himself was out throwing in
his lot with Holmes.

---

1. "Bull Pups and Literary Agents," BSJ (XA):54-57,
   1958.

Editor's note: For other non-caninical solutions to this
problem see the following article by George Fletcher and
page 127 of the June 1969 Journal, where we are told that
"The expression 'I keep a bull pup' is North-West Fron-
tier slang meaning that the user has fits of quick temper."

SIGHTING-IN ON WATSON'S BULL PUP

by George Fletcher

Dr. Watson's observation "I keep a bull pup" (STUD) has been subjected to various interpretations and speculation.[1] In the June 1967 BSJ (Vol. 17, No. 2, p. 114), Deal-Top Monographer Jerry Stockler was reported as having advanced the theory that Watson's "bull pup" was actually his "bull dog" (or short-barreled, large-calibre) revolver. This is close to the mark. There is, however, a type of firearm which _is_ a bull pup: this is a military rifle of unusual design, so constructed that the action is placed toward the back of the buttstock, with the trigger forward of the magazine. The result is a much longer barrel on a standard-length stock, or a standard-length barrel on a very short stock; thus, for example, the overall length of the weapon is the same, but the barrel is essentially longer than it could be in a similar rifle of conventional design. There is the benefit here of greater accuracy. This benefit, unfortunately, is badly offset by the inherent failing in this design: The shooter's ear is next to the action or at least close to the chamber—each shot reverberates through the firer's head like a blow on an anvil.

One of the earliest bull-pup rifles (the phrase apparently originated in the United States) of which we have substantial knowledge is a weapon designed by Harry Gamwell, a Liverpool gunsmith who flourished around the turn of the century.[2] His design was patented on April 16, 1904, and the prototype was soon fired and liked by King Edward VII (who had frequent occasion to avail himself of Holmes's skills[3]). Unfortunately for Gamwell, his patron—Admiral of the Fleet Sir Henry Keppel—who had induced Edward to try the rifle, died that same year, and the entire project came to nought.

We know Watson's proficiency with firearms,[4] and it is possible that during his army career he had realised the advantages which this type of rifle might have, and not just in Afghanistan. If he did attempt to design such a weapon, his attempts must have miscarried as surely as did Gamwell's later ones. (Or could "Gamwell" be Watson with a healed leg?) Watson's own wound(s) and new interests may have conspired to distract him from his experiments, or he may have been dissuaded from keeping a rifle of military calibre at 221B Baker Street. Imagine the damage which Holmes—who was an expert rifleman[5]—could have caused the wallpaper and plaster had he chosen this weapon for his patriotic target-shooting (MUSG)!

Notes

1. See, for example, The Annotated Sherlock Holmes, Vol. 1, pp. 151-152 at note 18; and D. A. Redmond's Cumulated Index, p. 62 s.v "Watson: bull pup."
2. F. W. A. Hobart, "Gamwell's 'Bull-Pup' Rifle," The American Rifleman 118:68-70, (October) 1970.
3. SCAN, BERY, ILLU, and at the time of HOUN and 3 GAR.
4. Robert Keith Leavitt, "Annie Oakley in Baker Street," Profile by Gaslight, pp. 230-242.
5. Ibid.

Gamwell's short rifle as used by King Edward VII

THE SUSSEX VAMPIRE   B. & G. Wells

Full-size (9" x 9") prints in any colour on any colour paper are available from Dr. George E. Wells, Jr., 727 Nottingham Road, Baltimore, Md. 21229; price $10.00.

by   D. A. Redmond

Fred Mende in the March 1971 BSJ ("Will the Real Watson Please Stand") makes a case for Surgeon-Major Preston as the prototype of Doctor John H. Watson. Mende
admits other theories to have been advanced—Major Wood,
Doctor James Watson, and Doctor A. C. Doyle. His own
theory bears some aMending, however, for his excellent
research seems to omit a significant item in one of the
sources he cites: S. H. Shadbolt's The Afghan Campaign
of 1878-1880.[1] This item is the biographical notice of
Surgeon George Watson, M.B., Bengal Medical Department.[2]
For comparison with that of Alexander Francis Preston,
as given by Mende, here is a summary of Shadbolt's note:

> Born 4th September 1844; M.B., Edinburgh, 1866
> House Surgeon, Dumfries and Galloway Royal Infir-
>   mary, 17 months
> L.R.C.S., Edinburgh, 1868
> Passed for the Indian Medical Service, 1872; com-
>   missioned, passed course at Netley
> Arriving India Autumn 1872, posted successively
>   to 33rd Bengal Native Infantry, 8th Bengal
>   Cavalry, 14th Bengal Lancers
> Permanently appointed January 1876 to 13th Bengal
>   Lancers
> Volunteered for active service in Afghanistan,
>   autumn 1878; present at capture of Ali Musjid,
>   21st November
> Proceeded with 13th by forced marches to the Kuram
>   Valley, autumn 1879
> Suffered repeated attacks of fever; moved to the
>   Peiwar Kotal in July 1880, but died of enteric
>   fever 25th July; buried at Fort Kuram

In many particulars the resemblance is too close to
be accidental. The writer of the scanty biographical
information about John H. Watson, "late Indian Army,"
must surely have known of Surgeon George Watson as well
as of Surgeon-Major Preston. Watson was dead; it would
be safer to use his name, and his ill health and enteric
fever would be a reason for invaliding him home, while
Preston was still on duty. It is striking to see Surgeon
George Watson's portrait in Shadbolt's record; the hir-
sute visage is much more reminiscent of John H. Watson
than is the youthful Preston. Clearly, our prototype is
plural, a blend of facts and faces; and Mende's suggestion that a recuperating Preston may have reminisced to

Doctor Doyle in the South of England between 1882 and 1885 is an attractive one. Doyle would not have dared to depict Preston as himself alone. Several "real" John H. Watsons must stand up.

It is perhaps irrelevant to the location of Watson's wounds, or to those of Surgeon-Major Preston, but it may be enlightening in relation to the frequent vagueness of Watson's own narratives to inspect the maps of the Battle of Maiwand as given respectively in official and unofficial accounts of the Afghan campaign. Shadbolt gives a map (see next page) bearing the ascription, "Drawn from a sketch by Lieut. Hon. M. G. Talbot, R.E., when the field was revisited in September." The attribution is also given to "Edwd. Weller, Lith." However, the official account, published by the Intelligence Branch, Indian Army, as The Second Afghan War, 1878-80, Abridged Official Account,3 bears the same legends; but differs in ascribing the "Position of troops, Major Leach, R.E," while only the "Ground" is from Talbot's sketch; and sundry points, particularly the retreat route of General Burrows, are different. It is evident that, as the official account admits:

The exact sequence of the incidents which followed and the precise time of their occurrence cannot be ascertained with accuracy, and protracted enquiries into and discussion of these points have not resulted in any satisfactory elucidation of the disputed questions. The main facts are, however, tolerably clear.[4]

This smacks somewhat of W. S. Gilbert's Grand Inquisitor:

> Which was which he could never make out
> Despite his best endeavour.
> Of that there is no manner of doubt—
> No possible, probable shadow of doubt—
> No possible doubt whatever.[5]

The subsequent narratives left for us by John H. Watson, M.D. (or was it M.B.?) seem to suffer from the aftermath of Maiwand. One can now understand his babbling to Mary Morstan of a double-barrelled tiger cub (and perhaps even his confusion as to when he was married and to whom) on the same basis as the prosthesis fixation which has already been demonstrated[6] to have resulted in Watson from the battle fatigue of Maiwand. He was too shaken, as were nearly all the British in that disaster, to know what happened; and his case was long in the cure. Surgeon-Major Preston may have been twice wounded somewhere; Surgeon Watson may have died of enteric fever;

SKETCH OF THE ACTION AT
MAIWAND
27th July, 1880.

0 100 200 300 400 500 600 700 Yards

Note. The Sketch shews the relative position of the Afghan advance and guns, at the time when our line gave way. The smooth-bore battery had retired from the front some time before.

Position of the Afghan Artillery

Dry Ravine 15' to 20' deep

Held by Ghazis throughout the A[...]

3 Armstrongs

4, 6 Prs

4, 6 Prs

4, 6 Prs

2, 9 Prs

wheel   tracks

Kabulis

Final Ghazi Advance

Grenadiers

Maclaine's guns (captured)

Sappers

2 Co. J.R.O.

E/B. R.H.A.

4 Co. Jacob's Rifles

66th

Ge[...]

3rd Cav[...]

Direction of Cavalry Charge after th[...]

2 Co. J.R.

Approximate final Position as shewn by Afghan Cavalry

loose camels

Afghan camp

Position occupied by Maclaine's guns at commencement of the action.

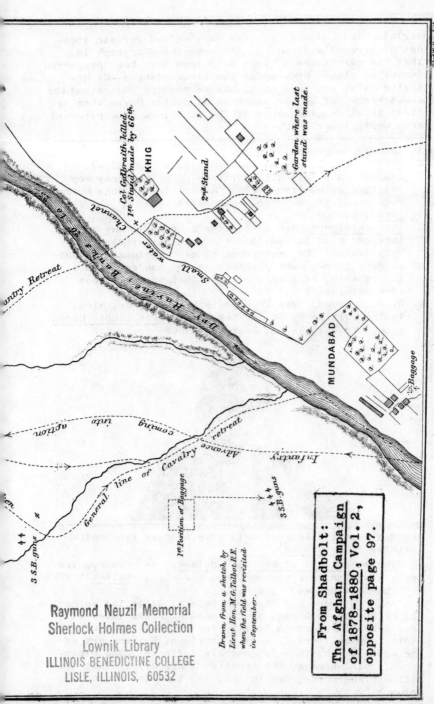

KHIG

Col Galbraith killed
1st Stand made by 66th

2nd Stand

Garden where last
stand was made.

Channet

Small water

Dry Haine's Home

MUNDABAD

Baggage

untry Retreat

coming into action

General line of Cavalry retreat

Advance

Infantry

1st Portion of Baggage

3 S.B. guns

3 S.B. guns

Drawn from a sketch by
Lieut. Hon. M.G. Talbot R.E.
when the field was revisited
in September.

From Shadbolt:
The Afghan Campaign
of 1878–1880, Vol. 2,
opposite page 97.

London: Sampson, Low, Marston, Searle, & Rivington.

Earl Weller Lith.

certain other medical men may have called certain incidents to recollection; but the wonder and triumph is that the narratives of John H. Watson have been preserved for us as clear and—under the circumstances—as detailed as we now have them. Can we perhaps understand the scratchings-out in the notebook of Doctor Doyle when he first tried to make sense of the ramblings of a returned army medical man?

---

1. London: Sampson Low, 1882.
2. Ibid., Vol. I, Biographical division, pp. 233-4.
3. London: John Murray, 1908. (Was Orderly Murray any relative of publisher John Murray? Is the John Murray version of the map more authoritative?)
4. Ibid., p. 504.
5. The Gondoliers, Act I. [Editor's note: It may be of interest also to recall a statement attributed to Mark Twain: "The researches of many antiquarians have already thrown much darkness on the subject, and it is probable, if they continue, that we shall soon know nothing at all."]
6. D. A. Redmond, "The Prosthesis Fixation; or, Stop, You're Pulling My Wooden Leg," The Devon County Chronicle," Vol. 4, No. 5, September 1968, pp. 4-6.

Hercule Poirot discusses detective stories (in Agatha Christie's The Clocks):

"The Adventures of Sherlock Holmes," he murmured lovingly and uttered reverently the one word, "Maître!"

"Sherlock Holmes?" I asked.

"Ah, non, non, not Sherlock Holmes! It is the author, Sir Arthur Conan Doyle, that I salute. These tales of Sherlock Holmes are in reality far-fetched, full of fallacies and most artificially contrived. But the art of the writing—ah, that is entirely different. The pleasure of the language, the creation above all of that magnificent character, Dr. Watson, Ah, that was indeed a triumph."

WHO WAS HURET?

by William E. Fleischauer

Prologue

After setting down the following article on the identity of Huret and the circumstances of his capture, I was, of course, anxious to determine if other members of the Sherlockian fraternity had investigated this singular case before. Upon consulting D. A. Redmond's incomparable Cumulated Index to The Baker Street Journal ("Good old index") I found that the only mention of the case in the Journal was made by the late Edgar W. Smith in "From the Editor's Commonplace Book," BSJ (NS) 9:245-255, (Oct.) 1959, pp. 254-255. I quote in part:

"Dr. Watson says, in The Golden Pince-Nez, that 'the tracking and arrest of Huret, the Boulevard assassin—an exploit which won for Holmes an autograph letter of thanks from the French President and the Order of the Legion of Honour' took place in the year 1894. I wonder if anyone has ever wondered which French President it was who showed this measure of gratitude?"

Mr. Smith, beyond the Reichenbach, knows the answer. I hope that it is the one which follows.

In The Adventure of the Golden Pince-Nez Dr. Watson lists some of the cases which occupied Sherlock Holmes after his miraculous return in 1894. Among these is "the tracking and and arrest of Huret, the Boulevard Assassin," an exploit which won for Holmes an autograph letter of thanks from the French President and the award of the Legion of Honour.

Why was a case of this magnitude never published? The award of the Legion of Honour is not an everyday occurrence. Obviously, it was for a considerable service to the French President, since he himself wrote a letter of thanks to Holmes. Was Holmes pledged to secrecy? Probably not, since he was awarded one of France's highest decorations. This could hardly be kept from the public. Holmes had, from time to time, been engaged in what would now be called "cloak-and-dagger cases." The Bruce-Partington Plans, The Second Stain, The Naval Treaty, and His Last Bow come readily to mind. Yet all were published after the facts could neither help nor harm anyone. The cases of the reigning family of Holland, the King of Scandinavia, the death of Cardinal Tosca, and the affair of the Vatican cameos may have involved information which could prove embarrassing to some prominent personages. We can understand the reasons for not committing these cases to print. But the present case names an assassin. What harm

can come of revealing the name of a murderer, no matter
how highly placed? Let us examine the facts.

Watson says the case occurred in 1894. This means that
the letter and award came, in all probability, from the
French President holding office in 1894. Upon checking
French history we find that not one, but two men held
that office in 1894. They were Marie François Sadi
Carnot, who had been elected in 1887 and who served until
24 June 1894; and Jean Paul Pierre Casimir-Perier, who
served from 24 June 1894 until 15 January 1895. These are
the basic facts found in any encyclopædia. Let us go deeper.

The term of Sadi Carnot was terminated abruptly on
24 June 1894. After addressing a public banquet in the
city of Lyons, he left the hall and, in the
boulevard outside, was stabbed to death by an
Italian anarchist named Santos Caserio. President
Carnot expired (a) immediately, (b) an hour later, or
(c) the next morning, depending upon which encyclopædia you
read. Ah, Watson, we progress. An assassin and a boulevard. But, alas, Caserio was captured on the spot. No
tracking and arrest. He gave revenge for the death of a
fellow anarchist, one Vaillant by name (who had hurled a
bomb into the French Chamber of Deputies some time before), as his motive. It appears that we must dismiss
this crime as sheer coincidence and proceed to the next
occupant of the Elysée.

Casimir-Perier was elected by the Chamber of Deputies
immediately after the death of Sadi Carnot. He was a
wealthy man and a director of the largest mining and
metallurgical cartel in France. His administration was
attacked immediately and throughout its duration by the
Radical Left. To add fuel to the fire, the celebrated
Dreyfus case came to light early in his administration.
He was a Dreyfus supporter and testified in the officer's
favour at the trial. This action was not calculated to
endear him to a large segment of the French populace.
His life and the lives of his family were threatened many
times, but there is no record of any attempt on his life.
He finally resigned on 15 January 1895 in a fit of pique,
not out of fear but because the opposition of the Radical
Left and the intransigence of his own ministers (who did
not keep him informed of affairs) made it impossible for
him to govern. He retired and devoted himself to his
mining interests and was forgotten by everyone.

Which, then, of these two men wrote the letter and
awarded the decoration to Holmes? Casimir-Perier appears
to be the more likely possibility. This view is taken by
no less redoubtable a Sherlockian than William S. Baring-

Gould. In a footnote in <u>Sherlock Holmes of Baker Street</u> Baring-Gould says of Casimir-Perier: "His unpopularity as President of the Republic was such that, in the autumn of 1894, threats were made to murder him, his wife, and his children. He had reason to be anxious, too; the previous President, Sadi Carnot, had himself been assassinated on May 30, 1894 [sic]. Unquestionably, it was the President himself, whose life Holmes saved from the Boulevard Assassin, Huret."

This sounds logical. However, in view of the fact that Baring-Gould says that Carnot was assassinated on May 30, rather than on June 24, as was actually the case, we must presume that he did not devote a great deal of research to this case and simply assumed that Casimir-Perier was a more logical recipient of Huret's attentions.

If it was Casimir-Perier, then why the secrecy? He was in office for only six months, and he left it an angry and disillusioned man. He would have had no interest in protecting or shielding anyone who had tried to kill him or his family. We seem to be no better off than we were at the beginning.

Let us return, then, to Sadi Carnot. I trust that we have overlooked nothing of importance. Ah, but we have. President Carnot's administration was not entirely devoid of interest. There was the Panama Canal Scandal which almost caused the fall of his government. Indeed, the only reason it did not fall was Carnot's own impeccable reputation for honesty. Not a breath of scandal ever touched his own personal or political activities. He came to office at a time when one General Boulanger (whose actions contributed the term "man on horseback" to the language) was attempting a <u>coup</u> d'état. One of Carnot's first actions was to banish Boulanger from France. He was tried <u>in absentia</u> for treason, found guilty, and sentenced to death. He fled to the Isle of Jersey for a time, and then went to Brussels, accompanied by some of his followers, all of whom vowed revenge against Sadi Carnot. After a few years Boulanger became despondent about his cause and finally, on 30 September 1891, shot himself on the grave of his mistress, in Brussels.

These are the ascertainable facts of the case. It is impossible to refute the Baring-Gould theory about Casimir-Perier. However, I would like to examine a possible alternative involving Sadi Carnot.

Boulanger's followers hated Carnot as much as their late leader did. They could not return to France for fear of imprisonment or the guillotine. They could not bribe their way in as long as Carnot, with his unassailable virtue, was in power. Nor could they hope for the banishment to be lifted as long as Carnot had anything to say about it. What then? Obviously, Carnot must be removed. They wait in hope that his government will fall, but his administration proceeds staunchly through crisis after crisis. Premiers are changed, but the President remains. Finally they decide that Carnot must be killed. But how? They cannot enter France to do the job themselves. They must find a man or an organisation that will do it for them. There was once an organisation which performed services of this type, but its leader perished in Switzerland in 1891. Their discreet inquiries reveal that this organisation still exists and that it is now headed by its former chief of staff, a former English army officer, Colonel Sebastian Moran. Possibly he can help them.

Now, the Belgian police, as a matter of course, keep themselves informed as to the doings of political refugees within their borders. They learn that the talk of the Boulangists has turned to assassination and that they have been inquiring as to the whereabouts of one Colonel Moran. The Belgians notify the head of the French Sûreté. His first idea is to dismiss it as just another of those unending émigré plots—until he sees the name "Moran"; he knows of this man.

The head of the Sûreté at this time is François le Villard, of whom we heard in The Sign of Four, when Holmes set him on the right track in a case involving a will. It will be recalled that he sent Holmes a letter full of "stray magnifiques, coup-de-maîtres and tours-de-force." Holmes said of him then: "He has considerable gifts himself. He possesses two out of the three qualities necessary for the ideal detective. He has the power of observation and that of deduction. He is only wanting in knowledge, and that may come in time." Holmes made this remark in 1888.

Now it is 1894, and le Villard possessed knowledge. He was able to unravel the tangled skein of Reichenbach and deduce that only Moriarty lay at the bottom of the Falls. Also, since the French police do not ignore the entry of foreigners into their country, he was aware that a tall, hawk-faced man had recently entered France, ostensibly to conduct some research at a laboratory in Montpellier. He respected this man's incognito but was not surprised when Holmes contacted him and revealed his identity. Le Villard would be a valuable ally in locating and keeping an eye on Holmes's nemesis, Moran.

Therefore, le Villard was instantly aware of the seriousness of the situation when he saw the name "Moran" in the message from Brussels. He immediately apprised Holmes of the possible plot. Since the Sûreté does not attempt

to use its powers outside French jurisdiction, would it
not be possible for Holmes to serve France while helping
himself? Holmes contacted Mycroft, who verified that
Moran was indeed in London and that he had been contacted
by a foreigner who appeared to be French. Holmes and le
Villard decided that no further time was to be wasted if
the best shot in the Empire was on the trail of Sadi
Carnot. Holmes left immediately for London. The results
of his trip are recounted in The Adventure of the Empty
House. After Moran's capture, le Villard informed the
President of the plot and the taking of Moran. Carnot
wrote a personal note to Holmes to express his thanks
and awarded him the Legion of Honour. Incidentally, this
decoration can be awarded by the French President on his
own. However, the award of the decoration was not made
solely for this case. This was not the first time that
Holmes had assisted M. Carnot. It will be recalled that,
in The Final Problem, in 1891, Watson read that Holmes
had been engaged upon a matter of supreme importance to
the French government. This could well have been an investigation of the Panama Canal scandal—and very interesting reading it might make, too. The Legion of Honour,
then, was awarded for both past and present services
rendered to Carnot and to France by Mr. Sherlock Holmes.

Holmes replied to Carnot's letter with a note of
thanks, and warned him that the danger might not be over.
Unfortunately, Carnot did not heed this advice, and two
months later he was struck down by Caserio, Moran's hire-
ling. Was Caserio avenging Vaillant, the arrest of Moran,
or simply carrying out orders? It does not matter. The
Boulevard Assassin had struck—through a hired killer.

Now, Holmes was left with another "Birdy Edwards." He
had stayed the assassin's hand for a while, but he could
not protect the intended victim forever. Small wonder
that the full story of Huret was not told, for it was
not a complete success.

"Huret," did I say? I thought it was "Moran." Where
did "Huret" come from? Obviously, Watson would not pub-
licise a partial failure, especially in Holmes's first
case after his return. But Watson had to explain the
case which returned Holmes to the living. So he wrote
The Empty House, concealing all the references to le
Villard, Carnot, and Caserio. To replace them he invented conversation to explain Holmes's wanderings. This
accounts for those maddening discrepancies in The Empty
House. Watson even went so far as to deny having ever
heard of Colonel Moran before; he had forgotten this
when he wrote up The Valley of Fear, some years later.
In that case Colonel Moran is discussed in great detail,

including his salary and position, all while Watson is present.

Watson, with pardonable pride, wanted to mention Holmes's decoration. So he invented a case and mentioned it in <u>The Golden Pince-Nez</u>, written in 1904. He could not truthfully call the assassin Moran, so he decided to use a pseudonym, a French one; hence Huret, a passable French name and a source of continual bewilderment to the Literary Agent, who scanned the French newspapers for any mention of someone by that name, without success. He never knew that he was a victim of Watson's pawky sense of humour.

Epilogue

Edgar Smith continued:

"The apprehension of Huret, by the text, could have occurred any time between early April, 1894, and the end of the year. <u>On June 24, 1894, President Marie François Sadi Carnot of the French Republic was himself assassinated</u> [emphasis Mr. Smith's]. If it was he who wrote Holmes, his satisfaction at Huret's arrest was, unfortunately, short-lived. If it was not he—that is, if the arrest took place after June 24th—the letter must have been from Carnot's successor as President: Jean Paul Pierre Casimir-Perier.

"The really challenging question this chronological problem raises is, of course, the identity of Huret's victim. Could it, perchance, have been President Carnot?"

Perchance, Mr. Smith, perchance.

The Legion of Honour

MYCROFT COME BACK; ALL IS FORGIVEN

by Benjamin S. Clark

I assume that you are all familiar with Father
(later Monsignor) Ronald Knox's brilliant paper on
Mycroft which is one of the highlights of H. W. Bell's
Baker Street Studies. As you will recall, the author
contends that the only rational explanation of the odd
rôle Mycroft Holmes played in The Greek Interpreter
is that he must have been working for and in the interests of Professor Moriarty. The validity of this explanation, Ronald Knox believed, was reinforced, if
not confirmed, by the assumption that Mycroft must have
had a source of income over and above his modest government salary in order to afford digs in the fashionable Pall Mall section as well as membership in the
Diogenes Club. Under Ronald Knox's theory, Mycroft is
seen as a sort of double agent. Presumably he was paid
by the professor as an expert furnishing organisation-
al aid in criminal enterprises while (obviously unbe-
known to Moriarty) leaking, within limits, information
to brother Sherlock to enable him at least to counter
the machinations of Moriarty. The professor, in turn,
so the Knox theory goes, was kept posted, within limits,
on certain of Sherlock's plans and activities.

One cannot help but admire the brilliance with which
this case against the Diogenes Club member is developed.
But over recent years I have been increasingly troubled
by the fact that if Ronald Knox's theory was indeed correct, it was a very large blot on the escutcheon of the
Holmes family. This revulsion on my part has led me to
re-examine the thesis to see if possibly the wrong conclusion had been drawn from facts which, while admittedly incontrovertible, might lend themselves to a different interpretation.

As noted previously, it was in the case of The Greek
Interpreter (which, of course, marked the first meeting
between Watson and Mycroft) that we see the seed and
partial bloom of Ronald Knox's theory. Let me now at
once concede that Mycroft's rôle in that case was indeed
an odd one. It was a rôle, as Ronald Knox points out,
which served primarily to make possible the escape of
the villains Latimer and Kemp through what amounted to
a timely warning from Mycroft, whose actions may well
in addition have been responsible for the death of Paul,
Sophy Kratides's brother. However, while I don't wish
to bore my readers with a well worn truism, neverthe-

less, it must be admitted that we are all fallible.
If the captain of the Yale team fumbles, I don't believe the authorities immediately rush in to examine
withdrawals from President Pusey's bank account.
Even if we assume that by the time of The Bruce-
Partington Plans Mycroft was a reformed character, it
is difficult to see the British government giving him,
let alone keeping him in, a position of high trust.
(On this score it might be added that if, as Ronald
Knox suggests, Sherlock was fully aware of the dual rôle
his brother had been playing would not he, whose loyalty to England was unquestioned, have been duty-bound
by conscience to put country above brother and apprise
the authorities of Mycroft's record?) Mycroft, according to the Knox theory, was willing, under orders from
Moriarty, to work closely with Wilson Kemp (a man of
the foulest antecedents) in order to further the fortunes and nefarious schemes of the grand commander of
crime. And do not forget that under the Knox theory
Mycroft, while not necessarily wishing the death of
his famous brother, did not scruple to put him in great
jeopardy, particularly when, as the Knox presumption
goes, he furnished Moriarty with certain details of
Sherlock's continental flight itinerary. Even if Mycroft's motive under the Ronald Knox assumption when
discussing The Final Problem was hopefully to lure Moriarty to his doom, the risk in the luring to Sherlock
was nevertheless enormous. As we know, he only just
did escape joining Moriarty in a fatal tumble into Reichenbach Falls. In brief, I find Mycroft in the rôle of
villain downright unthinkable. This is not to say that
he was not a man of mystery. On first speaking about
his brother to Watson, Holmes, you will recall, claimed
for Mycroft powers of observation superior to his
own. (He later revised this comment to include powers
of observation and deduction). Subsequent to this
statement, Watson gives us a demonstration of Mycroft's
power of observation as the two brothers sit in the bow
window of the Diogenes Club.[1] Holmes also told Watson
at that time that he had enlisted Mycroft's cerebral
help on many occasions and that his brother had referred
to him some of his most interesting cases. Unfortunately, we have no information on any of these. Leaving out Mycroft's assistance as cab driver in The Final
Problem, the only two cases in which we see him consulting with his brother—both cases introduced to Sherlock
by Mycroft—are, of course, The Greek Interpreter and,

some five or six years later, The Bruce-Partington
Plans. In the case of The Greek Interpreter Mycroft not only introduced Holmes to the case but himself played a rôle therein—a rôle, as previously
noted, which left much to be desired. In The Bruce-
Partington Plans he simply introduced the case to his
brother, stressed its desperate seriousness from the
standpoint of national security, and advised him to
get cracking. Let us return to the case of The Greek
Interpreter. Ronald Knox saw only one interpretation
of Mycroft's mishandling of this case, namely a criminal one. Adopting an a priori line of reasoning, he
then examined all facets of Mycroft's story as revealed
or possibly suggested in the Canon to build up a
documented charge of connivance with Moriarty. As I
said earlier, I believe there is an alternate interpretation. It is not complimentary to Mycroft, but
it does remove the stigma of criminality. A careful
examination of both cases, The Greek Interpreter and
The Bruce-Partington Plans, furnishes, I believe, the
true reason why Mycroft himself did not, as a rule, go
"out into the field." I believe these cases furnish
incontrovertible proof that it was not because, as Mycroft claimed and Sherlock echoed, he could not
be bothered with the detailed leg-work necessary to
develop a case. I believe it was simply because Mycroft in action was a bumbler. As our late friend,
Lyttleton Fox, so brilliantly demonstrated, Mycroft
in a sense was a computer.[2] An armchair analyst, if
you will. But he was not a general. He did not know
where to look for significant clues and was incapable
of planning a course of action—unlike his brother
Sherlock, who could plan a campaign which time and
again brilliantly resulted in the capture of the criminal.

Turning now to The Bruce-Partington Plans: In this
case, as I said, Mycroft played no rôle other than to
drop the problem in Sherlock's lap and to tell him to
solve it. However, while he thus left all the active
work to Sherlock, is it not astonishing that he did
not even do what he could have done from his armchair?
A glaring example of ineptness over and above sheer
physical laziness can be found in the fact that it was
Sherlock who had to ask by wire for a list of foreign
agents operating in England. Since the case involved
the theft of vital plans for the construction of the
Bruce-Partington submarine, and since foreign powers
only would be interested in effecting such a theft,

why in the world didn't Mycroft at the very start give
his brother what Sherlock later asked for, namely a
complete list of all foreign spies or international
agents known to be in England, along with addresses?

And what of the meeting at 221B Baker Street after
breakfast on the day following Sherlock's discovery of
advertisements in the agony column of The Daily Telegraph? You may recall that Mycroft and Lestrade joined
Holmes and Watson on that occasion, and Holmes read
off to his audience the messages that he had arranged
in chronological order. To refresh your memory, here
they are:

1st message: "Hoped to hear sooner. Terms agreed to.
Write fully to address given on card. Pierrot."

2nd message: "Too complex for description. Must have
full report. Stuff awaits you when goods delivered.
Pierrot."

3rd message: "Matter presses. Must withdraw offer unless contract completed. Make appointment by letter.
Will confirm by advertisement. Pierrot."

4th message: "Finally: Monday after nine. Two taps.
Only ourselves. Do not be suspicious. Payment in
hard cash on goods delivered. Pierrot."

Holmes, it might be mentioned here, having discovered
the advertisements and arranged them chronologically
the day before the post-breakfast meeting referred to,
then commented to Watson that they represented a fairly
complete record. But if only they could get at the man
at the other end! After a little thought he stated,
"Well perhaps it won't be so difficult after all," and
he immediately took Watson around with him to the office
of The Daily Telegraph. The next day, when he had
heard the four messages read, Lestrade's only comment
was one of disapproval of the Holmes-Watson burglary
of Oberstein's house. Mycroft's reaction on the other
hand was enthusiastic. "Excellent! Admirable! But
what use will you make of it?" Can you believe that
this question is asked by a man whose powers of observation and deduction are supposed to be superior to
Sherlock's?

Sherlock in replying to Mycroft's question asked if
he and Lestrade had seen Pierrot's advertisement that
day. "What," said Mycroft, "another one?"

"Yes, here it is. 'Tonight. Same time. Same place.
Two taps. Most vitally important. Your own safety at
stake. Pierrot.'"

"By George" cried Lestrade, "if he answers that we

have got him." "That was my idea when I put it in!"
said Holmes.

Now we expect Lestrade to be obtuse, but if one
sticks to the traditionally accepted appraisal of Mycroft's abilities as observer and deducer, one cannot
help but wonder. Surely if Mycroft did indeed possess
superior talents, when Sherlock asked whether they had
seen Pierrot's advertisement for that day, wouldn't he
have immediately deduced it was from his brother's fine
Italian hand? In which case what one would have expected would have been some remark such as "I wager I can
surmise what little birdy is responsible for this one!"
But Sherlock has to spell out, not only to Lestrade but
also to his brother, "That was my idea when I put it
in." A remark which, so far as both listeners were concerned, was not superfluous.

Where, then, did we get the impression of Mycroft's
mental brilliance? From Sherlock, of course, and from
Mycroft himself who did not suffer from false modesty
and was quite willing to toot his own trumpet. You may
remember that at the start of The Bruce-Partington Plans
he sends his brother into action with these words, "Give
me your details, and from an armchair I will return you
an excellent expert opinion." As a matter of fact, Mycroft contributed exactly nothing to the case other than
the list of all foreign spies and international agents
together with their addresses. This information obviously required only the opening of a file drawer, and,
as we have noted, it was not volunteered immediately,
but had to be requested by Sherlock.

Once again we must return to The Greek Interpreter.
The first words spoken by Mycroft to Watson when they
were introduced were "I hear of Sherlock everywhere
since you became his chronicler." It is obvious, and
Ronald Knox made a note of the point, that Mycroft must
indeed have been jealous of his brother's fame. Hence,
where he could, Sherlock did his best to see that Mycroft via Watson's pen got a good press.[3] In addition
to helping Mycroft share in some of his glory, it would
be my strong suspicion that to the extent Mycroft found
his government salary insufficient for a Pall Mall—Diogenes Club way of life, Sherlock undoubtedly came a-
cross with the difference.

One further and final point to support my thesis.
In the chronology of the cases, or at least the chronology that I find the most likely, The Greek Interpreter occurred in September 1888. The Naval Treaty
was presumably in 1889, while The Second Stain came

later in that year, probably in the month of December. Once Watson had been introduced to Mycroft, is it not inexplicable that in neither the case of The Naval Treaty nor in the case of The Second Stain, both cases of critical national importance, that Mycroft, if he had the abilities he and Sherlock claimed he had, should not have been called in to help, particularly if at times he was the British government? I think in my interpretation we have the answer. Both the cases referred to came to Sherlock in confidence from others, not from Mycroft, and required handling under conditions of extreme secrecy. If in Sherlock's view Mycroft would have been able to make a significant contribution towards solution in either case, I am sure he would have called on his brother, but I am afraid that Sherlock was well aware of Mycroft's limitations and realised there was no point in bringing him in, particularly where the rating was top secret.

This cutting down of Mycroft to what I believe was his true mental stature may, after all these years, seem like an act of lèse-majesté. However, surely his family would rather have him go down in history as, at worst inept, not venal—not to mention his fellow members in the Diogenes Club who must have regarded the Ronald Knox theory as presenting them, in their association with Sherlock's brother, a bit of a sticky wicket.

---

1. Incidentally, however, how do we in fact determine the accuracy of the brothers' observations? I do not recall that the individual observed was ever stopped and questioned. Is ours the sort of faith that makes ventriloquism in the films possible?
2. "Mycroft Recomputed," BSJ (NS) 19:4-11, (March) 1969.
3. On this score, however, I must say Sherlock rather overdid it when he told Watson at the time of The Bruce-Partington Plans: "Occasionally he is the British government."

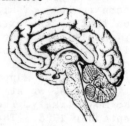

THE MYSTERY OF THE INDELIBLE PENCIL
by William G. Miller

Can a dying man attempting to write a final message
fail to complete his message but still find the strength
to return his pencil to his pocket? One would think not.

What then, is one to make of the Master's comment in
The Adventure of the Retired Colourman indicating that
this is possible? This was the case in which Josiah
Amberley gassed his wife and the amorous Dr. Ray Ernest
after luring them into a hermetically sealed strong-room.

When Holmes explained to a police inspector how he had
solved the case, the following exchange occurred:

Holmes: "Now, we will suppose that you were shut up
in this little room, had not two minutes to live, but
wanted to get even with the fiend who was probably mocking at you from the other side of the door. What would
you do?"

Inspector: "Write a message."

Holmes: "Exactly. You would like to tell people how
you died. No use writing on paper. That would be seen.
If you wrote on the wall someone might rest upon it.
Now, look here! Just above the skirting is scribbled
with a purple indelible pencil: 'We were——' That's all."

Inspector: "What do you make of that?"

Holmes: "Well, it's only a foot above the ground. The
poor devil was on the floor dying when he wrote it. He
lost his senses before he could finish."

Inspector: "He was writing, 'We were murdered.'"

Holmes: "That's how I read it. If you find an indelible pencil on the body——"

Inspector: "We'll look out for it, you may be sure."

At first reading, it would seem that Holmes was indicating that, when the doctor's body was recovered from
the well into which it had been dropped by the colourman,
the indelible pencil would be found. Was this really what
the Master intended to convey? Is it believable that,
with his extraordinary powers of observation and deduction, he could make such a blunder?

There were only two ways in which the pencil could
have been put into the doctor's pocket—either by the
dying man or by the colourman himself. Holmes, however,
knew that the pencil was not in the doctor's pocket. So
why his puzzling comment?

The mystery is cleared up if one re-examines the Master's comment, "If you find an indelible pencil on the
body——," and realises that it begins with "If" and is,
in fact, an incomplete sentence. Had not the eager in-

spector cut off Holmes in mid-sentence, the full statement would have been: "If you find an indelible pencil on the body I will be very much surprised."

With the policeman's eyebrows rising in puzzlement, Holmes would have added: "Instead, you will find the pencil in Josiah Amberley's <u>own</u> pocket." With considerable relish, he would then have explained how this could be.

In the first instance, Holmes rejected, as a physical impossibility, the notion that the doctor might have put the pencil into his pocket. Clearly, a dying man with strength enough to do so would have had sufficient strength to complete the message on the skirting.

The Master likewise rejected the possibility that the colourman, in removing the corpses from the strong-room and wishing to destroy all the evidence, stuck the pencil into the doctor's pocket, consigning bodies and pencil to the waiting well. Why? Because, had the colourman seen anything unusual in the presence of the pencil on the floor, he would have known that a message had been written and would have searched the small room until he found the purple markings on the skirting, and he would have erased the message. However, the partial message remained for Holmes's eyes to discover—and no pencil was found in the strong-room.

With these facts before him, Holmes knew that the pencil did not belong to the doctor. Instead, it was the property of the colourman himself and was inside the strong-room before the foul deed was committed. The indelible pencil was probably used by Amberley in the strong-room to keep his records. In his last moments the doctor found it and began his indictment.

After the murders the colourman carried the bodies to the well and re-entered the strong-room to remove his deed-box in order to blame the "theft" on the missing couple. Seeing the pencil on the floor, and knowing it to be his own, he simply picked it up and thrust it into his own pocket.

Dr. Watson does not record whether the pencil was recovered, but one may rest assured that when the colourman was charged at the police station and his pockets emptied, their contents included one indelible pencil.

BAKER STREET INVENTORY

BARZUN, JACQUES and **TAYLOR, WENDELL HERTIG**
  A Catalogue of Crime
    New York: Harper & Row, 1971; $18.95.
    "Being a Reader's Guide to the Literature of Mystery,
    Detection, & Related Genres," this great work is of
    obvious interest to all those interested in the field
    —and may well be the last word on the subject. In
    addition, the amount of space devoted to Sherlockian
    literature makes it an important book in our special
    sphere of interest. (The bibliography is a great one.)
    For a discussion of this work, see BSJ 21:44-48, 1971.

BERMAN, RUTH
  Sherlock Holmes in Oz
    Oziana #1, International Wizard of Oz Club, 1971.
    The Master is brought to the land of Oz to solve the
    mystery of the missing pearl—which he does, of course.

HARDWICK, MICHAEL and **MOLLY**
  Sherlock Holmes' Privatliv
    København: Martins Forlag, 1971.
    This is the Hardwick book about Billy Wilder's film,
    translated into Danish by Peter Jerndorff Jessen, and
    with a Foreword by A. D. Henriksen.

HOYLMAN, DOUG
  Moriarty and the Binomial Theorem
    Proper Boskonian, No. 6, 1970.
    The author believes that Holmes was ignorant of higher
    mathematics and really didn't understand what that
    famous treatise was all about.

KISSANE, JOHN M., M.D.
  Two Victorians Look at Science
    Pharos, July 1971.
    The two Victorians are the author and Sir Arthur Conan
    Doyle. Discusses the relationship between practical
    and applied science, and concludes that the "fusion
    between abstract theory and practical application of
    the scientific method" is embodied in Sherlock Holmes.

LEWIS, ARTHUR H.
  Copper Beeches
    New York: Trident Press [1971]; $6.95.
    A novel in which the leading characters (as well as
    the author) are members of The Sons of the Copper
    Beeches. Not only is it of great interest in its own
    right, but it is doubly so because so many Irregulars
    are closely identified with it. We have had nothing
    like it since the late, great Anthony Boucher's The
    Case of the Baker Street Irregulars.

NORDBERG, NILS, editor.
  Sir Arthur Conan Doyle: Hunden fra Baskerville
    N.p.: Gyldendal Norsk Forlag [1971]; Kr. 17,50.
    Another attractive Norwegian production, with a schol-
    arly introduction and informative notes. (Re previous
    Sherlockian works from the same editor and publisher,
    see BSJ, Sept. 1970, p. 186, and June 1969, p. 122.)

PAGE, ANDREW
  A Canonical Handbook
    N.p. [1971.]
    A useful, scholarly compilation of Canonical data under
    many headings. Obtainable from the author at 3130 Irwin
    Ave., Bronx, N.Y. 10463, for $1.00.

TRACY, JACK
  Conan Doyle and the Latter-Day Saints
    N.p.: Privately printed; n.d.
    An excellent short monograph on the Mormons, with il-
    lustrations and maps, designed to correct the errors
    in A Study in Scarlet. Obtainable for $1 from Jack
    Tracy, 955 E. Boone St., Frankfort, Ind. 46041.

WERNETTE, J. PHILIP
  Holmes and Watson Were Wrong
    Michigan Quarterly Review, Vol. X, No. 2, Spring 1971.
    Professor Wernette shows that Holmes's knowledge in
    all fields was much greater than Watson indicated in
    that famous tabulation in A Study in Scarlet; Holmes
    did not ignore information that might crowd out other
    data but acted on the principle that "All knowledge
    comes useful to the detective."

            *   *   *   *

  Recently announced are two works on our favourite subject:
Trevor Hall (author of Sherlock Holmes: Ten Literary Studies):
The Late Mr. Sherlock Holmes and Other Literary Studies, Lon-
don: Duckworth Books, 1971 (£2.10); and Michael Harrison ("The
Camberwell Poisoning Case"): In the Footsteps of Sherlock
Holmes, New edition, Newton Abbot, Devon: David & Charles,
1971 (£2.50).

  Ron De Waal is endeavouring to have reprints made for the
Irregulars of "the longest and most valuable catalogue of
books by Doyle published to date": "Sir Arthur Conan Doyle,"
The National Union Catalog, Pre-1956 Imprints . . . [London:]
Mansell, 1971, Vol. 148, pp. 237-286; and The National Union
Catalog, 1956 through 1967, Totowa, N.J.: Roman and Little-
field [1971], Vol. 31, pp. 44-46.

  Peter Blau reports that Adventures of Sherlock Holmes
(Basil Rathbone reading SCAN, REDH, SPEC, and BLUE), #GL-611,
on 5 7", 16 rpm records, is available for $6.95 from Audio
Book Co., 301 Pasadena Ave., South Pasadena, Calif. 91030.
Also, Listening Library, Inc. (One Park Ave., Old Greenwich,
Conn. 06870) has some Sherlockian items on their sales list—
records, filmstrips, a paperback, and a tape casette.

  From Capt. H. M. Hacksley of the Canadian Air Force, now
stationed in Germany, we have the last installment of a comic
strip that has been appearing in the German TV magazine, Hör
Zu, Sherlock Holmes und das Geheimnis der blauen Erbse [Sher-
lock Holmes and the Secret of the Blue Pea (Carbuncle?)]. All
thirty-five strips are being printed in one volume, obtainable for DM 8,50 from Bärmeier & Nikel, Buchdienst 2001, 6
Frankfurt/M., Postfach 2173, Germany.

  The following are obtainable from Andrew Page (3130 Irwin
Ave., Bronx, N.Y. 10463: An Introduction to Sherlock Holmes (25¢);
Priory Papers, A Study in Examinations (50¢); a new, revised
edition of A Case of Bishopsgate Jewels (40¢).

  The 1971 Annual Edition of The Pontine Dossier is now on
the press and copies may be obtained from Luther Norris (3844

Watseka Ave., Culver City, Calif. 90230) for $3.00. A few
copies of the First Annual Edition are still available ($3.00).

Fred Mende writes that a new eight-volume series, The History of London, is being issued, and he believes that the volume covering 1870-1914 may be purchased separately. A brochure is available from University of California Press, 2223 Fulton, Berkeley, Calif. 94720.

The November 1970 issue of The Library Chronicle of the University of Texas at Austin contains "The Writer as Bookman: Christopher Morley's Library," by Anna Lou Ashby. The library included many Sherlockian and Irregular items, of course. The illustrations include an excellent full-page photograph of Morley in his library.

Best Detective Stories of the Year—1971, edited by Allen J. Hubin (Dutton; $5.95), is an excellent collection, and many Sherlockians are mentioned in it.

*   *   *   *

PERIODICALS RECEIVED

THE BAKER STREET PAGES, New Series, Vol. 1, No. 1, June-July 1971. A bimonthly publication of the recently reactivated Baker Street Pageboys; subscription $1.00 a year, to be sent to Andrew Page, 3130 Irwin Avenue, Bronx, N.Y. 10463.

THE DEVON COUNTY CHRONICLE, Vol. 7, Nos. 2-4, January-May 1971. Published by the Chicago BSI and edited by R. W. Hahn, 938 Clarence Avenue, Oak Park, Illinois, 60304.

THE HOLMESIAN OBSERVER, Vol. 1, Nos. 4-7, June-September 1971. Published by The Priory School, of New York, and edited by Andrew Page (address above). Subscription, $1.60 a year in U.S.A.; $2.50 a year overseas.

INVESTIGATIONS, An Irregular Journal of Atlanta-Area Sherlockians, Vol. 1, Nos. 1-3, January, March, and May 1967. This is the publication of The Confederates of Wisteria Lodge, a newly resurrected Scion Society. Subscription: $1 a year (approximately six issues), to be sent to the Editor, E. M. Hughes, 538 Burlington Road NE, Atlanta, Ga. 30307.

SHERLOCKIANA, Nr. 2, 1971. The publication of Sherlock Holmes Klubben i Danmark, edited by Henry Lauritzen.

THE VERMISSA HERALD, Vol. 5, No. 2, April 1971. The official publication of the Scowrers and Molly Maguires, edited by W. A. Berner, 4712 17 Street, San Francisco, Calif. 94117.

*   *   *   *

EXTRA-CURRICULAR ACTIVITIES

The latest book by Walter Klinefelter ("The British Barque Sophy Anderson"), A Further Display of Old Maps and Plans (La Crosse, Wisconsin: Sumac Press, 1969), is a desirable work in a distinguished format, and has to do with two of his (and my) favourite subjects, philately and cartography. A few copies are available for $4.00 from the author (R.D. 1, Dallastown, Pa. 17313). Also available from the same source: The Case of the Conan Doyle Crime Library, $1.50; and the offprint of his "Surveyor General Thomas Holme's Map of the Improved Part of Pennsilvania" (Winterthur Portfolio 6, 1970), $3.00.

Reviewed in The Times Literary Supplement, London, 7 May 1971, but not yet seen is The Long Road West (London, Chatto and Windus, 1971; £2.25), by Frank Morley ("The Three Garridebs").

LETTERS TO BAKER STREET

From the Marquis of Donegall ("The Manor House Case"),
 Editor of <u>The Sherlock Holmes Journal</u>:

I am most honoured, nay, overwhelmed that The Baker
Street Irregulars should have considered me worthy to be
invested with their highest honour, The Two-Shilling
Award, in the Edgar W. Smith Birthday Honours (April 1st,
1971). Honestly, the letter with the Award came as a most
enjoyable surprise, and I feel that Mr. Holmes cannot have
experienced greater joy or well-being than mine, on the
occasion of his receiving that "fine emerald tie-pin" at
Windsor, or on a less commendable occasion, when he
"patted affectionately" the Duke of Holdernesse's cheque
for £12,000. I was particularly touched by this Award, in
view of the fact that it has been impossible for me to
join you all at a BSI Annual Dinner for far too many
years. This has been a great disappointment to me; and it
is always nice to be reminded that, though an enforced ab-
sentee, a fellow-BSI is not forgotten.

Should any student of the Master propose (which is, I
feel, highly improbable) to re-name the Award "The Ten-
New-Pence Award," I am sure that you can be relied on,
Mr. Editor-Commissionaire, to treat the heretic in much
the same way as Mr. Holmes dealt with Mr. James Windibank!

Please express my very warmest thanks to all concerned
in the conferment of the Two-Shilling Award upon myself.
                With best Sherlockian greetings to all BSI,
                                [Signed] Don.

     *   *   *   *   *

From Bartlett Dale Simms, D.C., of St. Louis:

I read with interest Dr. Rauber's "The Immortality of
Sherlock Holmes" in the June BSJ. I first became aware of
the importance of Zadig et <u>al</u>. upon reading an article in
the July 1906 issue of <u>The Strand Magazine</u> entitled "Fore-
runners of Sherlock Holmes" (no author). It mentions that
Holmes achieved that rare place in literature where all
deduction is synonymous with Sherlock Holmes.

This article points up Zadig from the Persian book,
<u>Negarestan</u>, who possessed the talent of deduction to a re-
markable degree, as did Dupin and Gaboriau (<u>File No. 113</u>, where
Lecoq cut out letters and pasted them on a sheet of paper to
form words, similar to what was done in <u>The Hound of the
Baskervilles</u>). There were many more likenesses, pre- and
post Sherlock Holmes, but these I think are the ones who
influenced Arthur Conan Doyle. Mayhap Sir Arthur wrote this!

     *   *   *   *   *

From Miss Margaret F. Morris, of Arlington, Texas, <u>Third
Mate</u> of The Barque <u>Lone Star</u>:

I must comment on one new feature of the BSJ, the delightful verses in the last three March issues wherein
Dr. Ezra Wolff comments on the annual dinners. I hope he
has as much fun writing them (and in doing his research)
as I do reading them.

*   *   *   *   *

From Nicholas Utechin, University College, Oxford:

What an excellent article is that one by Dr. Naganuma,
"Holmes and Communication"—that's some really good original research.

*   *   *   *   *

From Katherine Karlson, of Seaford, New York:

It was certainly a pleasure to see so many fine articles
in the Journal's one-hundredth issue, especially Glenn
Holland's "The 'Small, but Very Efficient Organization.'"

*   *   *   *   *

From Andrew Page, of the Bronx, <u>Saltire</u> of The Priory
School, of New York:

I feel that the Scion Society section in each issue of
the Journal takes up too much room. I would much rather
see the 3 or 4 pages reduced to one, and the others used
for another article. To be sure it is always enjoyable to
read about the goings-on at different Scion meetings, but
this can be done through personal correspondence. One solution might be to list only the titles of the Scions and
whom to write to if interested. In the December issue of
each year a short one- or two-paragraph news-brief could
be included, listing the main events of each meeting that
year. If this method is used correctly, we would be able
to read 3 or 4 more articles each year, while at the same
time join other Scions on our own.

*   *   *   *   *

From Morris Rosenblum, A.B., M.A., Ph.D., <u>etc.</u> ("The Greek
Interpreter"):

Thank you for sending me that item from <u>Abstracts
of English Studies</u> about my "Reflections on 'a Hebrew
Rabbi'" (in BSJ, March 1970). "How far that little candle
throws its beams." It's amazing to see how little articles
like that one on the Hebrew Rabbi are picked up by other
journals. How much enlightenment our Journal spreads in
other fields!

My wife and I have just returned from six weeks in
Israel. I'm busy making my way through the accumulation
of mail and was delighted to see the centenary issue of
the Journal. We should do something about the apparent
lack of interest in Israel in reference to the Sherlock
Holmes stories. Looking for available editions in Hebrew,
I enlisted the aid of friends in the book field there,
searched in the book shops of Jerusalem and Tel Aviv,
visited book fairs and sales, showed my list of Doyle
works in print there (only six in all), and could find
only two books containing in all translations of twelve
stories! Most of these stories are not among those considered the better ones. One bookseller, queried in Yiddish as to why there is so little Holmes available, said
that he does not "relate" to Israeli life. I dismissed
that as balderdash because on his shelves the bookseller
had Mickey Mouse, Popeye, <u>etc.</u> in abundance.

*   *   *   *   *

From Irving Fenton ("The Singular Tragedy of the Atkinson Brothers"), of Brooklyn:

The One-Hundredth issue of the Journal arrived today without fanfare. The postman delivered it quietly as if it were one of the numberless magazines I receive every year. But for all that, it was an eventful occasion—even a sad one—for the realisation has come upon me that I shall not be here to receive the Two-Hundredth issue. Sufficient unto the day, however.

The first hundred have given me as much pleasure as one is entitled to in the most fragmented of all possible worlds, and I want to express my appreciation and gratitude at having been here to receive it. And mixed-metaphorically speaking, long may it wave, or be published or extol the doubtful virtue of the Victorian Age, and long may Julian Wolff be around to see that it does.

*   *   *   *   *

From Henry Lauritzen ("The Royal Family of Scandinavia"), Vicepræsident of Sherlock Holmes Klubben i Danmark and Editor of Sherlockiana:

Thank you very much for the June Journal—excellent as always. To think that this is the one-hundredth issue! Congratulations for your fine work. There are three articles that got my highest mark—10—and they come in a row: "A Coming Plague," by Dudley; "The 'Small, but Very Efficient Organization,'" by Holland; and "Some Notes on the Name of the Brothers Moriarty," by Skene Melvin. "The Identity of the King of Bohemia," by Blackburn, also got a 10 —but without the underlining stroke.

*   *   *   *   *

From Kevin Cook, of Fort Worth, Texas:

I feel that many of the articles in the Journal are very good, like Roy Pickard's "Sherlock Holmes on the Screen" (June 1971) and Dr. Naganuma's "Holmes and Communication" (March 1971). I much prefer articles that talk about interesting facts, like those I mentioned. Articles like "The Immortality of Sherlock Holmes" (June 1971) and "The Relationship of a Physician and a Master" (December 1970) are very boring and seem to be far from saying anything of importance. The reason I read the Journal is to gain facts and knowledge about the times and happenings of Sherlock Holmes, not theories about him.

*   *   *   *   *

From Glenn Sowell, of San Marcos, Texas:

I received my first issue of the BSJ and compliment you and the authors supplying some very well written articles on the Canon and other related subjects. A majority of the pieces provided excellent reading material, excluding the article by Dr. Kohki Naganuma. My impression received from reading this article was of a degrading effect toward the Master's creator. True, Sir Arthur was a literary genius, but not a mathematical one. An author such as

he comes but once; let us hold on to what is left, not
dissect his excellent penmanship, searching for minute
"impossibilities." Nothing personal is directed toward Dr.
Naganuma, and may he receive my deep apologies if it was
taken this way.

The Journal was nicely edited, and I am looking forward
to my forthcoming issues.

*   *   *   *   *

From Jack Tracy, of Frankfort, Indiana:

My compliments on the one-hundredth issue of the BSJ
[June 1971]—a worthy addition to its continuing excellence. I was particularly struck by David Skene Melvin's
fine article, which I believe has solved the problem of
the Moriarty name once and for all.

I like the format of more and shorter articles per
issue, but I sincerely hope that worthy contributions will
not be excluded on the basis of length.

Re "Early Decimalisation (?)" on page 83, the five-
shilling dollar appears not to have been part of a formal
decimalisation scheme, but the florin was. A Special Report
of the British Record, published by the British Information
Services and dated 25 January 1971, states: "Proposals for
decimalizing the currency were first made about 150 years
ago. A Royal Commission in 1841 recommended such a change,
and the florin, the two-shilling piece, was in fact introduced in 1849 as a first step. After these first steps,
successive Royal Commissions recommended against change"—
for which we may be Canonically grateful. "The controversy," the Record goes on, "continued in a desultory fashion
for the next fifty years or so until a 1918 Commission
recommended no action, after which little was heard about
a decimal currency until 1951."

The florin is mentioned once in the Saga (in The Crooked
Man), but we do not have Holmes's opinion of the decimalisation agitation. One cannot help wondering whether his
romantic and traditionalist side or his calculating logic
would have prevailed. Watson, good fellow, would have been
dead set against it.

*   *   *   *   *

From A. D. Henriksen ("A Case of Identity"), President of
Sherlock Holmes Klubben i Danmark:

An odd misunderstanding! In his treatment of the topic
"Sherlock Holmes on the Screen" in the June issue of BSJ,
Roy Pickard makes the same mistake as did Ordean A. Hagen
in his great work, Who Done It? Both authors mention the
first Danish creator of Sherlock Holmes as Forrest Holger-
Madsen. They might have seen a photo from one of the films
showing Holger Madsen as Sherlock Holmes in the front of
the picture, which in Danish is expressed so: "Forrest:
Holger-Madsen." Please, let the late Holger-Madsen from
now on be released from this curious first name, "Forrest."

Another Danish creator of Sherlock Holmes, Viggo Lar-
sen (1910), seems unknown to both of the above-mentioned
authors. Readers of our Danish quarterly, Sherlockiana,
may remember a still, reproduced in No. 1-2, 1963.

The Scion Societies

THE RESIDENTS OF BASKERVILLE HALL
of Northern Illinois

Correspondence: Mrs. Gayle Lange Puhl, Lady Henry,
11301-B Lange Road, Hebron, Ill. 60034.

The first meeting was held at Puhl Hall, Lange's Farm, 17 April 1971. Officers were elected and a constitution was adopted.

This Scion, the only one of its kind, is devoted to the study of both Sherlock Holmes and Solar Pons.

The next meeting will be held at the home of Greg Gerrard in Wonder Lake, Illinois, after the corn is planted.

* * * *

HUGO'S COMPANIONS
of Chicago

Correspondence: Robert W. Hahn,
938 Clarence Ave., Oak Park, Ill. 60304.

The Companions met at the Baker Street Pub on 28 April (the April Carousal, at which 34 were present) and on 10 June (the reception for Holmes and Watson, in which 85 participated).

The April meeting was featured by an important announcement confirming the Holmesian exhibit at the Royal London Wax Museum and the tape recording and films of the Queen's birthday celebration. In June, wax figures of Holmes and Watson were at the head table; Matt Fairlie, an Irregular of long standing, was formally presented with the Irregular Shilling (see page 116 of the June BSJ); Gordon Jewkes, the British Acting Consul General, was introduced; and the writer-director and cast of a new Sherlockian musical for children were also on the agenda.

* * * *

MYCROFT HOLMES SOCIETY
of Syracuse

Correspondence: Gerald R. Clark,
2712 Midland Ave., Syracuse, N.Y. 13205.

The first meeting, attended by 30, was held at Lawrinson Penthouse, Syracuse University, on 21 April, and received considerable TV and newspaper coverage. It was topped off by a display of Sherlockian items and books.

* * * *

THE SIX NAPOLEONS
of Baltimore

Correspondence: Steve Clarkson, Harker,
69 Straw Hat Rd., Apt. I-D, Owings Mills, Md. 21117.

22 Napoleons were at The House of Welsh on 12 May to toast the woman and discuss The Retired Colourman. Following musical tributes to Aunt Clara and the awarding of the quiz prizes, it was announced that arrangements had been made for a large display of Sherlockiana at the Enoch Pratt Free Library, in commemoration of the Silver Anniversary of the Napoleons.

* * * *

THE STUDENTS IN SCARLET is a new Scion organised by Old Irregular Paul S. Clarkson ("The Red Leech"), Curator, Special Collections and Rare Books, Goddard Library, Clark University, Worcester, Mass. Surely, we shall be hearing great things of it.

* * * *

THE GREEK INTERPRETERS
of East Lansing, Michigan

Correspondence: Donald A. Yates, Melas,
537 Wells Hall, Michigan State University,
East Lansing, Michigan 48223.

The Interpreters held their second spring meeting on 12 May.
Robert Brunser distributed hand-printed copies of Vincent Starrett's "221B"; communications from corresponding friends were
read; there was a quiz on The Sign of Four; and the Melas read a
monograph on the "locked room" in detective literature.

*   *   *   *

CREW OF THE BARQUE LONE STAR
of North Central Texas

Correspondence: Margaret F. Morris, Third Mate,
472 Westview Terrace, Arlington, Texas 76013.

The spring cruise was held 14 May with nine members aboard.
The reading of communications from corresponding members and
some routine matters took up the first leg of the cruise. Then
the Crew quizzed itself on The Five Orange Pips; the honours went
to Laverne Prewitt and Bill Beeson. After the members approved
a joint meeting with the Fort Worth Corral of the Westerners,
the cruise ended with the ceremonial signing of the ship's log.

*   *   *   *

THE BROTHERS THREE
of Moriarty, New Mexico

Correspondence: John Bennett Shaw,
1917 Fort Union Drive, Santa Fe, N.M. 87501.

The Brothers had their first annual Colonel Sebastian Moran
Trap Shoot on 15 May, and 14 attended. (Unfortunately, the prize
was won by a lawyer.) This was followed by a cocktail party
and dinner, attended by 28. There were four well researched
toasts and papers by John Bennett Shaw and Saul Cohen. The next
meeting will be held on 10 September in the town of Moriarty
(pop. 520) to celebrate the 127th birthday of Prof. Moriarty.

*   *   *   *

MAIWAND JEZAILS
of Wayne, Nebraska

Correspondence: Richard D. Lesh, Commandant,
505 East 10th Street, Wayne, Nebraska 68787.

The meeting at The Radisson Blackstone in Omaha on 29 May
was featured by an excellent programme. The Canonical Toasts
were followed by a sumptuous meal, and then there were three
scholarly papers, the main one being "The Adventure of My Fair
Philologist," by Jason Rouby.

*   *   *   *

THE CONFEDERATES OF WISTERIA LODGE
of Atlanta

Correspondence: Robert S. Gellerstedt, Jr.,
2551 Meadow Lark Drive, East Point, Ga. 30344.

The regular meeting was held at the home of Robert Gellerstedt on 30 May with 15 in attendance. As always, there was a
lively Sherlockian discussion, and then Donald Webster gave a
quiz on The Retired Colourman. After a tie-breaker, W. M. Rapp
was declared the winner and was designated to give the quiz
(on The Devil's Foot) at the next meeting, a picnic on 25 July.
Interested Sherlockians are welcome at our gatherings.

THE RED CIRCLE

of Washington

Correspondence: Peter E. Blau,
2201 M Street NW, Washington, D.C. 20037.

The Red Circle convened on 11 June at Blackie's House of Beef, with 25 in attendance, for a discussion of (Napoleonic and other) busts. Also featured: a report on Russian travels, by Barbara Shickman; a communiqué on the scheduled auction of the Doyle estate, from Joe Daniloski; and a reading of two Sherlockian poems composed by the late Ogden Nash ("Never Mind the Overcoat, Button up That Lip" and "Just Holmes and Me, and Mnemosyne Makes Three," New Yorker, 24 July 1954 and 17 April 1965; also see BSJ 13:215, 1953).

* * *

THE NON-CANONICAL CALABASHES

of Los Angeles

Correspondence: Stephen Verebelyi, Secretary,
4559 Lexington Ave., Los Angeles, Calif. 90029.

The First Annual Basil Rathbone-Nigel Bruce Memorial Dinner took place at the Ram's Horn Restaurant in Encino. We drank the Canonical toasts and special ones to Rathone and Bruce, and after dinner President John Ball spoke of our intention to become the largest and most complete repository of Sherlockiana in sight and sound productions. Then we heard from our contest winners, and the deerstalker prize was awarded to Harold Stanislow. There was an announcement of the soon-to-be-produced Sherlock Holmes watch, and then we heard a eulogy of Nigel Bruce by Dr. Ronald Lawrence, as well as talks by David Millar, noted film collector, and Ron James, author of the forthcoming book on Sherlockian films. Mrs. Ouida Rathbone, who was unable to be present, wrote a very gracious letter.

As to our future plans: We are now conducting negotiations with several radio stations to begin our own Sherlock Holmes programme, which we hope will have as guests from time to time great Sherlockians from all over the country.

* * * *

THE SCANDALOUS BOHEMIANS

of New Jersey

Correspondence: Martin J. King,
1113 Sylvan Lane, Mountainside, N.J. 07092.

A record number attended the third annual dinner at The Dickens Pub, in Union, New Jersey, on 25 June. The Commissionaire of The Baker Street Irregulars was present with his lovely wife, and he greeted the society with a few well chosen words. Presiding were two of the three Founders, Keith Paulisen and Martin King, with Norman Nolan as programme chairman for this meeting. Thanks to Chris Steinbrunner, two Sherlockian films were shown; the traditional toasts were drunk; and Dan Morrow spoke learnedly of Mr. Barker, private detective, from his boyhood days as an original irregular to his professional work as a competitor of Holmes. The quiz on The Bruce-Partington Plans was hotly contested but clearly won by Lisa McGaw.

* * * *

At the last meeting of THE BAKER STREET UNDERGROUND, of Ithaca, Andrew J. Peck was elected Politician and Trained Cormorant. All correspondence is to be addressed to him at: 306 Highland Road, Ithaca, New York 14850.

* * * *

The recently inactive BAKER STREET PAGEBOYS has been revived with Glenn S. Holland (10469 Lindbrook Drive, Los Angeles, California 90024) as President and Andrew Page (3130 Irwin Ave., Bronx, N.Y. 10463), <u>Saltire</u> of The Priory School, as Vice-President. This is a junior (members under 20) Scion, and correspondence is invited from all those who are interested.

* * * *

The correspondence society organised by Rose Vogel (1041 Camelot Gardens Drive, St. Louis, Mo. 63125) and Steve Clarkson (69 Straw Hat Road, 1-D, Owings Mills, Md. 21117), and which was announced on page 53 of the March 1971 BSJ, is named THE BOARD-SCHOOL BEACONS. A rule has been made that each member must write to another at least once a month. All Sherlockians, young or old, are welcome and are invited to write.

* * * *

THE SCION OF THE FOUR
of Morgantown, W.Va.

Correspondence: Andrew G. Fusco, <u>Commissionaire</u>,
      643 Trovato Drive, Morgantown, W.Va. 26505.

After a great hiatus of approximately nine years, the Scion held a reorganisation session at the Flame restaurant in Morgantown on 7 July. Of the eight present, there were several new <u>aficionados</u>, in addition to the old stalwarts. The traditional Canonical toasts consumed a good portion of the evening, and Mrs. Stephen A. Crocker, widow of the founder, was honoured <u>in absentia</u> as <u>the</u> woman. A very Irregular business session ended with the election of officers, and then we heard Basil Rathbone's reading of <u>The Final Problem</u>, which was followed by much serious discussion of the Saga.

* * * *

TRIFLING MONOGRAPHS

Correspondence: Susan M. Rice, <u>Magnum Opus</u>,
      380 Lone Pine Road, Bloomfield Hills, Mich. 48013.

This newly organised Scion of young Sherlockians consists of five founding members at present, with several others in view. Communications by mail or telephone (313-642-1198) will be eagerly received.

"Stand with me here upon the terrace..."

AUGUST DERLETH, appropriately Investitured as "Inspector Baynes, Surrey Constabulary" (for he indeed did have instinct and intuition, and he did rise high in his profession), died on July the fourth. He was a prolific writer and a great one, well known and much admired in the literary world—and especially well known to Irregulars as the creator of Solar Pons, the greatest serious imitator of the Master.

WANTS AND OFFERS

David Galerstein (51 Fall Lane, Jericho, N.Y. 11753) is anxious to rent the Rathbone-Bruce and the Clive Brook versions of The Hound of the Baskervilles for a private showing to be run on a cooperative basis.

Thomas O. Smallwood (P.O. Box 61, Aptos, Calif. 95003) invites offers for two bound volumes of The Strand Magazine—III and V, containing the original appearances of twelve of the tales.

Christian Hamilton (Leysin American School, 1854 Leysin, Switzerland) wishes to sell: Maurice Leblanc: Sherlock Holmes versus Arsene Lupin: The Case of the Golden Blonde (paperback), New York, Atomic Books, 1946; Christopher Morley, ed.: Sherlock Holmes and Dr. Watson: A Textbook of Friendship, New York, 1944; Edgar W. Smith: Appointment in Baker Street, Pamphlet House, 1938; Profile by Gaslight, 1944; The Baker Street Journal, Original Series, Vols. 1-3, 1946, 1947, 1948; Vincent Starrett: The Private Life of Sherlock Holmes, New York, 1933; 221B: Studies in Sherlock Holmes, New York, 1940.

Vernon Lay (52, Oakleigh Gardens, Whetstone, London, N.20, England) offers: 221B: Studies in Sherlock Holmes, 1940, $24.; Starrett's The Private Life of Sherlock Holmes, London, 1934, $24.00; Profile by Gaslight, New York, 1944, $12.00; Gavin Brend: My Dear Holmes, $12.00; Baker Street Studies, 1934, $24.; Sir Arthur Conan Doyle: Centenary 1859-1959, $12.00.

Professor Arthur Coleman (104 Searington Road, Albertson, N.Y. 11507) wants a copy of Basil Rathbone's autobiography, In and Out of Character.

William Hyder (14 E. Hamilton St., Baltimore, Md. 21202) has Memoirs of Sherlock Holmes, Harper, 1905, with 23 illustrations by Hyde and one by Paget; spine discoloured, hinges cracked, two plates loose. He offers it for the best bid received by 1 February 1972.

Noah Andre Trudeau (11 Ogden Ave., Peekskill, N.Y. 10566) is engaged in research on the Basil Rathbone-Nigel Bruce films produced by Universal and would like to hear from anyone with information (casts and actors, screen-writers, music writers, shooting location, etc.) or available memorabilia.

The Scowrers and Molly Maguires, of San Francisco, now have their own Scion pin, intended for members, but collectors may acquire one for display (but not for wear) for $4.25. Orders are to be sent to Dean Dickensheet, 244 26th Avenue, San Francisco, Calif. 94121, and cheques should be made out to "Scowrers' Book Fund."

John E. Cimisi (231-10 147th Ave., Rosedale, N.Y. 11413) wants to buy old radio records or tapes, especially those starring Basil Rathbone and Nigel Bruce.

Mrs. Alla T. Ford (114 South Palmway, Lake Worth, Fla. 33460) announces: "20% off my old list of Sherlock Holmes and detective books. List available, but it has to be returned."

Marvin Norton (990 Sarazen Drive, Rockledge, Fla. 32955) wants to start a Scion Society in the central Florida area, and would like to hear from interested Sherlockians. Telephone number is 305-631-0753.

A Sherlock Holmes watch is to be made available by The Non-Canonical Calabashes, of Los Angeles: one-jewel, $19.00; 17-jewel, $22.00. Orders (but no remittances as yet) should be sent to: Sherlock Holmes Watch Order, c/o Miss Glenna Dunning,

542 S. Coronado, Apt. 5, Los Angeles, Calif. 90057.

Paul Uzarowski (6747 N. Campbell Ave., Chicago, Ill. 60645) wants to buy Sherlockian movie posters, scripts, sound-tracks, stills, and recordings of Sherlockian radio and television shows.

Robert L. Boone (388 E. California, Pasadena, Calif. 91106) offers copies of two papers by Irving Fenton: "An Analysis of the Crimes and Near-Crimes at Appledore Towers in the Light of the English Criminal Law" (BSJ, April 1956) and "Holmes and the Law" (BSJ, April 1957). Just send him a stamped and addressed envelope. Also: He is interested in corresponding with any Sherlockians who are in the law-enforcement field.

Charles Roberts (2425 Greenwood, Pueblo, Colorado 81003) wants photographs of Holmes as portrayed by Wontner, Barrymore, Rathbone, Brooks, Norwood, Cushing, and Lee. He is also interested in English-language versions of the Holmes films—Rathbone's in particular.

Walter Klinefelter (R.D. 1, Dallastown, Pa. 17313) offers a copy of the Heritage Press edition of The Adventures, as new, in slip-case, for $7.50.

Glenn J. Shea (5 Pine Hill Road, Jewett City, Conn. 06351) is looking for: Sherlock Holmes, the play by Doyle and Gillette; The Incunabular Holmes and Introducing Sherlock Holmes, both edited by Edgar W. Smith; A Sherlock Holmes Almanac, by Petersen; The Sherlockian Atlas, by Wolff; Montgomery's Christmas Annuals for 1950 and 1951; the recordings of Arthur Conan Doyle, c. 1939, and of John Gielgud and Ralph Richardson in dramatisations. Also, he would welcome correspondence from England.

Stanfield D. Hill (82 Florence Road, Riverside, Conn. 06878) wants to dispose of many copies of The Sherlock Holmes Journal and The Baker Street Journal from the early and mid-1960's and a few from the 1950's; My Life with Sherlock Holmes; The Sherlock Holmes Companion; The Man Who Was Sherlock Holmes; Seventeen Steps to Baker Street.

William J. Walsh (6, Ernst Drive, Suffern, N.Y. 10901) has had some pencils made up with the inscription, "Baker Street Irregulars," and offers them (no more than 2) for 10¢ each.

THE CHRISTMAS CARD OF THE SHERLOCK HOLMES SOCIETY OF LONDON

For 1971 the Society's Christmas card will be illustrated with Sidney Paget's portrait of Silver Blaze (much larger than shown below), and the text will consist of quotations from the story of the same name. The price will be the same as last year: 30¢ each for quantities of fewer than 12; 25¢ each for 12 or more. Prices include envelopes and postage.

From the Editor's Commonplace Book

The September issue of each year contains the final notice of our annual Silver Blaze festivities, and this issue is no exception. It is still possible to participate in this great event, which will be run at Belmont on 17 September; write to the Benefactor of the Race, Thomas L. Stix, Jr., at 34 Pierson Avenue, Norwood, N.J. 07648.

*   *   *   *

Henry Lauritzen reports that the Danish Silver Blaze, which took place on 19 June, was a great success. It was won by Graaskæg with Miss Paris second by half a length in a breath-taking finish. Henry adds: "Silver Blaze came in last, I am sorry to say." But everybody had a great day and a beautiful and nice evening full of fun.

*   *   *   *

From Cornelis Helling ("The Reigning Family of Holland") we have Televizier (a Dutch periodical) for 20 March, containing an item about "Avroskoop," a television programme consisting of fragments of Sherlock Holmes films with comments by Anthony Howlett, Peter Cushing, Christopher Lee, and Cornelis Helling.

*   *   *   *

I hear of Sherlock everywhere. William Walsh reports that Joseph Gerard Brennen, in The Meaning of Philosophy, devotes half a page to a short discussion of the Master's deductive processes—and "Watson, John" appears in the index.

Also, Albert Silverstein writes: "In communications-seer Marshall McLuhan's The Mechanical Bride there is a section called "From Da Vinci to Holmes" in which he contrasts the homebodiness of Western Man's daily life with the vicarious identification with heroes who search and hunt. The Master is his No. 1 exemplar."

And it seems to me that I did have a Sherlockian reference by Toynbee to include here, but if I did I have mislaid it. Perhaps it was a Freudian slip, since I do recall the words of Edgar W. Smith (on page 191 of BSJ for July 1957): "There are those, of course, who think that Dr. Toynbee's own books are among the least remarkable ever penned."

*   *   *   *

Many of us may remember that Thomas Gomez, who died on 18 June, played Moriarty in Rathbone's short-lived production, Sherlock Holmes (by Ouida Rathbone), in 1953. But it will come as news to most of us that Gomez also appeared in the 1942 Universal Sherlock Holmes and the Voice of Terror as Meade, the leader of the saboteurs. We are indebted to Peter Blau for this information.

*   *   *   *

An article in the Washington Post for 9 April reveals that it was our own Tom Mahoney ("The Case of John Vincent Harden") who, as public relations agent for the Blood Banks organisation, persuaded then Postmaster-General Blount (a blood donor himself) to issue a commemorative stamp honouring blood donors.

* * * *

An article titled "Resplendent Regalia" appeared in MD for March 1971, and in it one finds: "In earlier times the kings of England, like those of other lands, regarded their regalia as a personal treasure; to relieve their acute financial distress, both Henry V and Edward III pawned their crowns." Perhaps Alexander Holder's client (the future Edward VII ?) was merely acting in accordance with an old English custom when he pawned the Beryl Coronet.

* * * *

Don Redmond sent me a book list from the Old Authors Farm, Morrisburg, Ontario, and it contained some remarks: "Reading Hound of the Baskervilles again reminds me of kid days when I made pocket money as a Niagara Guide. Memory Holds the Door as my old Friend John Buchan put it.

"After two-hour Tour with Conan Doyle (. . . about 1923) he paused to scratch 'SH' on a rock. Gazing out over the Canadian Falls, he said to Lady Doyle, 'A Glorious Trail's End for anyone . . . I should have killed Holmes over there, not the Swiss Alps.'

"Dear Old Client Christopher Morley paid tribute to Sherlock with greater skill, but this is mine. Anyhow, search Goat Island with a large Glass and you will find the last of 'SH' . . . he is there."

* * * *

F. Dennis France has furnished the programme of the Goodman Children's Theatre Company of the Art Institute of Chicago for the world premiere of The Marvelous Misadventure of Sherlock Holmes. ("The story concerns Holmes's call to Bohemia to search for the lost Black Pearl of the Borgias.")

* * * *

Probably only Rex Stout will be happy to learn that Dr. Watson is a woman:

Joanne Woodward as Dr. Watson (a psychiatrist) and George C. Scott, who thinks he is Sherlock Holmes, in They Might Be Giants

WHODUNIT

JOSEPH MERRIAM, Jr., M.D., a member of The Speckled Band, of Boston, is a pathologist at the Boston Veterans Hospital and a sometime instructor at Harvard Medical School. His hobbies include gardening, versifying, and dreaming about travel—particularly to places associated with Holmes. 85 Belknap Road, Framingham, Mass. 01701.

EDWARD A. MERRILL, a retired Colonel of Engineers, is a member of the Scowrers. He previously appeared here in March 1970, and his paper, "Holmes and Brunton: Civil Engineers," won the Morley-Montgomery Award. 840 Powell Street, Apt. 102, San Francisco, Calif. 94108.

NICHOLAS UTECHIN is a student at Oxford, majoring in modern history, and he hopes to go into the News and Current Affairs Section of the B.B.C. (He adds: "Basil Rathbone was a distant cousin of mine; he and my grandfather were second cousins.") 6 Jubilee Gardens, Bearsden, Glasgow. Scotland.

BENJAMIN GROSBAYNE, who previously appeared in the Old Series Journal, is a great expert in the field of music. He has conducted in New York and many European cities; has written much on music; and was Chairman of Brooklyn College Music Department. 50 Harvard St., Newtonville, Mass. 02160.

J. S. (Jud) CALLAWAY has been an attentive Sherlockian for many years, but this is his first writing on the subject. At present he is on a tour of duty in Alaska, after studying communications at the Navy Training Center in Pensacola. Box 278, New London, Missouri 63459 (mark "Please Forward").

JACK TRACY was a film producer for an Indianapolis TV station until recently. After that he wrote a novel which is awaiting production. Although passionately interested in Holmes since childhood, he has not previously contributed to the literature. 955 East Boone St., Frankfort. Ind. 46041.

GEORGE FLETCHER ("The Cardboard Box"), a scholarly Sherlockian, is senior Editor at Fordham University Press, and, as expert proofreader, is of great help in the production of this Journal. 241 Battery Ave., Brooklyn, N.Y. 11209.

D. A. REDMOND ("Good Old Index"), Librarian of Douglas Library, Queen's University, Kingston. Ontario, Canada, has made many scholarly contributions to Sherlockiana and has rendered immortal service by preparing our annual subject indexes and the great, indispensable Cumulated Index. 178 Barrie St., Kingston, Ontario, Canada.

WILLIAM E. FLEISCHAUER, Commissionaire XII of The Six Napoleons, of Baltimore, is a Management Analyst with the Social Security Administration. Now retired from the army, he has served in Military Intelligence in Iran, Austria, and Switzerland. 4914 Canvasback Court, Ellicott City, Md. 21043.

BENJAMIN S. CLARK ("The Retired Colourman"), a knowledgeable Sherlockian of long standing, has contributed much to our literature. He is a member of The Five Orange Pips and, in the non-Sherlockian world, a partner in White, Weld and Co. 20 Broad Street, New York, N.Y. 10005.

WILLIAM G. MILLER, self-described as "a very amateur Sherlockian," has been a newspaperman for twenty years and is now Assistant Managing Editor of the Boston Globe. 142 Storey Avenue, Newburyport, Mass. 01950

Sherlock Holmes is Coming Back

TWO more "reminiscences" by Dr. Watson of the Great Detective are to see the light. The first one is entitled "The Singular Experience of Mr. J. Scott Eccles." It will appear in COLLIER'S for August 15th, which will be a "SHERLOCK HOLMES" Number. There will be an intimate sketch of Sir Arthur Conan Doyle, creator of Sherlock Holmes, of his old teacher, Professor Bell of Edinburgh, who was the original of the Great Detective, and many anecdotes and illustrations of the unique place in literature and on the stage achieved by "the greatest character in fiction since *Monsieur Dupin*."

Here is what Collier's Fiction Editor wrote:

"I think I can safely say that it is one of the most remarkable detective stories of modern times. Not only is the plot novel, but the author brings to this tale all of the atmosphere of mystery and the extraordinary character drawing which long ago made him famous. I consider the story a great asset for any periodical. It is one of those cases where an author wins success along a certain line, creates a band of imitators, drops out for a time, and then comes back as if to show just how good he really was."

Collier's
The National Weekly

Sherlock Holmes Number—August 15th

Volume 21, Number 4
(New Series)

December 1971

THE BAKER STREET JOURNAL

An Irregular Quarterly of Sherlockiana

Editor: JULIAN WOLFF, M.D.

THE BAKER STREET IRREGULARS
NEW YORK, N.Y.

THE BAKER STREET JOURNAL

An Irregular Quarterly of Sherlockiana

ATTENTA! . . . PERICOLO!

Our Commonplace Books tell us that your subscription to THE BAKER STREET JOURNAL expired with DEC 1971

In order to avoid any untidy gaps on your Sherlockian shelf, please write your name and address below and return this notice with your remittance.

NEVER HAS SO MUCH BEEN WRITTEN BY SO MANY FOR SO FEW!

• • • • • • • • • • • • • ` • • • • • • • • • •

Please continue my subscription to the JOURNAL for   years at $4.00 per year. My remittance is attached.

NAME:

ADDRESS:

Zip Code:

If new address, please check ☐

Send to: Julian Wolff, M.D.
33 Riverside Drive
New York, N.Y. 10023

DEC 1971

THE BAKER STREET JOURNAL

AN IRREGULAR QUARTERLY OF SHERLOCKIANA

PRODUCTION

Our records show that your
subscription to THE BAKER STREET JOURNAL
expired with

In order to avoid any delay please
put Sherlockian shelf, sign both your
name and address below and return this
notice with your remittance.

NEVER HAS SO MUCH BEEN WRITTEN
BY SO MANY FOR SO FEW

Please check one or more of the following:

□ ANNUAL for_____ years at $6.00 per year.
No remittance is enclosed.

NAME

ADDRESS

ZIP Code:

□ If box address, please, mark □

Send to: Julian Wolff, M.D.
34 Riverside Drive
New York, N.Y. 10023

Volume 21, Number 4
(New Series)

December 1971

THE

BAKER STREET

JOURNAL

Founded by **EDGAR W. SMITH**, Esq.

"Si monumentum quaeris, circumspice"

Subscription $4 a year

All communications and remittances should be sent to the Editor

Julian Wolff, M.D.

33 Riverside Drive, New York, N. Y. 10023

CONTENTS

THE SECOND MASTER

(On the passing of August Derleth, 4 July 1971)

by Howard Lachtman

Now the light grows dark at Praed Street,
Speak not of beekeeping or rheumatic ills;
Their greatest adventure is just begun
For all the closing of their chronicles.
The Second Master and his Agent pass
To that Celebrated Detective Kingdom above,
Imitative figures who performed
Original labours of love.
And two others appear before them,
Brothers akin as heraldic emblem:
"Dr. Watson?" "Dr. Parker, I presume?"
Colleagues, the Agents warmly join hand.
"Holmes!" "Your arm, if you please, my dear Pons."
Four immortals go forth in that better land,
Hand in hand, arm in arm, brethren complete.
Now the light grows dark in Praed Street.
And the Second Agent's agent is made glad
By Sir Arthur's cordial comradeship:
"Well and bravely done, August lad!
Now if we can give our sleuthing chaps the slip,
We'll toast the end of business at Baker and Praed."
Yet even as these Fathers signal the B&S attendant,
Their children find the old game freshly afoot,
And ride eternal hansoms through fogs resplendent
(For Heaven is complete with London cabs and soot).
And though that City admits no possible flaw,
Still they serve the cause of Immutable Law
Against the mathematical possibility of evil,
Since Moriarty and his twin serve the Devil
(The Most Dangerous Man in that princely seat,
Though not entirely unknown at Praed Street).
Thus hail and farewell, Parker and Pons,
Worthy Master, honest Agent, detectives elite,
Seconds who recaptured that notable First feat,
The delight of schoolboys and the dispute of dons:
The Light will never go out on Praed Street.

'TWAS THE SECOND MORNING AFTER CHRISTMAS
A Tale in Verse

by Edgar S. Rosenberger

John Watson stopped around to greet his dear old
friend in Baker Street, and wish him Merry Christmas,
though precisely two days late. Said Sherlock Holmes,
"The same to you! And likewise, Happy New Year, too. On
that, at least, we might as well anticipate the date."

The Great Man, only slightly fazed, lay on the sofa
as he gazed upon a battered billycock, while Watson
snugly sat hard by the fire in his old chair, and warmed
his chilly fingers there; and, looking at his friend, he
asked, "Where did you get that hat?"

Said Holmes, "This hat has gone astray. It came to
me on Christmas day. It is the find of Peterson, the
good commissionaire. This is the story that he told: On
Christmas morning, in the cold, he headed home from
celebrating at some small affair. A band of hoodlums,
on the loose, attacked a man who had a goose. He swung
his cane at them, but smashed a windowpane instead. Our
friend stepped in and tried to stall this crazy, mixed-
up free-for-all, but when they saw his uniform, they
all picked up and fled. So Peterson now has the goose.
I have the hat, but what's the use? The science of deduction really doesn't mean a lot. The owner of this
hat, I think, has had hard luck and takes to drink.
There's much more I could tell you, but I merely say,
'So what?'"

His discourse got no further, for there came a pound-
ing at the door, and Peterson came bursting in and clat-
tered to a stop. Cried he, "It's all about that goose!
Will you please tell me how the deuce this sparkling
diamond ever found its way into its crop." Holmes whis-
tled and exclaimed, "By Jove! This certainly is treas-
ure-trove. It is the blue carbuncle of the Countess of
Morcar. The thing was pilfered from her purse. As you'd
expect, it bears a curse. How sad for such a pretty
thing! It glitters like a star."

"The papers state the facts," he said; and, picking
up The Times, he read, "A plumber named John Horner
seems to be the guilty man. He is the one, at any rate,
who, asked to come and fix the grate, apparently un-
earthed the stone, and pilfered it and ran. The evidence
hangs by a thread. It rests on what James Ryder said,
the head attendant at the Cosmopolitan Hotel. The Countess's own maid supports the simple facts that he reports: The lady's bureau rifled, and the culprit gone

as well."

"Well, well," said Holmes, "this is a case! Our little problem is to trace the course of this carbuncle from
the Countess to the goose. The simplest method is, I'm
bound, an insert in the 'Lost and Found.' If that should
fail to do the trick, we'll try another ruse. I'll notify
the owner that he can regain his goose and hat. The tag
said Henry Baker, and his friends should note it well.
Here, Peterson, just take this down to sundry papers in
the town—the Globe, St. James's, Evening News, the Echo,
and Pall Mall."

The doctor left to make his round, and, coming back
that evening found none else than Henry Baker 'neath the
fanlight at the door. His nose was red, he had a twitch,
confirming the deductions which the Master had presented
just a little while before. The two ascended to the room.
"Ah, Henry Baker, I presume," said Sherlock Holmes, with
easy geniality and grace. "Here is your hat. We ate the
bird, but here's another. On my word, you could not find
a better, plumper one to take its place. Perhaps you'd
like the other's craw?" The caller gave a loud guffaw.
"No, thanks," said he, "I'm pleased with that replace-
ment that I see." Holmes said, "The goose you lost was
fine. Perhaps it's just a quirk of mine, but could you
tell me who the seller of that bird might be?"

"Why, certainly," the man replied. "I haven't anything to hide. I patronise the Alpha Inn, where I'm a
frequent guest. The owner of my favoured pub has organised a Christmas club. I paid my dues, received my
goose, and you know all the rest."

The caller, having had his say, bowed out and strode
upon his way. "So much," said Holmes, "for Henry Baker,
and I think that we would miss a trick if we did not
pursue this clue while it is hot. So bundle up, old boy,
and we'll be off to Bloomsbury."

'Twas bitter cold, the stars were bright upon that
far-off winter night. Their breath blew out like pistol
shots, their steps rang loud and clear. They deftly
threaded through a maze of London's ancient, storied
ways, and walked into the Alpha Inn, to have a glass of
beer. Holmes said, "Good evening! Greetings! Peace! I
came to talk about your geese. I spoke to Henry Baker,
and he thinks they're really fine." The landlord said,
"You'd better see the man who sold the geese to me. It's
Breckinridge at Covent Garden—them's 'is geese, not mine."

They left the cheery warmth and light and sallied
forth into the night. They zigzagged through the slums
and reached the famed old market-place. They shortly
spotted, at his stall, the man on whom they came to

call, a horsy gent with trim side-whiskers and a ruddy
face. Holmes said, "Good evening. Rather cold. I see your
geese have all been sold. The landlord of the Alpha Inn—
I think you sent him some? I had a talk with him, and he
has recommended you to me. And, by the way, could you inform me whom you bought them from?"

The surly fellow cocked his head and, standing arms
akimbo, said, "Let's have it straight. What's that to
you? What's more, why should you care?" Holmes asked,
"Why all the angry words? I'm asking where you got the
birds." The man replied, "That's my affair, and none of
yours. So there!"

Holmes shrugged his shoulders, yawned, and said, "I'll
bet those geese were country bred." The salesman snapped,
"Now ain't you smart! Well, sir, you've lost your bet.
I've handled geese since I was small, and you come here
and have the gall to tell me you know better. Man, I tell
you you're all wet!" Holmes countered, "Want to bet a
pound?" The dealer brought his books around. Said he,
"They came from Brixton Road, see? Oakshott is the name.
It reads, 'Sold to the Alpha Inn.' So, Mr. Big, you lose,
I win!" Holmes tossed a sovereign on the slab and shrunk
away in shame.

"Not bad, eh, Watson?" chuckled he. "That's what you
call psychology. If I'd put down a hundred pounds—but
what's this all about?" They turned and saw a noisy brawl
in front of Breckinridge's stall. The salesman seized a
rat-faced runt and hoarsely yelled, "Get out!"

"Aha!" said Holmes. "I heard their words. He wants to
know about those birds." He overtook the little man who,
terrified, had fled. "Good sir, if you will pardon me, I
think, perhaps, that I may be of help to you in clearing
up this mystery," he said. The stranger asked, "But who
are you?" Holmes said, "I know you're in a stew. You're
trying to locate some geese, but don't know where they
went. Well, you can stop your worrying, for I can tell
you everything. I know just where they came from, and I
know where they were sent." The little man exclaimed,
"Oh, sir! I've longed to know just where they were. But
how do you know who I am? You seem to know me well."
Holmes said, "I think that I can guess. You are James
Ryder, none the less, the head attendant at the Cosmopolitan Hotel."

They took a cab to Baker Street. Said Sherlock Holmes,
"Pray take a seat. We'll get down to the matter that we
came to talk about. The goose you want was brought to me.
It laid an egg, as you can see. This bright blue stone is
what you seek—of that I have no doubt." The suspect
staggered to his feet, his pallid face white as a sheet.
"Hold up!" cried Holmes. "Collect yourself, or you'll be
in the fire!" The caller, overwhelmed with care, sank

weakly back into his chair. The doctor poured a slug and said, "This is what you require."

Holmes said, "There's little you need tell. I know the story pretty well. The lady's maid-in-waiting hit upon a nifty deal. You both worked out a clever plot to put John Horner on the spot. I think, James Ryder, you are an unmitigated heel." The little wretch sprang from his seat and threw himself at Holmes's feet. He pleaded, "Oh, have mercy, sir! I won't go wrong again." Said Holmes, "You may well cringe and crawl, but you had better tell us all. By that alone can you avoid more suffering and pain."

Said Ryder, "Here's where it began. I had the stone, but had no plan. I hurried to my sister's place—she lives out Brixton way. I smoked a pipe in her back yard, and thought it over long and hard. And then a neat solution dawned upon me, plain as day. I went and seized a barred-tail goose, laid hold its bill and pried it loose. I forced the stone into its throat, but then it flapped away. My sister, hearing something queer, came out and asked, 'What goes on here?' I said, 'I picked the goose you promised me for Christmas day.' 'All right,' she said. 'It's yours to keep.' I said, 'Thanks, Maggie, thanks a heap.' I killed the goose and trudged to Kilburn, where I knew a fence. We opened up the bird, but oh! For me it is a tale of woe. There was no blue carbuncle, and I nearly lost my sense. I only had one thought, to race at top speed to my sister's place. I asked about that barred-tail goose. She said, 'Yes, there were two.' But now the flock had all been sold; the dealer left me in the cold. So that's my story, gentlemen. Oh dear, what shall I do?"

A silence followed; minutes passed. The culprit's breath came short and fast. Then Sherlock Holmes strode to the door and curtly said, "Get out!" "What? Heaven bless you!" Ryder cried, and, leaping from his seat, he hied at top speed down the stairway, like an army put to rout. Holmes said, "It's not my normal rôle, but maybe I have saved a soul. It is the season of forgiveness; let us mark it well. Now, doctor, it is time that we indulged in some gastronomy. Once more the feature is a bird—if you will touch the bell."

The author writes: "I have long thought it regrettable that that magnificent tale, The Adventure of the Blue Carbuncle, has never been set to verse. I read it every year at Christmas, and each time I read it the stern voice of duty tells me I should make a poem of it. After several false starts and much blood, sweat and tears, I finally came up with the above."

REFLECTIONS ON CANONICAL VEHICLES
AND SOMETHING OF THE HORSE
by Henry C. Potter

In a colour story on New York City, in a recent edition
of an evening paper, the decrepit horse-drawn victorias at
the entrance to Central Park were blithely misidentified
as "hansom cabs." To this long-time equiphile one portent
was clear: The last vestige of the horse-drawn world was
about to sink without a trace. Before some younger Irregular should come upon "a tall dog-cart" in the Canon and
wonder what in the world that could have been, it is high
time to memorialise the Holmesian vehicle and something of
its lore.

Baring-Gould's Annotated, aided by the fine Sidney Paget
Strand illustrations, has already striven to aid my project. But one senses that, except in the case of hansom cabs
and four-wheelers, his familiarity with the other vehicles,
the horses themselves, the actual mechanics of driving, was
predominantly scholarly and literary. My own knowledge being just the reverse, my hope is that between us a more
three-dimensionalised picture may be handed on of that by-
gone but still fascinating world.

The first vehicle (chronologically speaking) mentioned
in the Saga turns up in The Gloria Scott and is the dog-
cart. Baring-Gould notes that: "The dog-cart was not a cart
drawn by a large dog, as some might think, but a sportsman's vehicle, a two-wheeled, one-horse cart with two double seats, back to back, the rear seat being so constructed that it could be shut to form a box for carrying a dog."

Actually, it was not the rear seat that shut but the
tail-gate, which normally was in the let-down position,
supported by chains to form a footrest for the occupants of
the rear seat. While occasionally seen in London, the dog-
cart was usually to be found in the country. Its wheels
were some four feet in diameter, and the bottom of the body
was well off the ground so as to clear the bushes and rough
going on shooting parties. A larger and higher version will
turn up shortly in The Man with the Twisted Lip.

Perhaps it would be wise at this point to distinguish
between cart and carriage: A cart is a two-wheeled vehicle, a carriage always four-wheeled.

A more aristocratic dog-cart appears in The Musgrave
Ritual. Baring-Gould reproduces a good Sidney Paget illustration of it, complete with footman on the rear seat, arms
correctly folded. Musgrave holds the "ribbons" (jocular for
reins) correctly in his left hand, the whip in his right.
Not as correct, however, is the absence of driving gloves,
which—aside from their pro forma aspect, were really necessary with a horse of any spirit. Was the presence of the
liveried footman sheer swank? Not at all; he was a vital
necessity at the horse's head when Holmes's train pulled in.

The next vehicle mentioned by Watson, which reappears
throughout the Canon—and why not, since at that time there
were 8,000 of them in London?—is the hansom cab. It took
its name from its original designer, the carriage maker,
Joseph A. Hansom. Says Baring-Gould: "'The Gondolas of London' was the felicitous title conferred on the hansom cabs

by the great Benjamin Disraeli. [Editor's note: See "The Victorian Gondola," by James C. Iraldi, in BSJ (NS) 1:99-103, (July) 1951.] They were the fastest vehicles devised up to that time for negotiating the narrow and congested streets of London at high speeds. The top-hatted driver sat high up at the back of the hansom with the reins passing through a support on the front of the roof. The front of the hansom was open, except for two folding doors which came about halfway up and protected the traveller's feet and legs against the weather. To ride in this type of cab, with its brightly polished lamps and brasswork, its jingling harness and smartly trotting horse, was a highly pleasant experience."

One might add that the later models had a large rectangular glass window, suspended flat against the ceiling in fine weather and let down by the driver after one was aboard and the doors closed on a rainy day. There was, however, no protection for the driver; there was not the slightest provision made for the protection of any hired driver on any vehicle in that era of unthinking indifference.

Those folding doors! They were actuated by a lever operated by the cabby, one who could not see what he was doing; when entering the cab, it was wise to sit as quickly as possible to avoid getting pinched between them when they closed.

Communication between driver and passenger was through a little trap door which he opened when one got his attention by poking at it with cane or umbrella.

A vivid recollection: the feeling one had on sitting down that one's weight, so far abaft the centre of gravity, was about to lift the horse from the ground!

In point of time, the hansom cab was the predecessor of that other ubiquitous conveyance, the four-wheeler cab. Also known familiarly as a growler—why, no one remembers—it was a lineal descendant of its French predecessor, the coupé, which also inspired the English brougham, about which more later. The French carriage maker, in devising the coupé, revolutionised carriage design. Up to that time sharp turns were impossible because the front wheel would encounter the side of the body and seize, resulting in the overturning of the vehicle. By cutting away the body beneath the driver's seat and creating a sort of tunnel for the wheel, the carriage was enabled to turn within its own length. From that point on, all carriages, except for light traps like the American buggy, were designed with the "cut-under" feature.

I am indebted to one John R. Meader's article, "The Evolution of the Carriage" (in Metropolitan Magazine for 1905), for the four-wheeler's genealogy, and I cannot resist quoting his confident forecast for the continuing prosperity of the carriage maker of 1905: "The demand [for carriages and coaches] is so constantly increasing that carriage makers see little reason to fear the inroads of the power conveyances." As Ring Lardner used to say: "Could he but knew."

The four-wheeler carried four passengers; almost any amount of luggage could be carried on top, lashed to the guardrail. One of the strongest—and I use the word advisedly—memories of the four-wheeler passenger is the pungent smell of the livery stable from which it hailed; no passenger can ever forget it.

An interesting difference between the Jehus of hansoms and four-wheelers: The former's top-hat has already been noted; the growler's cabby would have none of that—his badge of office was the bowler hat (or derby).

The corresponding privately owned carriage, the gentleman's brougham, is our next exhibit. It makes its first appearance in A Study in Scarlet—but by reference only. Holmes's categorical statement that "the ordinary London growler is considerably less wide than a gentleman's brougham" can be challenged; the reverse was, more often than not, the case. Holmes could be right about the family brougham, which required a pair of horses to pull it, but the smaller bachelor's brougham—well portrayed in John Leech's drawing in the Annotated—was most certainly no wider than the cab. Question: Did Watson mis-report Sherlock? Why?

The brougham, named for its designer, Lord Brougham, who just about copied the French coupé, was lavishly appointed in its interior. Often it sported rich upholstery, a speaking tube to the coachman, a bud vase, a silver box for lucifers, and sometimes a bell-pull to sound a warning clang to dawdling inferiors on the roadway ahead. There were shades for all the windows and—a thoughtful touch—an arc-shaped piece of woven wickerwork which was placed over the forward edge of the rear wheel by the footman to guard Milord's finery from the muddy wheel as he alighted.

By way of more plebeian contrast, your attention is directed to a furniture van. So similar to today's vans, but for the driver's seat—exposed, as always—perched high in front, that there would be no reason to include it here except that it offers the only opportunity to memorialise that truly splendid animal, the draught horse.

About the only place you can see him today in all his glory is in the TV commercial for Anheuser-Busch, where you can admire eight beautifully matched examples in a well schooled, skillfully driven eight-in-hand.

The top breeds were the Percheron, the Clydesdale, the Suffolk Punch, and the Belgian Punch. Often standing "17 hands" (six feet eight inches from top of withers perpendicularly to the ground), he weighed close to one ton and was able to take off with an incredible load. He stands apart from all others, not only because of his size, weight, musculature, and strength, but also because he alone sports the so-called "feathers"—flowing hair about six inches long which grows profusely on the back sides of all four legs, from fetlock (ankle joint) to knee, or hock.

Passing from the realm of the working man to that of a ruler, we next come upon "A nice little brougham and a pair of beauties." This is Holmes's enthusiastic (and astute) appraisal of the King of Bohemia's turnout. Sherlock valued the pair (probably high-stepping hackneys) at "a hundred and fifty guineas apiece." Enough has been said about the vehicle itself, which makes its appearance in A Scandal in Bohemia. But there are curious errors on Watson's part as he describes the world of the horse in this case. When Holmes talks of the horse, the vehicles, and the men around them, we are on sure ground. But when Watson does, discrepancies begin to emerge. A theory will be enunciated later. But it begins here.

"Drunken looking groom" is Watson's (not Holmes's) description of the disguise adopted by Sherlock in his quest for information about Irene Adler, in the Serpentine Mews of St. John's Wood.

First, it must be realised that in the world of the horse there were two main subdivisions: riding and driving. They were sharply--often acrimoniously--divided. If the master indulged in both, very often it meant maintaining two separate operations; coach-house and riding-stables personnel simply did not mix. A groom, strictly a member of the riding side, who tried to fraternise in the Mews behind Irene's villa, a part of the driving world, would hear no gossip. Holmes would have had to assume the guise of an hostler, or stableman, if he hoped to obtain anything but the toe of someone's boot. Conclusion: Beyond question, Holmes knew the difference; equally beyond question, Watson should have known--but didn't.

Watson's next gaffe is his misuse of the term coach house. While many of the mews in today's West End still have their share of converted coach houses, the more modest and suburban St. John's Wood--where dwelt many another Mme. Pompadour since the days of the Regency--very likely did not contain anything grand enough to call a coach house. The mews here was a collection of carriage houses. These were large enough for several types of carriages, stalls for about four horses, tackroom, hayloft above, and living quarters for coachman and footman-hostler. But they were by no means large enough to house a coach or any other type of four-in-hand rig.

By contrast, observe Holmes's accurate description of Miss Adler's turnout, a "neat little landau." This was a covered carriage, named for its German designer and builder, drawn by a pair of horses. Unlike the square-cornered and box-like brougham, its general profile was gracefully rounded. Originally designed with C-spring suspension, it later had the ellipsoidal leaf-springs in general use. The leather-covered top was divided into two parts, over the centre door on each side; the rear half retracted into a well behind the rear seat; the forward half retracted behind the front seat, which faced rearward in the style known as vis-à-vis. In the "little" model everything was scaled down, and it could be drawn by light, rather than heavy, harness horses. Irene Adler must have cut a fine swathe in this, the toniest rig in the Canon, during her afternoon drive ("as usual, at five").

In the daily "Easter Parade" of fashionable vehicles in Hyde Park and Rotten Row, the "neat little landau" must have been a standout, its top lowered, its black-lacquered body glistening like a treasured Bechstein piano, its red wheels flashing in the sun, and full-liveried coachman with cockaded top-hat, driving a pair of matched hackneys, well groomed bays with docked tails, highstepping in unison, their necks proudly curved; and, gracefully poised in the rear seat, dressed in the latest French creation, her parasol raised--the woman.

Regretfully, one must turn away to our next exhibit,

"a tall dog-cart"—Watson's term, not Holmes's, for the vehicle used in the journeys in The Man with the Twisted Lip. It is difficult to believe that Neville St. Clair, in his circumstances, would own it. Its wheels were over five feet in diameter, its seat some seven feet above the ground. It was rarely seen in London, except in Hyde Park, driven by a well-heeled member of the upper classes. Its chief use was in tandem driving, when its high box enabled the driver to see over his wheel horse (or "wheeler") and thereby exercise better control over the leader. The leader trotted free and clear of the shafts and required a nice dexterity on the driver's part to keep him under control and in line. Such a posh vehicle would have attracted considerable attention in the disreputable East End; its driver, Holmes in the disguise of an addict, would have drawn crowds.

Two more bits of evidence of Watson's (resolute?) unfamiliarity with vehicles and the horse appear in The Man with the Twisted Lip. Can this be pathologic?

Item: After "dashing away"—evidently a high-spirited mare, this—and travelling a few miles, a minor miracle occurs: Holmes lights his pipe! Nothing is said about Watson taking the reins. Yet Holmes manages to load the pipe, strike the lucifer, shield it against the breeze created by the mare's fast gait, and get the pipe going—while he drives. Holmes, extraordinary man though he was, did not possess three hands. Conclusion: Watson's harrowing few minutes at the reins was a traumatic experience, blissfully buried in his subconscious, never to be exhumed.

Item: It must have been well past midnight when they arrived, yet, according to Watson, at "twenty minutes past four" A.M. they were on their way back to London, in the same cart, with the same horse. Granted that Holmes is indefatigable, but what about the poor horse? Conclusion: A fresh horse must have been between the shafts. Question: Was Watson merely indifferent, or was it his active dislike of equipage that blinded him to the change?

Carriage or cab: Turning now to The Greek Interpreter, we find Watson reporting Mr. Melas as testifying: "I say into the cab, but I soon became doubtful as to whether it was not a carriage." This is not a reasonable doubt. Almost anyone would have known the difference at first glance. The most slovenly of private coachmen maintained his carriage, his horse, and his harness in a far better condition than did any cabman. Melas's confusion would appear to be also Watson's.

Further evidence: In The Sign of Four, Watson uses the term "four-wheeler" when he means "carriage," and later states that "our cab was waiting," misusing the term applied only to a vehicle for hire.

For a refreshing change, in The Hound of the Baskervilles Watson names the vehicles accurately, beginning with the gig. Baring-Gould defines it properly: "A light, one-horse, two-wheeled carriage." The aficionado of equipage would add "or chaise" (and would feel impelled to list the American corruption, "shay," made immortal in the poem by another Holmes). It was also a convertible and was the favourite self-driven conveyance for the country doctor. It is with some surprise that one views the photograph in the <u>Annotated</u> of Dr. Bell, Sherlock's prototype, seated in prosperous splendour in his very posh, pair-drawn, coachman-driven victoria. His practice must have been indeed a rewarding one.

Also in <u>The Hound</u> appears the wagonette. Baring-Gould writes: "A <u>wagonette</u> was a four-wheeled carriage, open, or made with a removable cover; furnished [in the rear] with a seat or bench at each side, facing inward; and with one or two seats or benches arranged laterally in front [one may add "and higher"]. The 'cobs' [this is Watson's term] which drew it were short-legged, strong horses, usually reserved for heavy carriage work."

Here I must differ with Baring-Gould. The word "cob" was only used to designate a lighter type of harness horse which could be used in light driving rigs, but was also kept for hacking (ordinary, non-fox-hunting riding about the countryside). Horses reserved for heavy carriage work were a much heavier type, known as coach horses. Later in this Adventure, when Watson goes to Coombe Tracy, he is driven there by Perkins, the coachman, in the same wagonette.

But Watson's mission to Coombe Tracy was a highly secret one; coachman Perkins and the full panoply of the wagonette were certainly to be avoided. The inevitable conclusion must be that, not only was Watson unable to drive himself (a rarity in that day), but also that he must have disliked the very idea. The following question arises: Was Watson an equiphobe?

Mr. Stuart Palmer has already raised interesting questions in his "Notes on Certain Evidences of Caniphobia in Mr. Sherlock Holmes and His Associates" [BSJ (NS) 5:199-204, 1955]. It is suggested that one can change "Cani-" to "Equi-" and make out a strong <u>prima facie</u> case against Dr. Watson. Further evidence follows, but first let us turn to the next vehicle in the Canon, a drag (again Watson's term).

Baring-Gould defines the drag as "a private stagecoach with seats inside and on top," and he is 80% correct. From about 1890 on, "outside seats" were installed on top, but the earlier, classic drag had only one outside bench, high in the rear, for the footmen; passengers sat inside. More probably, Colonel Ross's party viewed Silver Blaze's victory from the top of a "brake" (from the German <u>Breike</u>) which had no seats inside for the simple reason that there was no inside. It was rather like an enlarged wagonette and was drawn by a four-in-hand. There were two, sometimes three, rows of forward-facing, upholstered benches, some eight feet above the ground. Behind these, as in the wagonette, were the two lower, inward-facing benches for the coachman, footman, and other servants who would lay out the elaborate picnic lunch at the racecourse. Once there, the horses would be unhitched, "rugged up" (blanketed), and tied under a nearby tree. The brake's pole would be removed and the vehicle pushed up close to the rail of the track, near the finish line. From the top of the brake a magnificent view of the races was assured.

This equiphile is forced to agree with Red Smith's estimate of the goings on at the track that day. Smith charges that "Holmes was the architect of an extraordinary piece of skulduggery." One must add that it was also a bold-faced swindle against British racing and the entire British betting public—to say nothing of the bookmakers. If, as the Mafia does in America today, Professor Moriarty controlled British off-track bookies, Holmes's Silver Blaze coup may well have been the final straw. Surely this is the day that the Professor issued a "contract" on Holmes and decreed "Hit him!"

Two more bits of evidence in the indictment of Watson must be recorded before we come to the final vehicle in the Canon; first the empty dog-cart. This turns up in The Solitary Cyclist and is noteworthy because, as usual, it is Holmes, not Watson, who halts the runaway horse. Watson says he abetted, but his rôle was probably only a hesitant waving of the arms from the safety of the verge. Secondly, we have a stately carriage belonging to Charles Augustus Milverton, cited here only because of Watson's comment on the horses' "glossy haunches." Quarters is the word, the only permissible word. Haunches indeed! The noble chestnuts would have blanched a dead white.

The final horse-drawn vehicle is the open, yellow barouche seen in The Adventure of Shoscombe Old Place. Baring-Gould writes: "A four-wheeled vehicle with seat in front for driver, with two double seats behind; with folding top which may be raised to cover the occupants but not the driver." One might add that the seats were vis-à-vis and that, since the top was open in front to the elements, the occupants of the rearward-facing seats got precious little cover also. The barouche was very similar to the landau, except for the arrangement at the top. It was the progenitor of the victoria.

Envoi

The compendium of vehicles terminates abruptly, with something of a shock. Perhaps it is fitting that the last reference coincides with the last Adventure. In His Last Bow, the "huge 100-horse-power Benz car was blocking the country lane."

Bibliography

The Evolution of the Carriage, by John R. Meader, New York: Metropolitan Magazine, 1905.

Carriages and Coaches, by Ralph Straus, London: M. Secker, 1912.

Driving, by His Grace the Duke of Beaufort, London: K. G. Longmans, Green & Co., 1890.

The English Carriage, by Hugh McCausland, The Batchworth Press, 1948.

A Manual of Coaching, by Fairman Rogers, London: J. P. Lippincott, 1900.

HOLMES AND WIMSEY:
A Study in Similarities

by John Linsenmeyer

The career of the Master, though essentially inimitable, has been followed by a host of overt or tacit disciples. Of these, perhaps the most significant is Lord Peter D. B. Wimsey, whose exploits have been publicised by the worthy Sherlockian, Dorothy Sayers.[1] Wimsey and Holmes exhibit surprising similarities of character, method, and taste, despite the great disparities in their social and financial circumstances.

Lord Peter[2] was born at Duke's Denver, Norfolk, in 1890, the second son of Mortimer Gerald, 15th Duke of Denver. He was educated at Eton and Balliol College, Oxford, at which latter institution he achieved great fame at cricket. He served in the Great War as a major in the Rifle Brigade and as an intelligence officer, and was decorated for gallantry. His amateur detective career commenced in 1921 in connection with the famous theft known as the Attenbury Emeralds Case. In 1935 he married a writer of mystery stories, the former Harriet Vane, M.A. (Oxon.), having a few years previously secured the release of that lady from a charge of poisoning her lover.

The points of similarity between Holmes and Wimsey, despite the 36-year difference in their ages, are striking. Both were offshoots of the English gentry—Holmes the younger son of a Yorkshire squire[3] and Wimsey the younger son of a duke. Both had French blood; Holmes was descended on his mother's side from the artist Vernet and Wimsey from the Delegardies, typified by the elderly raconteur and rake, Uncle Paul.[4] However, to digress briefly, it might well be said that Holmes and Wimsey alike exemplified that which has always been regarded as best in the character of the English "quality": an undemonstrative yet deep patriotism, sportsmanship, affection for the outdoors (including in both cases a devotion to blood sports, although with respect to Holmes this must be deduced from his exactness in the use of such terms as "hound," his reference to the excellence of the fishing and wild-fowling at Donnithorpe and Shoscombe Old Place, his possession of and affection for a loaded hunting crop, and his feeling at home in Trevor's gun room), chivalry, courtesy to social inferiors, and courage.

As to Holmes, his school is perhaps uncertain,[5] but both were "Oxbridge" men. Neither was in any sense a bookworm, but both were well-read and lovers of books _qua_ books;[6] Wimsey was a noted collector of rare editions and _incunabula_, and Holmes was sufficiently well versed to pass himself off as a book dealer.

Although of rural birth, both were confirmed Londoners (Holmes is in fact archetypical of _fin-de-siècle_ London); both lived in the West End and indeed both chose to live on busy, quasi-commercial streets: Holmes at 221B Baker Street, hard by the station and the telegraph office, and Wimsey about a mile or so away at 110A Picadilly, W. In their digs, both were attended by thoroughly stolid, British-bulldog types: Holmes by his Boswell and friend, and Wimsey by his superb man, ex-Sergeant Mervyn Bunter.

Holmes and Wimsey became detectives quite incidentally, the former through his association with Victor Trevor at Cambridge,[7] and the latter through Bunter's efforts to find something (in fact, the Attenbury Emeralds Case) to shake Wimsey out of the terrible depression induced by his war experiences and an unhappy _affaire de coeur_. Once entered upon their careers, both were highly successful—to the occasional annoyance of the more pedestrian members of the paid constabulary. In this connection, however, it should be noted that Wimsey's relations with the regular police were in large part cordial. Detective Chief Inspector Charles Parker of the Metropolitan Police was Wimsey's best friend and later became his brother-in-law,[8] and for the rest, Wimsey's relations with the provincial police were what one might expect of a duke's son in England between the wars. Holmes, while admitting the merits of Gregson and other regular police officers, could hardly be said to have been intimate with any.[9]

Physically, both men were fairly tall and slender, Wimsey being five-feet nine and Holmes a bit taller. Both men were, as the cliché goes, "well able to look after themselves" and skilled in self-defense. Wimsey, however, did not carry or use firearms,[10] either for defense or to aid in arrests.

Both men were fond of music and were indeed very capable musicians, Holmes on the violin and Wimsey on the piano. And both used music to relieve the tensions of a difficult case and to provide a climate for thought.

Alike, they were fond of good food and wine, although it must be conceded that Wimsey was the greater gourmet of the pair; indeed, he once established his identity against an impostor through a demonstration of winesmanship.[11] But Holmes was no slouch at the table: he described himself as "somewhat of a fowl fancier";[12] he served "a quite epicurean little supper . . . a couple of brace of woodcock, a pheasant, a _pâté-de-foie-gras_ pie,

-208-

with a group of ancient and cobwebby bottles";[13] and he renewed his energies with "a cold partridge on the sideboard . . . and a bottle of Montrachet."[14]

One detects the most meaningful similarities when one compares the two men's methods when attacking a difficult case. The critical reader can only establish this by a review of both the Canon and the Wimsey adventures, but a very cursory review of several episodes[15] might suffice to indicate the point.

In one of Wimsey's early cases, recorded in <u>The Unpleasantness at the Bellona Club</u>, an elderly retired general sitting for hours before the fire in his club was discovered to be dead of an apparent heart attack. Due to a peculiarity in the general's will, his exact time of death was crucial—and impossible to determine. Suspicion naturally fell upon the devisees under the will, one of whom was a shell-shocked war veteran with a serious nervous affliction. He eventually confessed to having killed the general by administering a lethal dose of digitalin.

Despite the intrusion of numerous red herrings, Wimsey established that, due to the limited number of occasions upon which the drug could have been administered, it was impossible for the confession to be true. He then established that the general's physician,[16] who was courting the only female devisee, had administered the drug. The one small detail of timing the effects of the drug after administration, overlooked by everyone, uncovered the murderer. "You know my method. It is founded upon the observation of trifles."[17] "It has long been an axiom of mine that the little things are infinitely the most important."[18]

Speaking of red herrings, in the case reported in <u>Five Red Herrings</u> Wimsey had occasion to investigate the murder of an artist in Galloway. The crime was brilliantly planned to look like an accident, even to the extent of counterfeiting a piece of the victim's work. Wimsey, however, penetrated the charade because his extraordinary powers of observation (<u>n.b.</u>!) revealed that one small item (a tube of white flake) was missing from the whole elaborate tableau, so the victim could not have fallen down the hill while painting the picture. In short, it was "one of those obvious things which nobody by chance ever observes."[19] Or: "Elementary. It is one of those instances when the reasoner can produce an effect which seems remarkable to his neighbour, because the latter has missed the one little point which is the basis of the deduction."[20]

The entire Wimsey family was involved in what may have

been Lord Peter's most challenging case, recounted in
Clouds of Witnesses. While he was touring southern
Europe, his brother, the Duke, his sister, Lady Mary,
her fiancé, Captain Denis Cathcart, and a variety of
other guests were at the Duke's "shooting-box," Riddles-
dale Lodge, in Yorkshire. The Duke had received a letter
from a friend informing him that Cathcart had been involved in card scandals. Later, the Duke was observed
next to Cathcart's body, the latter having been perfo-
rated through the lung by a bullet from the Duke's revolver. The Duke would not account in any remotely satisfactory way why he was out in the rain in the middle
of the night, and was accordingly held by the Coroner's
Jury to answer a charge of murder. Upon Wimsey's arrival,
a mysterious and significant set of footprints was found
at the lodge, following which provided clues to Lord
Peter, who told the police:

> "You just scour the railway-stations for a
> young man six foot one or two with a No. 10
> shoe, and dressed in a Burberry that's lost its
> belt, and with a deep scratch on one of his
> hands."

Echoes of the Master:

> " . . . the murderer was a man. He was more than
> six feet high, was in the prime of life, had
> small feet for his height, wore coarse, square-
> toed boots and smoked a Trichinopoly cigar. He
> came here with his victim in a four-wheeled cab,
> which was drawn by a horse with three old shoes
> and one new one on his off fore-leg. In all
> probability the murderer had a florid face, and
> the fingernails of his right hand were remark-
> ably long."[21]

It then appeared that Lady Mary was behaving in a
peculiar fashion, and had even attempted to remove
blood from her skirt. Wimsey, however, refused to let
this influence the investigation. ("I can discover
facts, Watson, but I cannot change them."[22]   "It is a
capital mistake to theorize before you have all the
evidence."[23] "There is nothing more stimulating than a
case where everything goes against you."[24])

Ultimately, it is established that Cathcart in fact
shot himself both to avoid exposure as a card cheat and
because of une affaire triste avec une parisienne demi-
mondaine.

Wimsey's next major case, reported as Strong Poison,
involved him personally as well. Harriet Vane, a writer
of popular mystery stories, was charged with poisoning

a rather irritating young man with whom she had been living in what is often called "sin." That he had been poisoned was clear; that she had done it appeared probable. Wimsey, however, besides growing infatuated with Miss Vane, retained enough of his wits to demonstrate that a dishonest solicitor could feed the victim the arsenic because the murderer had built up in his own body an immunity to the poison. Lord Peter arrived at the result simply because there was no other possibility. ("How often have I said to you that when you have eliminated the impossible, whatever remains, however improbable, must be the truth?"[25]

At the conclusion of this episode, however, Wimsey behaved in a most un-Holmesian fashion; he fell in love with Harriet Vane and asked her to marry him. She refused. Their long courtship, if such it can be called, involved their joint participation in more adventures. In Gaudy Night, the dons at Harriet's college sought her (and through her, Wimsey's) help in identifying a maniacal poison-pen vandal. In Have His Carcass, Harriet found the corpse of a dance-hall gigolo while on a walking tour of the coast.

Finally, in Busman's Honeymoon, the two marry (and naturally find a corpse in the basement of their house). One vignette deserves quotation; the local vicar is observed coming up the walk:

"This is magnificent," said Peter, "I collect vicars. . . . This is a very well-grown specimen, six foot four or thereabouts, short-sighted, a great gardener, musical, smokes a pipe——"

"Good gracious!" cried Miss Twitterton, "do you know Mr. Goodacre?"

"——untidy, with a wife who does her best on a small stipend; a product of one of our older seats of learning—in 1890 vintage—Oxford, at a guess, but not, I fancy, Keble, though as high in his views as the parish allows him to be."

[Harriet said] "But why the strictly limited High Church views?"

"The Roman vest and the emblem upon the watchchain point the upward way. You know my methods, Watson."

One is put in mind of the famous exchange between Sherlock and Mycroft as they sat in the Stranger's Room of the Diogenes Club and, by observation and deduction, identified a passer-by as an old soldier, very recently discharged, who had served in India as a non-commissioned officer in the Royal Artillery; and as a widower with children.[26]

The similarities and analogies can be drawn out indefinitely. But the Wimsey adventures are much too good to be scanned in capsules; enough has been said to indicate the very substantial similarities in character and method which can be verified only by critical reading of the texts themselves.

And it is submitted these texts are real. If one should think that this demonstration has consisted of quotations out of context or other verbal legerdemain,[27] it is respectfully suggested that he (1) reread the Canon; (2) read the Wimsey saga, or any substantial part of it; and (3) then attempt to draw such an analogy between Holmes and, for example, William Le Queux's Duckworth Drew, or R. Austin Freeman's Dr. John Thorndyke, or John Buchan's (Lord Tweedsmuir's) Brigadier Sir Richard Hannay, or Sax Rohmer's Sir Denis Nayland Smith.[28] This is not to say that other characters are necessarily without life or credibility; the point is that no other substantial character (prescinding from the merely imitative or parodistic) exhibits such solid similarities to the Master. Indeed, it could be said that, perhaps uniquely, if one is truly devoted to the Master, one will almost certainly admire Wimsey. In fact, one might even say, along with the solicitor Murbles, to Wimsey, "you're turning into a regular Sherlock."[29]

Did they ever meet? By the time Major Lord Peter Wimsey, D.S.O., was demobbed in 1919, Holmes was 65 and retired (save for emergency government service) to the Sussex Downs. One would certainly like to think that they did, and do, meet; Holmes would so enjoy Wimsey's library, and the prospect of their violin-piano duet is Elysian. But "_Vitae summa brevis spem nos vetat incohare longam._"[30] We can only muse.

*   *   *   *   *   *

LORD PETER WIMSEY
LAURITZEN

From *Gaudy Night*, by Dorothy L. Sayers (pub. 1935), chap XV

AS she turned back the worn calf cover the first thing she saw was the engraved book-plate with its achievement of arms: the three silver mice on a field sable and the "domestick Catt" couched menacingly on the helmet-wreath. Two armed Saracens supported the shield, beneath which ran the mocking and arrogant motto: "As my Whimsy takes me".

1. See, e.g., her "The Dates in 'The Red-Headed League,'" BSJ (OS) 2:279-290, 1947, and her "Dr. Watson's Christian Name," in Profile by Gaslight.

2. Although it is possible for a 20th-century American to lead a happy and useful life without understanding the complexities of British titles, there may be those who would be interested to know that the younger sons of a duke or a marquess, though not peers of the realm, bear a courtesy title of lord in conjunction with their Christian names, viz., "Lord Peter Wimsey," not "Lord Wimsey." (The latter style would be borne by a baron, and in customary address by other peers, except a duke, as well.) The wife of a younger son of a duke or marquess becomes (get this, now) not "Lady Harriet Wimsey" but "Lady Peter Wimsey"!

3. That Holmes's ancestors were country squires is Canonical (The Greek Interpreter). For Yorkshire, see Edgar W. Smith's Foreword to Profile by Gaslight and W. S. Baring-Gould's Sherlock Holmes of Baker Street, p. 11; but cf. Trevor Hall's Sherlock Holmes: Ten Literary Studies, pp. 18-35. Christopher Morley came down flatly in favor of Yorkshire in "Clinical Notes by a Resident Patient," in Profile by Gaslight. See also the discussion at Vol. I, pp. 51 et seq. of The Annotated Sherlock Holmes.

4. Of the recorded Wimsey episodes, Busman's Honeymoon is perhaps the richest in biographical data.

5. Monsignor Ronald Arbuthnot Knox, M.A. (Oxon.), holds that Holmes's college was Christ Church, Oxford ("Studies in the Literature of Sherlock Holmes," reprinted in Seventeen Steps to 221B at pp. 30-45; see pp. 41-42). Miss Dorothy Sayers opts for Sidney Sussex, Cambridge ("Holmes' College Career," in Baker Street Studies). Among later Sherlockians, Gavin Brend votes for Oxford ("Oxford or Cambridge," chapter 2 of his My Dear Holmes: A Study in Sherlock), and Trevor Hall makes a well documented and well reasoned case for Trinity, Cambridge—coincidentally his own college (Sherlock Holmes: Ten Literary Studies, pp. 56-85). Baring-Gould, following a hint given by Elmer Davis in 1933, comes down in favour of Holmes's having attended both universities (The Annotated Sherlock Holmes, Vol. I, pp. 59-63). If this author might be permitted to stick his own oar in, it seems that the Canonical facts are inconclusive, but Holmes's tendencies to Bohemianism and the physical sciences weigh the scales in favour of Cambridge.

6. See "Ex Libris Sherlock Holmes," by Howard Collins, in Profile by Gaslight, citing numerous Canonical texts.

7. Pace, then Oxford! See note 5 on Holmes's college.

8. Lord Peter's brother, Gerald, then Duke of Denver, was tried for the murder of his sister Mary's fiancé, Captain Cathcart. Wimsey, with Parker's assistance, proved that Cathcart had in fact committed suicide. Parker thereupon courted and married Lady Mary Wimsey (he being, no doubt like Watson, attracted to a damsel in distress). Most of the foregoing is chronicled in Clouds of Witnesses.

9. Nor could one possibly imagine Holmes capping quotations with the jolly Inspector Kirk in Busman's Honeymoon.

10. Under the Firearms Act of 1920, he would have required a police certificate to do so (though he could doubtless have procured one with ease). Holmes was under no such inhibition (see "Sherlock Holmes: His Arsenal and the Law," by John Linsenmeyer, BSJ (NS) 18:74-77, (June) 1968.

11. In "The Bibulous Business of a Matter of Taste."

12. The Blue Carbuncle.

13. The Noble Bachelor.

14. The Veiled Lodger.
15. Some of Lord Peter's adventures are not at all suitable. *Gaudy Night*, for example, dealt largely with the future Lady Peter's experiences on a visit back to her woman's college at Oxford; the criminal was an obviously psychotic scout, and Wimsey was only incidentally involved. And *Murder Must Advertise* was a prolonged undercover operation in an ad agency to expose a murderer, with the principal emphasis on other than detection techniques. It is proposed in the instant article to consider only the few most significant of Wimsey's detective adventures.
16. "When a doctor does go wrong he is the first of criminals" (Sherlock Holmes, in *The Speckled Band*).
17. The Boscombe Valley Mystery.
18. A Case of Identity.
19. The Hound of the Baskervilles.
20. The Crooked Man.
21. A Study in Scarlet. Ch. 3; cf. Holmes's analysis in *The Red-Headed League*: "Beyond the obvious facts that he has at some time done manual labour, that he takes snuff, that he is a Freemason, that he has been in China, and that he has done a considerable amount of writing lately, I can deduce nothing else." But see the amusing, non-Canonical incident where this technique goes awry because the subject of Holmes's analysis is wearing someone else's clothes (Maurice Baring, "From the Diary of Sherlock Holmes," in *Seventeen Steps to 221B*, pp. 23-24).
22. Thor Bridge.
23. A Study in Scarlet.
24. The Hound of the Baskervilles.
25. The Sign of Four.
26. The Greek Interpreter. See the quotation from *The Red-Headed League*, supra.; cf. the notes in *The Annotated Sherlock Holmes*, Vol. I, p. 594, esp. note 18.
27. Of the sort used in frivolous attempts to prove that Watson was a woman, or that Bacon wrote Shakespeare, or that Shakespeare wrote Bacon, or that Holmes and Watson were Rosicrucians, or any such nonsense.
28. Such a comparison could easily be essayed with nothing more than a quiet evening, an ounce or two of shag, and a copy of Sir Hugh Greene's new book, *The Rivals of Sherlock Holmes*, which contains a literate introduction, a map of central London in 1898, and a selection of 13 contemporary stories.
29. The Unpleasantness at the Bellona Club.
30. Roughly, "Life is short and forbids us to expect too much." (There is as much sense in Horace as in Hafiz.)

———•◦•———

Editorial addenda to the notes:

2. "... the great detective's attainments certainly suggest that he was educated at a college which offered exceptional facilities for mathematical and scientic studies ..." (*Sidney Sussex College—A Short History*, by C. W. Scott-Giles, as quoted in Bruce Kennedy's "Alma Mater, or Two Unexplained Years," BSJ 19:158-160, 1969, at page 160).
6. Also see Madeleine B. Stern: "Sherlock Holmes: Rare Book Collector," BSJ (NS) 3:133-155, 1953; and Julian Wolff: "A Catalogue of 221B Culture," in *To Dr. R.*, Philadelphia, 1946.
10. Lord Peter did have a pistol in "The Learned Adventure of the Dragon's Head," and in "The Bibulous Business of a Matter of Taste."

THE ABBEY GRANGE

or

Who Used Eustace?

by H. W. Starr

When reading <u>The Adventure of the Abbey Grange</u> most of us probably accept the account of the death of that bold bad bart., Sir Eustace Brackenstall, as unhesitatingly as did the good Watson when he uttered his verdict of "Not guilty." But let us step back for a moment and view this case with the cold and fishy eye which an intelligent inspector from the New York Homicide Squad or 20th-century Scotland Yard would cast upon it. When a veteran detective finds a slaughtered spouse untidily draped across the hearth rug, his immediate impulse is to install the surviving husband or wife as a prime suspect—and it is likely that he will be right. We should attempt his approach, for poor Stanley Hopkins, alas, cannot sustain that rôle. Despite the hopes of Holmes, Hopkins only too consistently carried on the tradition of Scotland Yard bunglers so nobly inaugurated by Lestrade, Gregson, & Co.

Our initial step, obviously, is to regard with suspicion any accounts given by the deeply interested parties, the witnesses and near-witnesses of the tragedy. Then, what reliable data are available? First we have the facts observed by the Master and most—but not all—of his deductions, for the outcome did not invariably prove him right. I do not refer to that negligence which he later remedied by intensive observation, but to his description of the killer: "remarkably quick-witted, for this whole ingenious story is of his concoction."[1] But we know from Captain Crocker himself that he was not responsible for the whole story; he says: "Theresa was as cool as ice, and it was her plot as much as mine" [p. 759].

The second body of fairly reliable data is that collected by Stanley Hopkins from local knowledge. From it we may certainly conclude that Sir Eustace looked upon the sauce with a kindling eye and that when under the influence his conduct was not impeccable. It is established that he heaved a decanter at Theresa, unfortunately missing her; but we have only her word for the provocation. Nevertheless, even if he was boiled to the gills, setting fire to a petroleum-saturated dog is not the behaviour of a really <u>nice</u> man. Still, we are not told how long his nastiness had been in evidence. The only incidents which we can date with any certainty, those referred to above, occurred <u>after</u> his marriage, and these may have been the episodes which Hopkins says could have brought Sir Eustace to the attention of the Yard. It is quite possible that originally he was merely a bit of a souse who behaved fairly decently. Theresa, far from his warmest admirer, speaks of him in his pre-marital period and stresses his "false London ways"—a phrase which we may confidently translate as "sophisticated and courteous conduct." Now if Sir Eustace were a notorious lush and an overt ravening sadist when he met Miss Mary Fraser, it does seem that she would have observed some trifling eccentricity or heard some ghost of a rumour during the half year of close acquaintance which preceded their marriage. If a chap lurches hither and yon chucking heavy decanters at people and touching off bonfires of pet dogs, he is likely to be gossiped about a little. Nor is he the sort "a sensitive and high-spirited woman" [746] marries. So, if he were as bad as all this, why did she marry him? Her stoutest defenders tell us. Theresa says, "He won her with his title and his money and his false London ways. If she made a mistake, she has paid for it, if ever a woman did" [754].[2] Captain Crocker himself admitted it: He was happy that "she had not thrown herself away on a penniless suitor" [759]—a pretty broad-minded reaction for a disappointed lover. Mary Fraser thus married "one of the richest men in Kent" [746] for his title and wealth. She may have done it coldly in the complete realisation that he was a raging sadistic drunkard. If he was, she knew it, for she half admits such knowledge when she says, "To be with such a man for an hour is unpleasant" [746]. The implication is clear that she could easily have perceived his frailties before marriage. Yet perhaps he was then only a genial heavy drinker. Hopkins calls him "a good-hearted man when he was sober" and adds that he seldom "went the whole way"; he usually got only "half-drunk" [749].[3] If so, after his marriage, Sir Eustace may well have discovered that he had acquired a frigid wife who wanted only his money and who profoundly shocked him by her behaviour. Lady Brackenstall's remark that the failure of the marriage may have been partly her fault because she could not stand the "proprieties" and "primness" of county society and preferred a "freer, less conventional atmosphere" [746] has an unsavoury implication. (Once more, we have a startling example of unconscious self-revelation.) So unhappy a marriage may well have brought out a vicious side to Sir Eustace's character which he had formerly succeeded in repressing. In any event, whatever our theory concerning the true behaviour of the deceased, Lady Brackenstall had a much unwanted husband on her hands. In those days a wife with no special influence did not find it easy to obtain a divorce with a hefty settlement. Lady Brackenstall, again giving us an unintentional insight, admits her motive

when she passionately denounces England's "monstrous
[divorce] laws," which, she raves, will bring God's
"curse upon the land" [746]. And, above all, our fair
Australian liked money.

The solution to her problem was elementary, for in all
probability the victim's widow would inherit his fortune.
He was childless, and there is no mention of an entail or
close relatives. (Incidentally, the second step of our
Homicide Squadman would have been an examination of Sir
Eustace's will. Since it had not yet reached probate, and
ultimately, Somerset House, Holmes could not have done
this without spending more time than he could afford to
squander, in view of Crocker's imminent departure from
England.)

But the means? Here the girls stumbled on a brilliant
improvisation. On the way out from Australia, Mary Fraser,
just for practice and a bit of girlish fun, had cold-
bloodedly reduced a ship's officer to such a state of
drooling imbecility that he devoted his spare time to
crawling on his hands and knees mopping up the deck in an
insanitary manner which neither maritime nor medical
authorities would approve. Suddenly he turned up in the
neighbourhood, and Theresa bumped into him—accidentally
or not?—in a country lane. Whether the girls already
knew of his presence and contrived the meeting with their
full plan in mind, or whether the encounter was genuinely
fortuitous with Theresa dripping a bit of venom concerning Sir Eustace just on general principle, we cannot say.
(In the latter event, the campaign must have been con-
cocted soon afterwards.) Here, they realised, was exactly
the tool they needed. Crocker was madly in love with Mary,
"wild, desperate . . . off the deck of his ship [and sometimes pretty goofy on it], hot-headed, excitable, but
loyal, honest, and kind-hearted" [756]—and he was im-
mensely strong and active. All that was necessary was to
get him in the proper frame of mind and to induce Sir
Eustace to attack him in a place where there was some
such handy implement of self-defense as that nice big
poker down in the dining-room. Note how beautifully they
played this poor fish. Says Captain Crocker:

> One day out in a country lane I met Theresa. . . . She
> told me all about her, about him, about everything.
> I tell you, gentlemen, it nearly drove me mad. This
> drunken hound, that he should dare to raise his hand
> to her, whose boots he was not worthy to lick! [The
> captain seems to have had some sort of licking com-
> plex.] I met Theresa again. Then I met Mary herself—
> and met her again. Then she would meet me no more.
> But the other day I had a notice that I was to start
> on my voyage within a week, and I determined that I

would see her once before I left. Theresa was always
my friend, for she loved Mary and hated this villain
almost as much as I did. From her I learned the ways
of the house [759].

The really skillful touch lay in Mary's telling him
that she would see him no more. We can be sure that if he
had not made another attempt to meet her, she would have
arranged the proper or, rather, improper rendezvous. But
she knew her man! The "farewell meeting" is stage-managed
superbly. Crocker is brought into the dining-room, the
presence of the poker is subtly indicated to him, and he
is carefully worked into a frenzy by the display of the
hatpin punctures, probably self-inflicted, since Mary revealed them only inadvertently to Holmes. ("Again I heard
from her own lips things that made my blood boil, and
again I cursed this brute who mishandled the woman I
loved" [759].) Theresa is on the alert and when she is
sure Mary has had time to set the scene, slips into Sir
Eustace's bedroom, wakes him up, and shoves into his hand
his heavy blackthorn stick, a cudgel unlikely to be kept
in a bedroom. Here we might point out that this last act
shows how well Mary knew both her men: The fundamentally
decent Crocker was quite capable of stopping an unarmed
husband without killing him and thus must be given enough
incentive to strike hard with a dangerous weapon. Theresa
then hisses, "There's a burglar in the dining-room. Hurry
and you'll catch him!" Sir Eustace, as usual a trifle be-
fuddled, naturally does not pause to reflect that a revolver or shotgun might be a better weapon than a cane
and rushes downstairs. A bit before Mary thinks he is
due, she probably places her hands, "in all innocence,"
as the gullible Crocker believes [759], on his upper arms
or shoulders as she pleads with him to be a good boy and
coolly leave her to a fate worse than death. When Sir
Eustace charges in, he finds that wife of his, who goes
in for the "freer, less conventional" life, apparently
embracing an extremely handsome young man. So he applies
the appropriate term to her and bops her with his cane,
but not hard enough to kill. The rest is inevitable.
Mary's little scream, which was not loud enough to awake
any other servant, gives Theresa the excuse to enter and
get the excitable Crocker down to the practical business
of laying a false trail.

Here we should pause in admiration. Other wives have
enlisted a lover to aid in the murder of a husband, but
only by revealing to him that the slaying is premeditated
by them. In this plot, despite minor flaws spotted only
belatedly by Holmes himself, we have a real masterpiece
in the history of criminology. The two murderers have not
struck the fatal blow. The man who did strike it sincerely

believes them innocent. Indeed, if by some oversight the
matter comes to a trial, he is the only witness who, despite his own peril, will give testimony that will ensure
their acquittal. Thus, even if their own outer defense
line falls, their second line of defense is still im-
pregnable.

We now approach an aspect of The Abbey Grange which is
much more difficult to analyse—just what went on in the
mind of the Master during the case. Mr. S. Holmes was
clearly having an off day; his initial failure to examine
the scene of the crime with care and his over-reaction of
attributing the concoction of the "whole ingenious story"
to Crocker indicate that he suspected the killer, and
probably Lady Brackenstall as well, of having deliberately planned and executed a murder. This was still his belief after he had identified Crocker at the steamship
office and directed his cabman to drive to Scotland Yard.
Knowing the slipshod methods of Stanley Hopkins when investigating a crime, he doubtless intended to have the
Yard take the fastest possible steps to seal and guard
the dining-room until the material clues there could be
legally recorded. He had left a note for Hopkins which
would keep him on the estate dragging the pond, incidentally thus making it difficult for Theresa to work up
the nerve to give the dining-room a careful checking
over. But on the way to the Yard he began to think about
Crocker's record. Here was a man who sounded much more
like the perfect fall guy for a beautiful and unscrupu-
lous adventuress than a criminal who would plan to kill
even a bold bad bart. for his money and his wife. So he
waited; after all, the material evidence might possibly
convict Crocker, but at most it would convict Lady Brackenstall of no more than being a frightened accessory after
the fact. Therefore he contented himself with giving
Hopkins a hint about a blind and waited until he could
size up Crocker.

We may surmise his conclusions from that interview.
Holmes was far too shrewd and experienced to be taken in
by a clever killer doing a first-rate job of acting at
very short notice and under the grave disadvantage of not
knowing how much Holmes had guessed. He would have been
bound to slip up over some detail. Furthermore, the captain naïvely recalled certain facts that a calculating
murderer would have suppressed. He revealed the full
series of meetings with Theresa and Mary as well as all
the propaganda with which they had saturated him.[4] If
he had had any doubts before, Holmes was now sure of
Mary's true rôle, but he was helpless. If he demanded a
full official investigation, he would accomplish nothing
but the utter ruin of a gallant, if fat-headed, young

ship's officer. Even if he were acquitted on grounds of self-defense, no reputable passenger line would ever again employ Crocker. As far as Mary and Theresa were concerned, there was no hope of convicting them of murder with Crocker the Gullible as their star defense witness. One thing, though, Holmes might do, possibly with the aid of Mycroft. From an exalted source a hint might be dropped into Lady Brackenstall's ear that she was strongly suspected, that she would be under close observation hereafter, and that her emigration to some such far-flung colonial outpost as Hongkong, Johannesburg, or Detroit would be appreciated. Perhaps she had sufficient self-control to be that rare type of killer, the one who gets what he wants from a single brilliant crime and has the wisdom to lead a blameless life for the rest of his days. Mary now had what she principally wanted—plenty of money without the encumbrance of her Eustace. She might not insist on marriage to that splendid stud, Jackie Crocker, even if she had ever seriously considered putting him on the matrimonial payroll. Meanwhile, Holmes had elicited a promise from the worthy captain to absent himself from the lady for a year. In that time Holmes might divert the susceptible youth into worthier channels. Finally—and this must have been a real trial—both discretion and the sheer vanity of the outfoxed expert (and for the second time by a woman!) forbade the Master to tell the truth to his worshipping Watson.

Consider the frustration, the repressed fury, and the wounded self-esteem of Holmes! He, the detective supreme, was at last in the very position that ordinary policemen, even Scotland Yard bunglers, had often found themselves in. Such men frequently know who committed a cold-blooded murder, but they can obtain no conviction. Clever defense counsels, lenient judges, inadequate evidence, and sentimental juries will safeguard the killer. Stupid, sentimental juries! When we reflect on this last consideration, a new and terrible intensity seems to lurk behind that only mildly double-edged statement which Holmes made at the final interview. Seething with hidden rage and a consciousness of utter futility, knowing full well what the verdict would be, he addresses his Boswell: "Watson, you are a British jury, and I never met a man who was more eminently fitted to represent one!"

---

1. P. 753 of The Complete Sherlock Holmes (Garden City, 1938), from which all subsequent quotations are taken.
2. In certain editions, notably the Garden City Return, p. 337, this last sentence has instead of "she has

(continued on page 223)

THE TWO LORD RUFTONS

by Philip José Farmer

Holmes, in <u>The Disappearance of Lady Frances Carfax</u>, notes that Lady Frances is the unmarried daughter of the late Lord Rufton. The famous Napoleonic soldier, Brigadier Étienne Gerard, also writes in his memoirs of a Lord Rufton. (Gerard's literary agent and editor, A. Conan Doyle, was also Watson's.) Lord Rufton, in Gerard's "How He Triumphed in England" (title by Doyle), was the English nobleman who, in 1811, was the host of Gerard while he was waiting to be exchanged for an English prisoner. In his autobiography, the Frenchman gives an account of his adventures which are, as usual, highly self-revealing and amusing. We need concern ourselves here only with the relationship of Gerard's host to Lady Frances, though we won't ignore certain implications or suggestions.

Holmes's case occurred 1 July to 18 July 1902, according to W. S. Baring-Gould in his <u>The Annotated Sherlock Holmes</u>. However, he admits that others have a good case for 1897. For our purposes any time between 1897 and 1902 is acceptable. Holmes says that Lady Frances was "still in fresh middle age," which would mean anywhere between 40 and 45 by late Victorian (or early Edwardian) standards. If she was 42 at the time of the case, she would have been born in 1855 or 1860.

Gerard's Lord Rufton seems to have been anywhere between 25 and 30, though he could have been older. Gerard does not mention any wife or child of his, and, while Gerard was one to stick to the essentials of his story, he surely would have said something about Rufton's wife if she had existed. The brigadier was too conscious of the fair sex not to have done so.

Gerard says that Lord Rufton came to Paris five years afterwards (in 1816) to see him, and Gerard does not mention any Lady Rufton in connection with this visit. Thus, it seems likely that Lord Rufton did not get married until after the visit, though he would have gotten a wife within a year or two if he were the ancestor of Lady Frances Carfax.

It's pleasing to think that Lord Rufton met and married Gerard's sister while in Paris, but we may be sure that this event would have been commented on at length by the Brigadier.

Holmes said that Lady Frances was "the last derelict of what only twenty years ago was a goodly fleet." He also said that she was the only survivor of the direct family of the late earl. Thus, a number of the earl's

children, and perhaps the earl himself, still lived in
1882 (or 1877). Any sons the earl may have had had pre-
deceased him. Lady Frances apparently did not begin
her wanderings in Europe until four years before the
case began. This would indicate that the last tie to
her ancestral home had died at that time and that this
tie was a sister or her father. I opt for the earl himself, since the money and, presumably, the ancestral seat,
went to the distant male relatives. Lady Frances would
have been forced to leave home sooner than four years before if the earl had died much earlier.

If Gerard's Rufton was the ancestor of Watson, he
would have been Lady Frances's grandfather. Her father
would have been born circa 1817-1840, and his father
would have been born circa 1785.

An objection to the theory of the Ruftons' being of
the same family is Gerard's reference to the lord's sister. He called her Lady Jane Rufton, whereas he should
have said Lady Jane Carfax, if she was of the same family as Lady Frances. But Gerard consistently shows in
"How He Triumphed in England" and in other chapters of
his memoirs, a deep ignorance of British titles. Indeed he displays a deep ignorance of other things British, especially British sports. It would not have occurred to him that the earl's sister would be called by
her family name, not her brother's title. And it is
likely that he had never heard Lord Rufton's family name.

Gerard's account and Watson's illuminte each other so
that what one lacks in data the other supplies. Thus,
combining the data, we know that Lord Rufton was an earl,
that the ancestral seat was High Combe, located near the
north edge of Dartmoor, and that it was near enough to
Tavistock to get there on the north-south highway in an
hour or two on a fast horse. High Combe is close to
Baskerville Hall, and it is possible that Lady Frances's
grandfather (or father or both) had married a daughter
of the Baskervilles.

Of course, neither "Rufton" nor "Carfax" is genuine.
Gerard doubtless gave the real title of his house in his
memoirs, but his editor, Doyle, changed it to avoid embarrassing an old and highly placed family. Later, as
literary agent for Watson (and, undoubtedly, a collab-
orator on some occasions), he recognised that Lady Frances was a descendant of Gerard's lord. Doyle had changed
the name of Rufton in editing the memoirs, and now he
could not resist changing Watson's original pseudonym for
Lady Frances's father to Rufton also. (No doubt, he did
so with Watson's permission.)

Doyle (or Watson) chose Carfax as the fictitious family name because of association with another name or object. I suggest that Doyle derived Carfax from the actual family's coat-of-arms, probably through a reverse use of canting, or punning, arms. The family's shield may have borne a quadriga (a Roman two-wheeled chariot with a team of four) and a fox, hence, car plus fax. Or perhaps, knowing that Carfax Square in Oxford is believed to be an anglicisation of the ancient Roman quadrifurcus, and knowing that the shield bore four shakeforks (or pitchforks or eel spears), or even a cross moline voided, Doyle chose the family name. At this moment I am going through Burke's Peerage for such arms in an effort to identify the real Carfaxes.

We know that the issue of the Carfax case was successful and even happy, since Lady Frances and the Hon. Philip Green were reunited. Apparently, they got married and had issue. Watson does not take the story that far along. But he may have referred to it, with typical Victorian obliquity, when he put into Holmes's mouth the comment that Lady Frances's middle age was "fresh." This would be another example of Watson's pawky humour.

THE ABBEY GRANGE

(continued from page 220)

paid for it" the odd phrasing "she was paid for it." One wonders if this apparent printing error is not what Theresa really said. If so, we have here a curious and rather sinister slip of the tongue.

3. In passing: There is something faintly contradictory about a man who seldom gets more than half-drunk, yet is so notoriously a confirmed drunkard that the whole neighbourhood knows about him. One wonders how much information—true or false—had been locally circulated by Theresa. Possibly even the dog-burning was done, not by Sir Eustace, but attributed to him when the cinders, originally ignited by Theresa, were found.

4. This was the one part Mary could not warn Crocker to suppress without running some danger of arousing even his suspicions.

A FEW TRIFLING PARAGRAPHS

by Jacques Barzun

1. A Note on Silver B----

The readers of this Journal will fill in the vacant place above without help from me or anybody else. But will they be right as they usually are? Let them decide. Leafing through, recently, the excellent memoirs, Cornish of Scotland Yard (Macmillan, 1935), my eye fell upon his description of certain frauds perpetrated in England with race-horses. One was run under a false name, another was somehow camouflaged, still another was dyed a new colour. One of the Superintendent's first cases in this series was that of Silver Badge (1920).

Who says that nature does not imitate art?

2. Holmes the Undergraduate

In the famous diary of James Agate, the English drama critic, one reads a letter from his friend George Lyttelton, dated October 29, 1946. One paragraph near the end runs as follows: "Here is a small point . . . the old question of Holmes's university. Well, in The Two Students[1] one of the clues is a small lump of black clay left on the chair[2] where the young man had put his running shoes. He had been practising the long jump. Well, in those days, whatever it may be now, it was only at Fenner's, Cambridge, where he could have jumped into black clay. The normal long-jump bed was of loose brown loam, but old Watts, the Fenner's groundsman, produced this stuff—probably from the fens—claiming (quite rightly) that, as there was no crumbling at the edges of a footprint, measurement of the jump was far more accurate. Surely this is proof positive. There is no doubt about the fact, because I was in the C.U.A.C. I often went to Oxford and saw their long-jump arrangements."[3]

At first blush, this document seems to raise one question and answer another. Though the writer is clearly

---

1. Mr. Lyttelton is evidently writing from memory: He means The Three Students.
2. The "small ball of black dough or clay" was on the tutor's table, not the chair, and it was the student's gloves, not his running shoes that had been left on the chair. There was, of course, a second pellet of clay in the bedroom.
3. The Later Ego, ed. Jacques Barzun (New York: Crown Publishers, 1951), p. 514.

trustworthy about the athletic information he reports from firsthand knowledge, what he tells us establishes only where Holmes was staying when, in 1895, he spent a little time studying early English charters. The sceptical critic will therefore demur to Mr. Lyttelton's inference that Cambridge was Holmes's university twenty years earlier.

But on second thoughts the reasoning becomes solid, however elliptical. The opening sentences of The Three Students lay great stress on Watson's determination that place and persons shall not be identified. Hence no reference to "Holmes's university," which would give away the college and the people as well. Yet it is clear that Holmes is on familiar ground. He knows his way to the athletic fields; he knows the character of the tutor Soames, poorly disguised as "an acquaintance," and treats him with a careless contempt Holmes never shows to strangers. Again, when Holmes goes out early the next morning it is to verify the colour and consistency of the lumps of clay which he has recognised at a glance—just like George Lyttelton.

Lastly, we ask ourselves, why did Holmes go to either of the universities to study English charters instead of the Public Record Office in London? Clearly, as a pastime of a few weeks in a congenial place. Clearly also, he knew beforehand what charters were there, even though he knew nothing about Thucydides: the ground had been staked out when he was an undergraduate. When, twenty years later, he set out before breakfast to hold a hearing on young Gilchrist, the only conceivable advantage of the Public Record Office would have been the proximity of the Master of the Rolls.

Trinity; the Tribune, 1682

THE DENTED IDOL
by David H. Galerstein

It is with a heavy heart that I switch on my electric typewriter to write these (not the last) words that I shall ever record about the singular gifts by which the Master, Mr. Sherlock Holmes, was distinguished. You too, dear reader, will feel the same heaviness of heart when you realise that the Master, great as he was, committed many grave errors during his twenty-three years in active practice. Reverence for a great person should never deter his admirers from noting his errors as well as his successes. Holmes would be the first to agree with this statement.

"Should you care to add the case to your annals, my dear Watson, it can only be as an example of that temporary eclipse to which even the best balanced mind may be exposed" (<u>Lady Frances Carfax</u>).

"You can write me down an ass this time, Watson" (<u>The Bruce-Partington Plans</u>).

"I have been very obtuse, Watson" (<u>The Solitary Cyclist</u>).

"That one word, my dear Watson, should have told me the whole story had I been the ideal reasoner which you are so fond of depicting" (<u>The Crooked Man</u>).

"Because I made a blunder, my dear Watson, which is, I am afraid, a more common occurrence than anyone would think who knew me only through your memoirs" (<u>Silver Blaze</u>).

The first of these series of blunders are the avoidable deaths.

"You cannot guard yourself too closely," Holmes warned young John Openshaw, adding that he would get on the case "tomorrow." Tommorrow! when the danger was immediate and the probability was that young Openshaw, one man alone, was being hounded by a gang. Moreover, the Master did <u>not</u> learn his lesson. He warned Mr. Melas, the Greek interpreter:

"I should certainly be on my guard if I were you, for of course they must know through these advertisements that you have betrayed them."

This, he said, to a middle-aged man who didn't possess a gun and who Holmes admitted lacked physical courage. How did Holmes expect Melas to guard himself?

Results so far: John Openshaw and Paul Kratides dead, and Mr. Melas lucky to be alive.

And despite Holmes's conceit that it was not easy to escape him, the murderers of Openshaw and Kratides did. Providence and not the law of England punished them for their misdeeds.

In The Resident Patient the danger was even greater. The men who sought Blessington actually penetrated his room, not once, but twice. Blessington hired Holmes because he was aware of the danger he faced. Holmes should not have walked out on him until he was told the truth.

With a client's life in danger, it was Holmes's duty to take immediate steps to save him—despite the lack of cooperation by Blessington.

The score is now three preventable deaths.

Also, since Blessington, not Dr. Trevelyan, hired Holmes, and since Openshaw did too, we now have to add —two lost fees.

Now we come to The Dancing Men. Once more Holmes neglected to come to the immediate aid of his client. He should have waited outside the house (as he did in Black Peter or The Six Napoleons). He should have scoured the countryside, pubs, and inns for the sole purpose of locating the writer of the mysterious characters.

The score is now four preventable deaths and two close calls (Mrs. Cubitt, like Mr. Melas, recovered). However, since it is doubtful that Mrs. Cubitt would pay Holmes for his blunder, and since it is equally doubtful that he would have the nerve to dun the widow after such an error, we now have three lost fees.

Holmes finally did learn his lesson. After Sir Henry Baskerville and Dr. Mortimer descended the hallowed seventeen steps, Holmes ordered Watson to don his coat, and they followed the two men. However, here too Holmes blundered and was outwitted by Stapleton. The latter saw, beforehand, the advantages of hiring a cab; Holmes didn't. He realised that he had blundered.

"Was ever such bad luck and such bad management, too? Watson, if you are an honest man you will record this also and set it against my successes!"

We cannot hold Holmes directly responsible for the death of the noble lady whom we shall call Mrs. Coram. He had no way of knowing she had poison. Still, he could very easily have prevented it.

Rather than rudely drop ashes all over a clean expensive carpet—something only a sloppy bachelor would do—to see if someone was hiding in the cabinet, Holmes could have simply walked over and opened the hidden recess. This would have prevented the lady from taking the poison—or if they weren't fast enough to stop her, trusty Watson was on hand for immediate and competent medical attention.

Also—suppose she remained in hiding and did not go out to eat lunch, what would Holmes have done?

The score is now five deaths (but no lost fee here).

The death of the great Birdy Edwards Douglas is perhaps the strongest blot on Holmes's record. He did have his chances—and I use the plural—to save this great retired colleague. He could have accepted, through Watson, the offer of Mrs. Douglas and Mr. Barker to speak to him in confidence, under a stipulation that he be the judge as to the disposition of the case. He made a similar type of agreement whith Sir James Damery in The Illustrious Client.

True, his first refusal came about because at that time he felt Mrs. Douglas and Mr. Barker were involved in the murder. That, too, was a temporary eclipse of a great mind.

Holmes knew that Moriarty had a hand in this job. How could Barker and Mrs. Douglas have been involved? Even if that possibility existed, a good detective always leaves himself an alternative, and if the widow and the friend were willing to talk to him in confidence, it was probably a sign that they weren't guilty of any murder.

Moreover, the alternative was very obvious and stated by Holmes when he told Mr. Mac and Watson that Moriarty ". . . may have been paid so much down to manage it."

Let us note this: In Boscombe Valley Holmes was willing to cover up for a former highwayman, multiple murderer, most wanted man in Ballarat, and an admitted killer. He also served as judge and had Watson as the jury to exonerate the gallant Captain Crocker, who killed a wicked, wife-beating drunkard. However, in the case of Birdy Edwards Douglas, a known target of the notorious Moriarty, Holmes admitted: "It may be that I am myself at fault for not following up the hint which you conveyed to me through my friend, Dr. Watson."

After admitting his blunder in thinking that they might have been involved in the crime, he added, "Now I am assured that this is not so."

Why not accept the confidence then? Abbey Grange reveals, once the police knew that Baldwin and not Douglas was killed, they had to disclose all or be traitors to their service. Holmes alone had the right to private judgment, a right he should have exercised, since he knew full well that Moriarty could not afford to fail because his whole unique position depended upon the fact that he had to succeed.

How simple it would have been for Holmes to have asked to see Mr. Douglas privately and let the world and Moriarty believe that Baldwin murdered Edwards-Douglas.

Most inexplicable of all was that, knowing full well Moriarty was after Douglas and after warning him about that, Holmes could not devise a better scheme to outwit the arch-criminal than a flight to Africa. In this case, the Napoleon of crime pulled a **coup de maître** on the master of criminal agents.

There can be no doubt that Holmes was aware of his shortcomings. That is why he asked the Chronicler, "I say, Watson, would you be afraid to sleep in the same room with a lunatic, a man with softening of the brain, an idiot whose mind has lost its grip?" (The Valley of Fear).

To summarise the deaths: There are sixty published cases; in these, six persons lost their lives through errors by the Master. If we take the published cases as a random sampling, then in one out of every ten cases persons involved with Holmes died through errors committed by the best and wisest man Watson ever knew.

Now for the lucky lapses—where death did not result.

In The Copper Beeches, Holmes repeatedly confessed that it was not a situation which he should like to see a sister of his apply for. He sat in his chair for hours demanding data, but it never occurred to him to get out of that chair, take a train for Winchester and investigate the strange actions of the Rucastles. To permit an impoverished Miss Hunter to go into a situation where he wouldn't permit his sister to go was not only an error—it was unconscionable.

However, the real error was in his deduction. When Holmes, Miss Hunter, and Watson broke into the room to find the ailing Miss Rucastle gone, the Master deduced that it was Mr. Rucastle who had spirited away the unfortunate lass. Common sense should have told him that Mr. Rucastle didn't have to kidnap her through a skylight, over a roof and down a long three-story ladder. Such a natural action when you come to think of it!

No, Rucastle could have sent Miss Hunter to Winchester on an errand and simply taken his daughter away. The presence of the ladder and the knowledge that Miss Rucastle had a man who wanted her, could mean only one thing—an elopement.

In his final summation of <u>The Hound of the Basker-villes</u>, Holmes told Watson ". . . we had no means of foreseeing the terrible and paralyzing spectacle which the beast presented, nor could we predict the fog."

What nonsense! What rationalisation! There was every reason to have predicted that the hound had a terrible and paralysing effect. Dr. Mortimer, in the initial interview, related that he cross-examined three different persons and all agreed that they saw "a huge creature, luminous, ghastly, and spectral." All told the same story without prior collusion, and all were hard-headed, reliable individuals.

The escaped convict Selden's death was preceded by "A terrible scream—a prolonged yell of horror and anguish . . . ." It turned the blood in Watson's experienced veins to ice. There were more cries, louder, more agonising, more urgent—then a last despairing yell and a dull heavy thud.

After discovering the most famous beard in literature, Holmes pondered, "There is one very singular thing however: How came Selden, in the darkness, to know that the hound was on his trail? . . . By his cries, he must have run a long way after he knew the animal was on his trail. How did he know?"

What else but luminescence could explain seeing a dog far off in the darkness? When all other possibilities are exhausted, whatever remains, however improbable , must be the truth. Here, all other possibilities did fail them.

The matter of the fog, too, was a mental lapse. Holmes couldn't predict the fog, but knowing it was very prevalent and that it moved, he should have had the foresight to plan for this, as well as other possible contingencies.

Result—one injured client, no lost fee, and a surprise round-the-world trip for Dr. Mortimer.

Now we come to what may be the greatest error of judgment committed by the Master. Holmes continually downgraded Watson's literary efforts. Considering the fact that untold millions of readers all over the world have enjoyed the narratives for over half a century— and the numbers keep increasing; considering the extraordinarily high level of scholarship these works have inspired, Holmes must be considered a very poor literary critic and judge. (His own two stories are definitely inferior to the poorest of those of John H. Watson, M.D.)

A brief discussion of the possible reasons for Holmes's errors will conclude this interminable piece.

For The Golden Pince-Nez, it would seem that Holmes
wanted to build up the case to a dramatic climax. He
needed money badly, since he hadn't completely recovered
from the financial drain of two years of travel without work, and he realised that a good ending would make
the story more saleable. It must not be forgotten that
he must have received a neat cut from Watson and the A-
gent for the rights to the stories. This was what Watson meant when he said that the stories were of some
practical value to Holmes.

For The Copper Beeches failure to investigate Rucastle immediately we must seek the explanation in the
nature of Miss Hunter herself. She undoubtedly made a
good impression on Holmes, as Watson shrewdly observed.
Had Holmes been in close contact with her, as required
by an investigation, he knew he would have fallen in
love with her. This would have endangered his great
powers of cold reason by diluting them with a flood of
emotion.

In the case of The Resident Patient, Holmes's great
conceit was offended by the obvious lie told to him by
Blessington and the Master's inability to get the man to
own up to his falsehood. Better it was to let a client
die as a warning to others to tell the truth, than that
the Master should not be able to elicit a confession.

As for The Greek Interpreter and The Five Orange
Pips, laziness explains Holmes's failure to act promptly. He was seized by a fit of it immediately after hearing the stories, and, interesting as these cases were,
he could not be roused from his mood.

The cause of this mood, which I euphemistically
call laziness, was drug addiction. This mood was the
black reaction that came upon Holmes after taking cocaine.

There can be little doubt that this drug did indeed cause a permanent impairment and that Holmes did
lose some of those great powers with which he was endowed.
This, and only this, explains the errors described
herein, Holmes's faulty deduction in The Copper Beeches
elopement, and his failure to foresee the horrible spectacle presented by Stapleton's pet. Drug addiction had
taken its toll, as it always does.

Let those of us who admire the great man wonder in
awe. Great as he was when in practice, to what untold
heights could Holmes have risen, had his great brain-
power been totally unimpaired?

A LETTER FROM DOCTOR WATSON

received by Mrs. Gayle Lange Puhl, née Gayle Lange

The Larches, Farmnott Lane
Trotsmouth, Sussex, England
3 May 1968

Dear Miss Lange:

My esteemed friend, Mr. Sherlock Holmes, has pressed me for years to tell the true story of why I wrote no more of his adventures after April of 1927. I have hesitated to do this because I thought there would be no interest in such stories, but due to the eager questions you put to me in your last letter, and your obvious interest, I have decided to relate to you all the details pertaining to the matter.

I had finished the last story, The Adventure of Shoscombe Old Place, in March of 1927, when my health failed suddenly, and I was placed on the critical list of the Charing Cross Hospital with pneumonia. I was, after all, nearly 75 years old, and the topsy-turvy life I had spent with Holmes, being roused out of bed at all hours of the night and investigating cases in all sorts of weather, along with my ill-fated campaign in Afghanistan, had left me in a precarious state of health for most of my life. My bout of illness was difficult, and convalescence was long and expensive. At my own request, I was admitted to a private nursing home in order to recuperate after my release from the hospital in August of 1927.

Holmes had retired to his little bee-farm in September of 1914 for the last time. He had broken up the suite of rooms which we had shared for so many years some time before, taking all his scrapbooks, indexes, papers, and documents with him to retirement. At that time he allowed me to remove all my notes of his cases, which were quite separate from his own. I always took the greatest care to guard these papers, since there were several plots afoot by some of the lower elements of London to get at these papers and destroy them. Holmes, living quietly in Sussex, was not bothered by these plots, since the criminals were never able to locate him.

When it became clear that I would not be able to keep up my rooms on Queen Anne Street because of my illness, the question arose of what to do with my notes. I had every intention of continuing with the stories after I was well again, and so I wanted them in a place from which I could obtain them at any time. For this reason, I disregarded the idea of handing them over to a governmental agency, which might be very reluctant to return

them to their rightful owner without a lot of fuss and
red tape and delay. I hesitated between putting them
with a dispatch-box full of notes I had deposited in
Cox's many years before and handing them over to Holmes.
I really disliked the idea of putting both copies of the
records together, for if anything were to happen, both
sets would be lost. It was at this point that my friend
and literary agent, Sir Arthur Conan Doyle, came to see
me in the nursing home with a request.

We sat on the sun-warmed veranda of the rambling
structure. I was pale and thin from my illness, and sat
with a warm blanket across my knees in the September sun.
Sir Arthur was dressed in travelling clothes, and his
ruddy face beamed across to mine.

"Now, Dr. Watson," said he, "is it true that you are
looking for a safe place in which to put your many notes
on Mr. Holmes's cases?"

"That is correct," I answered. "I will want to use
them again after I regain my health, but meanwhile they
must be well cared for."

"Would you lend them to me? I have been thinking for
some time that a complete list of Mr. Holmes's cases,
with a notation about each one, would be favourably received by the British public. If you would entrust your
papers to me, I could sort them out, index them, and make
my own notes. They would be available to you at any time
you wished."

I liked this idea at once, and handed over to Sir
Arthur the keys to my rooms where he would find the papers packed in two wooden trunks. He departed immediately, and I later received a note from him telling me that
he had the papers. Several notes were exchanged between
us during the next two years.

That interview occurred in September of 1927. Due to
the severity of my illness, my advanced age, and several
relapses which I suffered, I was unable to leave the
nursing home until 26 July 1931. Arrangements were made
before my discharge, and I went down at once to the
small village of Trotsmouth, where a little cottage was
outfitted for my retirement. I might mention that it was
between the years of 1927 and 1931 that rumours of my
death were begun. I made no effort at that time to refute them, since they made my slip into a quiet retirement all the easier, but I assure you they were false.

My finances were in a horrible state, due to the high
costs of my long illness and convalescence. I was eager,
therefore, to get out another batch of adventures, the
sale of which would relieve my skeleton bank balance.

I had learned of Sir Arthur's death some months before, and I was very much saddened by the occurrence. I wrote to the trustees of his estate on the subject of my notes, and I was much amazed to receive a letter informing me that there was no record of my papers in Sir Arthur's effects, and no trace had been found of them after an extensive search.

At once I made the trip to London to meet with them myself. I was cordially received, but they still denied any knowledge of the two trunks of notes Sir Arthur had carried from my rooms four years before. I asked to examine the boxes of papers they had removed from Sir Arthur's estate and stored in the family's bank vault. The trustees graciously agreed.

It was evident to me after an hour's search what the answer to the riddle was. I found perfect copies of my notes, carefully stored in cardboard boxes, all in Sir Arthur's handwriting! He had made exact copies of my notes against the day I would want them back. Either way, he would have the material for his proposed book. But where were my papers?

At this point I consulted Sherlock Holmes on the matter. Although he had been out of active practice for many years, he still maintained certain contacts with the London underworld. It was from these contacts that he learned that my notes had been destroyed by a band of burglars organised for that purpose in 1930.

Word had quietly gotten around the criminal underworld that Sir Arthur had possession of my notes, which, as I have written elsewhere, had been the goal of several British criminals for years. They had been unable to destroy them while I had them, and they found it equally impossible to do so while Sir Arthur was alive. But within three weeks of his death they broke into his house and found my notes in a downstairs cupboard, packed in my wooden trunks. They had been placed there after Sir Arthur had finished copying them. The thieves, however, knew nothing of the copies, safely hidden from them in the attic, and gleefully decamped with the trunks, which they burned. Nothing else was taken, and the occupants never knew there had been a burglary. Sir Arthur had told no one that he had my notes.

I realised that there was no possible way to recover my notes, and I was unable to use Sir Arthur's since they were part of his estate and were denied to me. My health was still bad, and the shock of the loss of my notes sent me back to bed for several months.

When I was on my feet again, my doctor forbade me to

(concluded on page 237)

THE BROOK STREET MYSTERY

by Andrew Page

"When a doctor does go wrong he is the first of criminals."
—Sherlock Holmes, in <u>The Speckled Band</u>

Much of the research done by Irregulars into inconsistencies in the Canon is sophistry. We all tend to put more weight on certain facts that support our theories and minimize those incidents that will question our monographs. There is nothing wrong with that, and this paper, at least in part, is a branch of that form of argument.

At the conclusion of <u>The Resident Patient</u>, Dr. Watson writes that "the proceedings against the page broke down for want of evidence, and the Brook Street Mystery, as it was called, has never until now been fully dealt with in any public print." The good doctor never states whether a final and unquestionable solution to the events of that morbid night was ever reached. I don't believe it was.

What do we <u>really</u> know about Dr. Percy Trevelyan? Besides what he tells Holmes and Watson, and what Holmes corroborates from his actions, we have very few confirmed facts. Is it possible that Doctor Trevelyan was, in fact, directly associated with the death of Blessington (Sutton)? It is more than possible, so let us examine the text.

When we first meet Dr. Trevelyan, Watson describes his manner as "nervous and shy . . . his haggard expression and unhealthy hue told of a life which had sapped his strength and robbed him of his youth." This description brings up two interesting questions. First, why should the doctor's appearance be such? His practice was, according to him, "from the first . . . a success." His work was not extremely taxing, and his situation was one of comfort. Maybe there was some personal, hidden reason for his nervous strain. Second, why should a doctor, especially one dealing in "obscure nervous lesions," be in such a pitiable state? One cannot imagine the Percy Trevelyan that Watson describes soothing a patient with a severe nervous disorder. Could it be that he was playing a part in the situation at hand and was nervous while in the company of such a great detective as Sherlock Holmes? It must be remembered that it was not Dr. Trevelyan's idea to take the matter to Holmes. "It was his [Blessington's] suggestion that I should come round to you . . . ."

If we approach the doctor's story from the angle that he is constantly lying to Holmes, we can build up a good case. What could be Trevelyan's reason for such treachery? Money, of course. Do we not detect a slight bit of bitterness in his voice when he says to Holmes, ". . .

during the last year or two I have made him [Blessington] a rich man." There he was, Percy Trevelyan, a rising young doctor, already established in a very handsome practice and paying over to Blessington three-quarters of whatever he earned. Unless he made a considerable sum, it would take him quite a while to build up enough capital to start out on his own. If Blessington was out of the way, he would still have the office and the practice, as well as full pay. Quite a nice setup. He would also have a good deal more time to himself, for he states that Blessington had a weak heart and "needs constant medical supervision."

Now we come to another point in question. If Dr. Trevelyan was an authority in his field, why was it so easy for the old man to fool him? It is possible that Holmes might have been able to imitate the disease close to perfection, but not an old and feeble man. The situation with Holmes is even doubtful, for Dr. Trevelyan gave his patient a complete physical examination, and even Holmes could not bluff his way through that. So what we have developing here is a theory that Dr. Trevelyan, goaded on by the remaing members of the Worthingdon gang and his desire to take over the practice, full-pay and all, helped out in the gruesome proceedings.

A few more ideas may be examined. Many chronologists date this case in late 1887, after Dr. Watson published his chronicle of A Study in Scarlet. If this is so, then it is entirely possible that Trevelyan was upstairs during the "trial" of Blessington. A Study in Scarlet relates to the readers how Holmes was able by the use of footprints to trace facts. If Trevelyan had read that, then he could have avoided being suspected by Holmes by simply not wearing shoes. Although this is entirely possible, it appears more probable that Trevelyan remained downstairs and kept watch for the gang, since he was aware that Holmes was interested in the case.

Furthermore, Trevelyan could have gained entrance to Blessington's room without causing any alarm, for he was a trusted member of the small household. If this is true, then the page, against whom the proceedings broke down, may have been innocent.

The speedy execution of Blessington may also have been one of Trevelyan's ideas. He may have realised that, with Holmes on the case, Blessington might crack and tell Holmes the true situation. If this did come about, it would mean the protection of Blessington and consequently the loss of Trevelyan's full-pay practice.

One may be tempted to ask why Trevelyan went to Holmes if it was his desire to keep matters quiet. If, instead

of going to Holmes, he had told Blessington that Holmes
had refused the case, Blessington might very well have
fled the country in terror. In order to secure money for
his flight, he most probably would have sold the house,
leaving Trevelyan out in the cold.

So now we may reconstruct the case as one where Dr.
Trevelyan's story from the outset was a fabrication. He
had worked with the Worthingdon gang and helped to ex-
ecute Blessington, receiving in return his own practice,
full-pay, and the satisfaction of outwitting the world's
only unofficial consulting detective.

W. H. Hyde

"'Blessington, I think, sat upright in bed'"

A LETTER FROM DOCTOR WATSON (continued from page 234)

do any work of any sort, including writing. My money was
practically gone, and it was only the revival of interest
in the sixty existing stories and the royalties resulting
from the release of a new edition of Holmes's adventures
that kept me from an impoverished old age.

I am quite elderly now, and it is out of the question
for me to use Holmes's vast amount of material in the
writing of new stories. My health has been poor for years,
and this does not help matters. Holmes and I are both
pleased that there is still interest in his adventures
after all this time.

I trust that this account answers the question that
you asked me, and I would like to wish both you and your
colleagues the very best in your pursuit of Sherlockian
scholarship.

Very truly yours,

[signed] John H. Watson, M.D.

LETTERS TO BAKER STREET

From Robert N. Brodie, ("The Gloria Scott"):

I note in the September issue an article by George Fletcher about the bull pup in which he quotes my colleague Jerry Stockler of the Deal-Top Monographers in the June '67 BSJ to the effect that the bull pup was a short-barrelled, large-calibre revolver. Mr. Fletcher then goes on to make an ingenious case for the bull pup's being a rifle.

Jerry and I consulted further on his speculation about the bull pup and published our conclusions in The Sherlock Holmes Journal, Summer 1969, under the title of "The Case of the Dog That Wasn't."

In that article we proved definitely that the bull dog was a revolver and were able to identify the calibre, thanks to Holmes's chance remark in The Speckled Band, when he said to Watson, "I should be very much obliged if you would slip your [my italics] revolver into your pocket. An Eley's No. 2 is an excellent argument with gentlemen who can twist steel pokers into knots."

That "Eley's No. 2" is conclusive. It is a cartridge made specifically for a .38-calibre revolver.

The September issue was, as always, excellent. I was especially glad to read the article by Nicholas Utechin.

* * * * *

From Professor John Boardman, of Brooklyn College:

I have recently run across a Holmesian reference in a rather unusual place. The March-April issue of Strategy & Tactics contains an article by Albert A. Nofi dealing with the situation in the Mediterranean on the eve of World War II. In it Mr. Nofi writes:

"Italian naval thought had accepted the theories of 'command of the seas' but had also realistically assumed that Italy was not likely to ever achieve the material superiority which such a philosophy necessitated. Italy had planned for many years for war with France, and Italian strategists had recognized the inherent, and unlikely to change, quantitative superiority of the French over the Italian fleet."

Needless to say, these observations reminded me of:

"The treaty...defined the position of Great Britain towards the Triple Alliance, and foreshadowed the policy which this country would pursue in the event of the French fleet gaining a complete ascendancy over that of Italy in the Mediterranean" (The Naval Treaty).

* * * * *

From the Marquis of Donegall ("The Manor House Case"), Editor of The Sherlock Holmes Journal:

I send you a correction to SHJ, Vol. 10, No. 2, Summer 1971. The penultimate paragraph of my editorial on page 37 should read:

"Holmes writes that Tuxbury Old Park, near Bedford, was 'inaccessible—5 miles from anywhere.' Yet, in the year of my birth (1903), it had a telephone. There was also a telephone (that worked) at the Railway Arms, Little Purlington, Essex (Reti)—the most primitive village in England, by which Dr. Watson was able, in 1898, to have an understandable conversation with Holmes, in Baker Street."

How is it possible for one man to make so many mistakes in eight lines? Not only have I no excuse; I haven't even an explanation!

    *   *   *   *   *

From Daniel J. Morrow of The Scandalous Bohemians:

I enjoyed J. S. Callaway's paper on the Bruce-Partington submarine in the September issue. I prepared a similar monograph for a meeting of The Scandalous Bohemians. My research showed that the Gustave Zede is a good bet. However, in 1895 two Englishmen, Silas and Rogers, built a cylinder-shaped submarine in Brighton. That same year John Holland was working on his Plunger. In 1896 France unveiled the "forward hydroplane" on her subs—a great stride in keeping them on a smooth course under water. Perhaps they got the idea from the Bruce-Partington plans. However, if the adventure actually took place after 1900 it would make more sense because England did have plans and submarines after that date.

As for the name Bruce-Partington: It may have come from the British firm, Vickers-Maxim (later Vickers-Armstrong), which eventually obtained the European construction rights to Holland's submarines.

    *   *   *   *   *

From Cornelis Helling ("The Reigning Family of Holland"), of Amsterdam, Holland:

The September issue was, as usual, splendid! I particularly appreciated "Hurlstone and the Ritual" and "Who Was Huret?" As to "An Enquiry into the Identity of the Bruce-Partington Submarine," I would point out that the submarine of 1893 was in fact the Gustave Zédé, in the article misspelt several times: Gustare Zede. This submarine was named after the famous French inventor of submarines. Then in the article, "The Mystery of the Indelible Pencil," there are two mistakes on page 175: "We were ——" should be "We we——"; "If you wrote on the wall someone might rest on it" should read ". . . some eye might rest on it." Minor faults, but somewhat disturbing. [Editor's note: Doubleday has "someone," and John Murray has "some eye."]

    *   *   *   *   *

From Rose Vogel, of St. Louis:

I really enjoyed the September Journal. Marvelous, I thought. I particularly liked Bill Fleischauer's article, "Who Was Huret?"

May I make a correction in the Scion Societies section? The correspondence society that Steve Clarkson and I organised back in March is called The Cavendish Squares, Ltd., and its publication is to be The Garroter. For entrance into this one may take an examination. The other scion that we started just recently is The Board-School Beacons, and the only requirement for this is that each member must write to another at least once a month.

I hope that everything is clear now.

*   *   *   *   *

From David Skene Melvin (new address: 36 Chapel Street, Brampton, Ontario, Canada), Chairman, the Sub-Librarian's Scion of the Sherlock Holmes Society of London within the Canadian Library Association:

If I may address you in your capacity as Commissionaire of the B.S.I., I feel I owe an explanation to the B.S.I. regarding our Sub-Librarian's Scion. Even though John Bennett Shaw had, with his blessing, allowed us to appropriate the name, we felt that, since his Scion within the A.L.A. was an official Scion of the B.S.I., that two almost identically designated Scions would be too much. Further, there was a feeling, tinged with nationalism, that since Canada's historical ties are across the Atlantic we should associate ourselves with that other fountainhead of Sherlockian wisdom. Besides, the B.S.I. has offspring enough of its own. Lastly, waxing philosophical, one can consider Canada as the bridge between the U.K. and the U.S. Consequently we formally associated ourselves as an official Scion of The Sherlock Holmes Society of London (England). I trust that the B.S.I. will not take this amiss. I assure you that this was not done out of any disrespect for the B.S.I. I do not presume to request that we be recognised as well by the B.S.I., but I would like to inquire if our Sub-Librarian's Scion might be granted associate status and if the BSJ would consider accepting reports on its activities. [Yes—to both inquiries; it is always a joy to include Canadians, as well as Englishmen.] Despite our formal ties being in Britain, I would like to think that we could retain ties of kinship with our American cousins. I know the Master would approve.

*   *   *   *   *

From Anne Giardina, of Lansdale, Pennsylvania:

As usual, the September issue is superb, but I feel I must protest against one article, "Sherlock Holmes's Honeymoon," by Benjamin Grosbayne. I don't deny that it was well written, but where in God's name did he get his facts? Or is he assuming the facts? I hope that Mr. Grosbayne is making the story up. How does he know that Holmes married Irene Adler or became a great conductor? No hint was ever given in the stories. Pray tell me, _where_ did he get his facts?

*   *   *   *   *

From Julian Blackburn, in Montpellier, France:

I am honoured by Henry Lauritzen's grading [on p. 182, September BSJ] of my "The Identity of the King of Bohemia" (June BSJ). I agree it did not deserve an "underlining stroke"; I sent it too hurriedly and without polishing. I particularly regret I omitted the principal reference, Corti's _Alexander von Battenberg_, from which the quotations and other details of Alexander's and Irene Adler's life were taken.

I regret that Benjamin Grosbayne's article (September

BSJ) is based on speculation, not on fact.

*   *   *   *   *

From Ted Bergman, of Lidingö, Sweden, Editor of <u>The Baker Street Cab Lantern</u>:

I would very much like to have Barbara Hodan's poem, "Seventeen Steps" (in the June BSJ), published in the next <u>Cab Lantern</u>, translated into Swedish, that is. She has allowed me to publish it, and I would very much appreciate your permission too. [Permission granted—Ed.]

Her poem seems to me to be the most serious and artistical piece of Sherlockian poetry that I have ever read. I will try to do justice to her excellent poem myself, interpreting rather than translating, I think.

*   *   *   *   *

From Susan M. Rice, of Bloomfield Hills, Michigan:

I thoroughly enjoyed the two most recent Journals. The article on film treatments of the Master (but seldom the Canon) was fascinating. In the September issue I enjoyed "Mycroft Come Back; All Is Forgiven." Please warn Mr. Clark, however, that I am working on a solution to the apparent discrepancy in Mycroft's character that will allow him to emerge as he really was: neither criminal nor incompetent.

I also found pleasure in reading the account of Holmes's honeymoon, but I advise Mr. Grosbayne to check again the love letters, press clippings, diaries, and official documents he quotes. It is my opinion that someone is attempting to perpetrate an elaborate hoax. I agree that Holmes was definitely capable of feeling and expressing love for Irene, but I believe that their affair was brief and bittersweet. My versified reply to Mr. Grosbayne is enclosed:

IRENE'S LAMENT

He has my picture still, I know,
Sandwiched in among his old files.
Am I <u>the</u> woman, or just a foe?
Does he see my cunning or just my smile?

I wonder if he thinks of me,
Drawing his bow across the strings,
Or sipping Mrs. Hudson's tea.
What memories does the snuffbox bring?

Oh yes, I'm Mrs. Norton still,
And still the lawyer's ring I wear.
But sometimes when alone I sense
A scent of shag upon the air.

I wish once more to cross his path
There 'midst London's spires and domes,
And as myself to say again
Good night to Mr. Sherlock Holmes.

"Stand with me here upon the terrace..."

William S. Hall

("The Blue Carbuncle")

Of necessity, we must be resigned to the fact that our noble Old Irregulars are gradually fading away, but the loss of Bill Hall, who died on 29 September 1971, was an unusually severe blow, especially hard to take, for our Irregular organisation in general and for each one of its members individually. Not only was he one of our Founding Fathers, but he was also a most knowledgeable and enthusiastic Sherlockian who had earned our highest honour, the Two-Shilling Award. But to those of us who knew him personally the loss is especially great, for he was a cherished friend who can never be replaced—or forgotten.

There ought to be space here for a personal tribute from your Editor-Commissionaire: It is well known that the purpose (and delight) of The Baker Street Irregulars is to pursue the study of that great body of Sherlockian literature. Now I hope that I shall not be impeached for heresy when I say that an equally great and delightful purpose is the forging of true friendships. In this respect I have been more fortunate than most, for I have made more than my share of very close and truly sincere friends—none closer, dearer, or more sincere than Bill.

WILLIAM K. LINDEMAN

William K. Lindeman, a long-time member of The Sons of the Copper Beeches, of Philadelphia, died on 21 October 1971. He was one of the senior Master Copper Beechsmiths, and was the Scion Toastmaster (a very good one) until his health failed during the last couple of years. In addition, he was Treasurer of the Publication Fund, and he had contributed quite a few papers to the Scion Society meetings.

ON FACING PAGE: Fred Dannay, Elmer Davis, William S. Hall, Christopher Morley, and Rex Stout at the dinner of The Baker Street Irregulars, 3 January 1947

The Scion Societies

THE DEPTFORD REACHERS
of Connecticut and Rhode Island

Correspondence: Rev. Henry T. Folsom,
338 Main St., Old Saybrook, Conn. 06475.

The first regular meeting was held on 30 April at the home of Prof. Harry D. Scammell, Davenport College, Yale University, and was attended by about a dozen members. Libations were enjoyed, and then the group proceeded to Mory's where a hearty meal in the highest Sherlockian tradition was enjoyed. A fitting climax was the sharing of Mory's traditional Green Cup, whose recipe used to be a generations-old secret.

Following dinner, the group returned to Davenport College, where the more serious discussions of the Canon took place.

Our membership at present consists primarily, but not exclusively, of members of the academic world, including quite a few faculty members from Yale and the University of Rhode Island. However, this erudition should not frighten away any who live in Connecticut and Rhode Island and who are interested in joining us. Membership is open to serious Sherlockians of both sexes.

* * * *

CREW OF THE BARQUE LONE STAR
of North Central Texas

Correspondence: Margaret F. Morris, Third Mate,
472 Westview Terrace, Arlington, Texas 76013.

The Barque took aboard the Sub-Librarians Scion on 21 June for a luxurious cruise. Other passengers included Bee-Keepers, Molly Maguires, Brothers from Moriarty, a trustee of the Garrideb Foundation, and friends, a total of 25. The 32nd floor of the LTV Tower became the crow's nest as all enjoyed a cold luncheon with chilled champagne and wine. Toasts were offered, and John Bennett Shaw presided as the papers were read. As befits a joint cruise, the gathering closed with a double tradition; all stood while Chairman Shaw read Vincent Starrett's "221B Baker Street," and then all signed the Ship's Log.

* * * *

THE CONFEDERATES OF WISTERIA LODGE
of Atlanta

Correspondence: Robert S. Gellerstedt, Jr.,
2551 Meadow Lark Drive, East Point, Ga. 30344.

The fourth meeting of the year, attended by 21, was held at the home of Doris Kennedy in Atlanta on 1 August. Sherlockian topics were hashed and rehashed, and there was a quiz on The Devil's Foot, won by Edwin Respess with a perfect score. Then a delightful picnic on the patio was enjoyed.

We meet every other month, and anyone interested is welcome.

* * * *

THE GREEK INTERPRETERS
of East Lansing, Michigan

Correspondence: Donald A. Yates, Melas,
537 Wells Hall, Michigan State University,
East Lansing, Michigan 48823.

The Interpreters met, for the third time this year, on 18 August at the Pretzel Bell, just off the MSU campus. The text under discussion was The Adventure of the Greek Interpreter, with which the membership demonstrated a laudable familiarity.

A prize was awarded for the best performance on an acrostic quiz based on that tale; correspondence from Sherlockians interested in becoming members was read; and the question of a qualifying quiz for prospective members was discussed. A fall meeting is planned.

*   *   *   *

THE RED CIRCLE
of Washington

Correspondence: Peter E. Blau,
2201 M Street NW, Washington, D.C. 20037.

Twenty-one members and guests of The Red Circle gathered at Blackie's House of Beef on 20 August (an appropriately blazing hot day) to discuss the results of their study of The Adventure of the Cardboard Box. A contest for the best Sherlockian limerick brought forth a number of entries and considerable evidence that the Circle encloses almost as many poets as punsters.

*   *   *   *

TRAVELLERS FOR NEVADA
of Las Vegas

Correspondence: W. E. Dudley, Prospector,
Box 2020, Las Vegas, Nevada 89101.

Through a curious incident, our first meeting was held at Caruso's Restaurant, Tucson, Arizona, on 22 September. Those who gave the proper countersign to the challenge, "Nine to seven," were admitted. Attendance was light at the first meeting, but we are asking those who wish to become associated with us to write. Several toasts, including one to Lucy Ferrier, our inspiration, featured the meeting.

*   *   *   *

THE NON-CANONICAL CALABASHES
of Los Angeles

Correspondence: Cecil Ryder, Interim Corresponding Secretary,
118 Carr Drive, Glendale, Calif. 91218.

Fifty-two fellows and ladies attended our first anniversary meeting on 18 September. We began proceedings with a toast to the Calabashes and a Sherlockian contest, won by Miss Jane Plotke. After a speech by Glenn Holland, which was heartily received, we sat spellbound by Mr. John Holmes, the Australian Trade Commissioner, who conclusively proved that he was the grandnephew of Sherlock and Mycroft. We then voted to find out if we could have personalised California license plates (cost $25). Those interested should write Sean Wright at 5542 Romaine St., Los Angeles, Calif. 90038. The Sherlock watch and plans for our proposed radio show were discussed, and then we saw Silver Blaze, with Arthur Wontner, followed by a vintage film. We then adjourned to meet on 9 January at the Scotland Yard Restaurant, the newest Sherlockian tavern. (The Scotland Yard, incidentally, plans a Sherlockian costume party on the Master's birthday, 6 January.)

*   *   *   *

THE SIX NAPOLEONS
of Baltimore

Correspondence: Steve Clarkson, Harker,
69 Straw Hat Road, I-D, Owings Mills, Md. 21117.

Forty-six Napoleons, Josephines, and guests assembled on 24 September at a gala Ladies' Night held in commemoration of our Silver Anniversary. An open bar and a fine prime-rib dinner were the gustatory features, while a variety of prizes were handed out to the winners of separate quizzes for ladies and gentlemen. The meeting was graced by the presence of Julian Wolff and his lovely wife, who came from New York to join us in our toasts to the woman and Mrs. Hudson. Congratulatory telegrams and letters were read, and the festivities lasted far beyond our usual adjourning time.

*   *   *

THE TRIFLING MONOGRAPHS

Correspondence: Susan M. Rice, Magnum Opus,
                        380 Lone Pine Rd., Bloomfield Hills, MI 48013.

The first official meeting was held on 25 September, at the home of the Magnum Opus. Besides the 5 founding members, there were 6 guests, most of whom participated in the quizzes given on titles of the Canon. Illustrators of the Sacred Writings and Billy Wilder's The Private Life of Sherlock Holmes were two of the topics discussed, after which the meeting was terminated, all concerned deeming it a great success.

*   *   *

Jack Tracy (709 West 6th, Bloomington, Indiana 47401) and Paul Cox announce the formation of THE UNANSWERED CORRESPONDENTS, the Sherlockian study group of Bloomington, Indiana, and Indiana University.

*   *   *

THE ARID AND REPULSIVE DESERT SOCIETY, a new Scion, has been formed in Phoenix, Arizona, and those interested should write to Richard A. King, 908 N. 5th St., Apt. #1, Phoenix, Arizona 85004.

*   *   *

The MYCROFT HOLMES SOCIETY, of Syracuse, is off to a flying start, with 45 members, and Jerry Clark, the founder, of 2712 Midland Ave., Syracuse, N.Y. 13205, is looking for more.

*   *   *

Diana Price (174 7th Ave., #2F, New York, N.Y. 10011) and Gail Goldsman (201 W. 21st St., #8E, New York, N.Y. 10011) are forming a female Scion Society in New York, and they would like to hear from interested Holmesians.

*   *   *

Brian Locke wants to start a Scion Society in southern New Jersey. Write him at 13 Sleepy Hollow Rd., Stratford, New Jersey 06084.

*   *   *

Thomas Hotz (1770 West 6th St., Brooklyn, N.Y., 11223) is interested in organising a Scion Society dedicated not only to the study of Sherlock Holmes, but also to a serious study of pastiches in general, with special emphasis on Solar Pons. He invites correspondence from those who want to join.

*   *   *

Valerie Hill (6760 South West 76th Terrace, South Miami, Florida 33143) and Renee Anastos have acquired eight additional members for their Scion, THE RESIDENT PATIENTS OF BAKER STREET, and invite more. All that is required is devotion to the study of the Canon. There are no restrictions as to age or sex.

*   *   *

Lloyd Alan Fradkin (1337 65th Drive, Lubbock, Texas 79412; telephone 806-747-0023) is planning a new Scion for both regular and corresponding members and invites applications.

The Silver Blaze(s)

CHICAGO

The 12th annual Silver Blaze Purse was held on 16 July at the Arlington Park track. It drew an enthusiastic crowd of 44 who lunched in the Classic Club and then set about the business of attempting to win a little on the next race.

The Silver Blaze Purse was the sixth race on the card and was won by the favourite, Tommy Bob, ridden by Jockey Richard Strauss.

Fred Townsend, PR man for the Royal London Wax Museum, graciously brought along the attire of the wax figures of Holmes and Watson, and Bob Hahn as the former and Jack Schrandt as the doctor joined other members of the party in the winner's circle, where Hahn presented the Silver Blaze Plaque to the trainer of Tommy Bob.

NEW YORK

The 20th annual renewal of the Silver Blaze was run at Belmont on 17 September. As usual, there was a good attendance, and all enjoyed the hospitality of The Players before proceeding to the track in a special bus. An excellent lunch was enjoyed in the clubhouse, and then the Irregulars cooperated in improving the breed (of race horses). The race was won by Royal Picnic, an odds-on favourite, so that even those who bet correctly did not profit too much. Then there was the ride back to The Players in our own bus, after which we disbanded, having had an enjoyable, even if not profitable day.

It would not do to discuss the Silver Blaze without mentioning a letter to the Editor that appeared in the sporting section of The New York Times on 12 September. This letter spelled out the history of the Silver Blaze and was quite authoritative because it was written by Tom Stix, Sr. ("The Darlington Substitution Scandal"), Benefactor of this Race, who founded this event and is the one who started Silver Blazes in so many cities.

From the Editor's Commonplace Book

What seems to have aroused the most interest among our readers in recent months is that much publicised English bank robbery—on Baker Street, of all places. The police were unable to prevent the crime in spite of the fact that the gang used a short-wave radio for communication, and the agents of the law were able to listen in on the proceedings (which included a tunnel in the approved manner of The Red-Headed League). Evidently these were not the best of a bad lot.

* * * *

There was good news for us New Yorkers in The New York Times of 8 October. Once more we shall be able to read those excellent columns by Red Smith ("The Netherlands-Sumatra Company").

* * * *

The St. Petersburg Times (of Florida), 21 October 1971, carried a long article about Rev. Leslie Marshal ("A Scandal in Bohemia"), our own non-conformist clergyman. It was devoted to his Irregular Sherlockian activities and was illustrated with an excellent photograph of him.

* * * *

Noel B. Gerson's Because I Loved Him, The Life and Loves of Lillie Langtry, which was recently published by William Morrow, may well be—as many believe—the life story of the woman, who has often been identified as the Jersey Lily. (Her autobiography, The Days I Knew, apparently omitted many of the most interesting events in her life, which did not occur during the days, of course.)

And, since we are speaking of the woman, I'd like to point out that a recent advertisement in The New York Times offered: "Lillie Langtry. A captivating cabinet photo of the 'Jersey Lily,' delightfully framed with signature $50." ("'Your Majesty has something which I should value even more highly,' said Holmes. . . . 'This photograph!'") I do not know the significance of the fact that the same ad offers an autograph note of Sir Arthur for only $15.

* * * *

Several Sherlockians have noticed the use of an unusual (but familiar) weapon in a current best-seller: In The Day of the Jackal, by Frederick Forsyth, an aluminum crutch is really a hunting rifle in disguise.

* * * *

W. E. Dudley, of Las Vegas, recently submitted an article which had to do with Sherlock Holmes to the magazine, Industrial Security. It was rejected with a note stating that Holmes was a "dope fiend." Mr. Dudley writes: "From the terrible handwriting [of the one who wrote the note] I would deduce that he is likely a medical gentleman or is suffering from palsy. His reference to the Master as a 'dope fiend' is like calling Winston Churchill an alcoholic."

Walter Pond ("Brunton, the Butler, of Hurlstone") found this in the letters section of the magazine, Opera, London, March 1971:

Singers of Fiction

Apropos 'Desert Island Dreams' (December), please ask Elizabeth Forbes: 'what about Irene Adler'?

S.H., c/o 221b Baker Street, London

ELIZABETH FORBES replies:

I should have been only too pleased to include Irene Adler in the singers mentioned in *Desert Island Dreams*, but unfortunately I do not know what she sang. The only clues we are given about her career are that she was a contralto, that she sang at La Scala and at the Imperial Opera of Warsaw and that she had retired from the operatic stage at the time of her involvement with Sherlock Holmes.

Personally I think Irene Adler would have made a superb Fidès, so perhaps there exists somewhere a disc (or a cylinder or a tape) of her singing 'Ah, mon fils' from *Le Prophète*.

And this is from The New York Times, 11 April '71:

To the Financial Editor:
Your treatise on bees (April 4) fill a long-neglected need. But how could any serious study of the subject fail to mention the most famous apiarist of them all?

I refer, of course, to Sherlock Holmes.

In his later years, the Master retired to Sussex where he devoted full time to keeping bees, and his knowledge of these busy creatures was every bit as extensive as his understanding of Professor Moriarty, the Napoleon of Crime.

Were Dr. Watson with us today, I feel certain that he would be the first to apply the needle to The Times for its gaffe. For shame that The Times should be the one to make bees Holmesless.

ROBERT L. JORDAN
New York

HOLMES IN RUSSIA

Sir Arthur Conan Doyles books are popular behind the Iron Curtain. More than 10 million copies of his books about the exploits of Sherlock Holmes have been sold in the Soviet Union.

There are 12 Federal Reserve System districts, each with a Federal Reserve bank.

John Bennett Shaw ("The Hans Sloane of My Age") has supplied this item from the Tulsa Tribune with the remark, "I knew they made money—but banks!!"

NORDBERG, NILS, editor
Sir Arthur Conan Doyle: De fires tegn
Oslo: Gyldendal Norsk Forlag [1971]; Kr. 17.50.
This Norwegian edition of The Sign of the Four is a
worthy addition to the Canonical series (see page 177
of the September BSJ) and contains an excellent introduction by the editor, "The Cocaine Bottle on the Man-
telshelf"—in Norwegian, of course.

STARRETT, VINCENT
Sherlock Holmes—One More Time
Chicago Tribune Magazine, 22 August 1971.
Our greatest Sherlockian discusses Billy Wilder's The
Private Life of Sherlock Holmes and remarks (but not
too unkindly) on the fact that the title was appropri-
ated without a by-your-leave from his own masterpiece,
the best book ever written about Sherlock Holmes outside of the Canon.

TITUS, EVE
Basil and the Pygmy Cats
New York: McGraw-Hill Book Company [1971]; $4.95.
The latest in that great series about Basil of Baker
Street (the "mouster," as he was dubbed by Edgar W.
Smith) which has been enjoyed by adults as well as
children and has received unanimous praise from Sher-
lockian and other critics. And it would not do to omit
mention of Paul Galdone's delightful illustrations.

WALSH, WILLIAM J., editor
A Curious Collection
N.p.: The Musgrave Ritualists Beta, 1971; $2.00.
This curious collection, well illustrated by Jon V.
Wilmunen, is indeed a good one, containing six essays
by recognised Sherlockian scholars, presented in an
attractive booklet. Obtainable from the editor at
6 Ernst Drive, Suffern, N.Y. 10901.

* * * * * *

SH-sf Fanthology 2, September 1971, is a collection of
writings on Sherlock Holmes, reprinted from science-fiction
magazines: "The Martian Who Hated People," by Edward Ludwig;
"A Letter (Mycroft to S.)," by Jon White; "Moriarty and the
Binomial Theorem," by Doug Hoylman; and a review of Billy
Wilder's The Private Life of Sherlock Holmes, by Dean Dickensheet. Copies are available at 50¢ from Editor Ruth Berman,
5620 Edgewater Boulevard, Minneapolis, Minn. 55417.

That famous pastiche, The Pursuit of the Houseboat, by John
Kendrick Bangs, has been reprinted by Scholarly Press, of St.
Clair Shores, Michigan. Dean Emeritus Herman C. Hesse, Distinguished Service Professor of Mechanical Engineering, College of Engineering, Valparaiso University, has prepared a
knowledgeable and scholarly review which is to appear in the
Vidette-Messenger, Valparaiso, Ind., as by "Carroll Lewis."

More Rivals of Sherlock Holmes, by Hugh Greene, was recently published by The Bodley Head, London; price £2.50.

The American edition of Trevor Hall's The Late Mr. Sherlock
Holmes and Other Literary Studies has been published by St.
Martin's Press at $7.50.

"Conan Doyle Looks at Medicine," by Harry S. Abram, M.D., a
discussion of Round the Red Lamp, appeared in Medical Times,
July 1971.

Abstracts of English Studies for April 1971 contains abstracts of the papers in March 1971 BSJ.

Heading our list of extra-curricular writings is Fanfare of Strumpets, by Michael Harrison ("The Camberwell Poisoning Case"), published by W. H. Allen, of London, at £1.25. Under the heading "Heyday of the Harlots" a review appeared in The Times Literary Supplement, London, 10 September, and the anonymous reviewer wrote: "Its title alone should guarantee the success of Fanfare of Strumpets."

The Saga of the Tin Goose, "The Plane That Revolutionized American Civil Aviation," a great book by Old Irregular David A. Weiss ("Crosby, the Banker"), has been published by Crown Publishers at $5.95. This is the interesting and definitive account of that famous old airplane, the Ford Trimotor.

Announced in October was The First Team, by John Ball ("The Oxford Flyer, published by Little, Brown; $7.95.

The brief (two pages) output of Pete Williams ("Old Abrahams") is XXII Reports, issued in a very limited edition and consisting of paragraphs on miscellaneous subjects.

*　　　*　　　*　　　*　　　*

PERIODICALS

THE BAKER STREET PAGES, New Series, Vol. 1, No. 2, August-September 1971. Edited for the Pageboys by Andrew Page, 3130 Irwin Avenue, Bronx, N.Y. 10463.

THE DEVON COUNTY CHRONICLE, Vol. 7, No. 5, June 1971. Edited for the Irregulars of Chicago by R. W. Hahn, 938 Clarence Ave., Oak Park, Illinois 60304.

THE ELLERY QUEEN REVIEW, October 1971. Edited by Rev. Robert E. Washer, 82 E. 8th St., Oneida Castle, N.Y. 13421. Contains much about Investitured Irregular Fred Dannay, of course, and a fitting tribute to the late Manfred Lee, the other half of the Ellery Queen team.

THE HOLMESIAN OBSERVER, Vol. 1, No. 8, October 1971. The publication of The Priory School, edited by Andrew Page.

THE HOOSIER HOT LINE, 30 July 1970. A periodical issued from time to time by L. C. Dobbins, 2025 Lincoln Ave., Apt. C-8, Evansville, Indiana 47714. Consists of the editor's interesting discussions of various topics, and includes much about Sherlock Holmes.

THE PIPE SMOKER'S EPHEMERIS, Winter-Autumn 1971. Edited and published by Tom Dunn, 20-37 120th St., College Point, N.Y. 11356.

THE PONTINE DOSSIER, Annual Edition, 1971, Vol. 1, No. 2, New Series. Published by Luther Norris, 3844 Watseka Ave., Culver City, Calif, 90230; $3.00. Contains much truly excellent writing about Solar Pons—and Sherlock Holmes, of course.

THE ROHMER REVIEW, No. 6, February 1971. Edited and published for The Sax Rohmer Society by Robert E. Briney, 245 Lafayette St., Apt. 3G, Salem, Mass. 01970. This issue contains "Letter to Sherlock," with Annotations by Julian L. Biggers. The letter is from Nayland Smith to Holmes and states that Moriarty was a tool of Fu-Manchu.

THE SCANDAL SHEET, Vol. 1, No. 2, September 1971. Published by The Scandalous Bohemians and edited by Robert A. W. Lowndes. Regarding subscriptions, write to Martin J. King, 1113 Sylvan Lane, Mountainside, New Jersey 07092.

SHADES OF SHERLOCK, Vol. 5, No. 2, 14 August 1971. Published by The Three Students Plus, edited by Bruce Kennedy, and

(continued on page 256)

WANTS AND OFFERS

Richard Minter (Box 4324, Eden, N.C. 27288) offers some back issues of BSJ at $5 each and requests want lists.

R. S. Gellerstedt, Jr. (2551 Meadow Lark Dr., East Point, Ga. 30344) wants the 4 issues of BSJ, Volume 3, Old Series.

Andrew Taylor (1345 Pembina Highway, Winnipeg 19, Manitoba, Canada) wants the following issues of BSJ (OS): Vol. 2, No. 3; Vol. 3, No. 4; Vol. 4, No. 1.

William Berner (4712-17th St., San Francisco, Calif. 94117) offers the first two Discourses, Ltd., Sherlock Holmes records at $4.95 each, postpaid. They are The Norwood Builder/The Disappearance of Lady Frances Carfax (DCO-1212) and Shoscombe Old Place/The Illustrious Client (DCO-1213). The next two are expected to be ready before this appears.

Victor Dricks (1547 E. 21st St., Brooklyn, N.Y. 11210) offers photographs of Holmes as portrayed by Rathbone. They are 8 x 10 inches and are priced at $2.25 each, or 5 for $10. Prices include postage and sturdy wrapping.

Miss Cindy McKoin (1725 Delachaise, Apt. 2A, New Orleans, La. 70115) wants pictures of Holmes and Watson for framing.

Miss Jinnefer Holmes (7547 Magnolia, Houston, Texas 77023) wants photos of Basil Rathbone and Nigel Bruce.

A solid silver (.999 fine) Sherlockian medal, 1¼" in diameter, is offered by The Scandalous Bohemians. The obverse bears a profile of the Master and the reverse a suitable quotation by Watson. It will sell for $12., postpaid in U.S. Foreign orders please add 50¢. A limited number of identical coins numbered serially to 100 are also available at $15. Orders for expected delivery in late December are being taken. Cheques should be made out to The Ostlers-SBNJ and sent to Martin J. King, 1113 Sylvan Lane, Mountainside, N.J. 07092.

Stanfield Hill (3927 Douglaston Parkway, Douglaston, L.I., N.Y. 11363) offers: Guy Warrack's Sherlock Holmes and Music, inscribed, $12.50; Sherlock Holmes and Dr. Watson, edited by Morley, $17.50; Starrett's Private Life of S. H., $10.00.

Eve Titus (11740 Wilshire, Barrington Plaza, Los Angeles, Calif. 90025) offers The Misadventures of S. H. for $15.00.

Andrew Fusco (643 Trovato Drive, Morgantown, W.Va. 26505) is looking for The Incunabular Holmes. Also, he has located some copies of Dr. Van Liere's A Doctor Enjoys Sherlock Holmes, and offers to procure them for $3 plus 14¢ postage.

Father Francis Hertzberg (Our Lady's Presbytery, 48 Shalmarsh, Prospect Hill, Hr Bebington, L63 2JZ, The Wirral, England) has a large range of Sherlockian items and many non-Sherlockian Strands and would welcome want lists.

The 1971 Annual of The Priory School (The Holmesian Observer) will be available after 30 January 1972 from Andrew Page (3130 Irwin Ave., Bronx, N.Y. 10463) for $1.25. It will appear in a limited edition of 100 and will contain articles by T. S. Blakeney, Julian Wolff, Lord Donegall, Father Francis Hertzberg, and others; 35 pp., 8 articles.

Charles W. Roberts (2425 Greenwood Ave., Pueblo, Colo. 81003) wants the Sherlock Holmes tales in Braille. Any helpful information would be most welcome.

(continued on page 256)

WHODUNIT

HOWARD LACHTMAN, a doctoral candidate in English at the University of the Pacific, is "a writer of sorts" and is on the bibliographical staff of Western American Literature. He won third prize in the 1971 Steven Vincent Benét Narrative Poetry Awards.
926 W. Mendocino Avenue, Stockton, California 95204.

EDGAR S. ROSENBERGER, a printer by trade, specialises in tales in verse and has made many notable contributions to the Journal over the years.
Apt. 5, Telford Gardens, Telford, Pennsylvania 18969.

HENRY C. POTTER ("The Final Problem"), a member of The Five Orange Pips, is a famous director-producer. He last appeared here in June 1970.
166 East 63rd Street, New York, N.Y. 10021.

JOHN LINSENMEYER, a member of The Sherlock Holmes Society of London, is an erudite attorney and a Sherlockian scholar. One Chase Manhattan Plaza, New York, N.Y. 10005.

H. W. STARR ("The Three Students"), a Founder and formerly Headmastiff of The Sons of the Copper Beeches, is a retired Professor of English and an authority on Thomas Gray.
300 Hathaway Lane, Wynnewood, Pennsylvania 19096.

PHILIP JOSÉ FARMER has been reading Doyle for over 40 years. Formerly an electromechanical technical writer, he is now a full-time fiction writer, and Doubleday is bringing out his biography of Lord Greystoke in 1972.
4106 Devon Lane, Peoria, Illinois 61614.

JACQUES BARZUN, University Professor of Columbia University, is a world renowned scholar, an expert in the field of the detective story (A Catalogue of Crime), and a knowledgeable Sherlockian. 1170 Fifth Avenue, New York, N.Y. 10029.

DAVID H. GALERSTEIN, Assistant Principal of a junior high school, is a serious student of the Canon who has made several valuable contributions to this Journal.
51 Fall Lane, Jericho, New York 11753.

Mrs. GAYLE LANGE PUHL, who previously appeared here in June 1968, has done Sherlockian illustrations for The Baker Street Pages and has lectured and exhibited at the local high school. She is a co-founder of The Residents of Baskerville Hall and was Editor of Baker Street Collecting and founder of Baker Street Collection, both now inactive.
Puhl Hall, 11301-B Lange Road, Hebron, Illinois 60034.

ANDREW PAGE, a college student and a new but very active Sherlockian, is Saltire of The Priory School and Editor of both The Holmesian Observer and The Baker Street Pages.
3130 Irwin Avenue, Bronx, N.Y. 10463.

SUSAN M. RICE teaches a special Greek studies curriculum. Her hobbies include Shakespeare, the theatre, travel, and reading of all sorts.
380 Lone Pine Road, Bloomfield Hills, Michigan 48013.

INDEX TO VOLUME 21 (NEW SERIES)

Articles

(Index continued on next page)

–––– ◉ ––––

BAKER STREET INVENTORY
(continued from page 251)

printed by Brad Kjell; 40¢ a year and 25¢ per issue. All communications should be sent to the editor at 80 Roaring Brook Road, Chappaqua, N.Y. 10514. This issue contains the paper delivered at the BSI dinner in January by John Bennett Shaw—a much discussed production, indeed.

THE SHERLOCK HOLMES JOURNAL, Vol. 10, No. 2, Summer 1971. Published by The Sherlock Holmes Society of London (The Studio, 39 Clabon Mews, London S.W.1, England) and edited by the Marquis of Donegall.

–––– ◉ ––––

WANTS AND OFFERS
(continued from page 252)

John Huegel writes that he is having a superb Inverness cape made made by a very talented young lady who is Capes for Men, 232 East 7th St., New York, N.Y. 10009. And Father Francis Hertzberg (address on page 252) also supplies capes as well as deerstalkers.

Sandy Harbin believes that many Sherlockians looking for rare books on Doyle, Rathbone, and others, may find this address helpful ("They no longer have In and out of Character"): Larry Edmunds Bookshop, Inc., "World's Largest Collection of Books and Memorabilia on Cinema," 6658 Hollywood Boulevard, Hollywood, Calif. 90028; 213-463-3273.

Terry Bellner (P.O. Box 817, Shalimar, Fla. 32579) has a large collection of Sherlock Holmes radio broadcast tape recordings which he offers for $175. Send an 8¢ stamp for list.

D. Martin Dakin (61, Suttons Lane, Hornchurch, Essex, England) wants The Incunabular Holmes, edited by Edgar W. Smith.

Mark Shepard (16947 Adlon Road, Encino, Calif. 91316) is making laminated wood decorations out of posters of the Rathbone-Bruce Holmes films, starting with an insert poster from the 1939 Adventures of Sherlock Holmes, offered for $57. The poster (14" x 34") is laminated on polished wood, then painted and stained. Woman in Green, a one-sheet poster, is $70.

Thomas Hotz (1770 West 6th St., Brooklyn, N.Y. 11223) wants to correspond with fellow Sherlockians in U.S. and abroad.

The only issues of the Journal available at the Journal office are the four issues of 1971, sold at the original price of $1 each. Copies of the Cumulated Index to the Journal, 1946-1969, inclusive, are $5 each. Inquiries relating to BSJ reprints should go to AMS Press, 56 E. 13 St. New York 10003. (The reprints appeared just before this issue went to press, and they are indeed very well done.)

SUBJECT INDEX TO VOLUME 21 (1971)

THE BAKER STREET JOURNAL

This subject index complements the
author and title indexes in Volume 21
No.4. Accounts of Scion Society meetings (except first mention of newly
formed scions), items in "Baker Street
Inventory" and minor small notes have
been omitted. (P) indicates a pastiche, (v) verse. Headings may be
Irregular. Compiled by D.A. Redmond.

Abbey Grange: Lady Brackenstall as
    murderer: Starr 215-220
Adler, Irene: as Georgiana Eagle,
    daughter of conjuror: Shreffler 25;
    career not known: Forbes 249; death
    leaving Holmes a son: Grosbayne 140-
    153; rebuttals: Giardina, Blackburn,
    Rice 240-241; memory of Holmes (v):
    Rice 241
Agate, James, places 3Stu at Cam-
    bridge: Barzun 224
Arid and Repulsive Desert Society
    (scion) 246   [162
Army, Indian, British officer in (ill.)
Astrology identifying Holmes: Fenton
    56

Baker Street: no plaque in: Ball 26-7
-- 221B: seventeen steps (v): Hodan 69
-- bank robbery, Sep.12, 1971: 248
Baker Street Irregulars (canonical):
    Holland 84-85
Baker Street Irregulars (U.S.A.):
    dinner, 1971: cablegram failed:
    Gore-Booth 57; (v) Wolff 49;
    investitures 54
Baker Street Journal: hundredth issue
    (edit.) 67-8; read for facts, not
    theories: Cook 182   [187
Baker Street Pageboys (scion) revived
Baker Street Underground of Ithaca
    (scion) 53
Bank robbery in Baker Street 248
Baring-Gould, W.S., Annotated Sher-
    lock Holmes, unfamiliar with horse-
    drawn vehicles: Potter 200
Battenberg, Alexander prince of,
    1857-93, as King of Bohemia (Scan):
    Blackburn 114-6
Bees: N.Y. Times omits Holmes 249
Bible, see Daniel   [12
Bicycle as public transport: Springer
Blanched Soldier: telephone in:
    Naganuma 21
Blue Carbuncle (verse paraphrase):
    Rosenberger 196-9
Board School Beacons (scion) 187
Bohemia, king of, as Alexander of
    Battenberg: Blackburn 114-6, 240
Bookplate of Lord Peter Wimsey 212

Boscombe Valley Mystery: telegrams
    in: Naganuma 16-17
Boulevard assassin, see Huret
Brandy, doctor's usual remedy, in
    Lamb, foretaste of Watson: Fletcher
    121
Brook Street mystery, see Resident
    Patient
Brothers Three of Moriarty, N.Mex.,
    (scion) 119
Bruce, Nigel, as Watson (port.) 9
Bruce-Partington Plans: Mycroft
    lazy in: Clark 169-74; submarine
    identified as French Gustave Zédé:
    Callaway 151-3; Helling, Morrow 239;
    telegram in: Naganuma 17
Bull pup, see Watson: bull pup

Cab, four-wheeler: Potter 201
Cadogan West, Arthur: name: Skene
    Melvin 95
Cambridge locale of 3Stu: Barzun 224
Canon: bibliography: Catalogue of
    crime by Barzun and Taylor (review)
    44-48
-- scarce in Israel: Rosenblum 181
-- verse paraphrases: Clarke 3-9
Cardboard Box, letter, package and
    telegram in: Naganuma 15-18
Carfax, disguised family name in
    Lady: Farmer 221-3
Cartwright (Houn) as Holmes' assis-
    tant: Holland 85
Catalogue of crime (review) 44-48
Cavendish Squares, Ltd. (scion) 239
Christmas card, Sherlock Holmes
    Society, 1971: 189
Cinema, see Films
Clay, John, henchman of Moriarty:
    Foster 97-99
Clerihew (verse form) epitome of
    Canon: Clarke 3-9
Cognac, see Brandy
Coining, see Counterfeiting
Collier's Magazine advt. for Wist:
    no.3, back cover   [14-21
Communications in Canon: Naganuma
Conjuror Bernard Eagle father of
    Moriarty: Shreffler 22-25
Contest, letter from Canonical
    character 54
Copper Beeches: Holmes errors in:
    Galerstein 229-31; letter in:
    Naganuma 19-20   [224
Cornish, Supt. George W.: Barzun
Counterfeiting in Engr: solution
    mentioned in Shos: Morrow 55
Crew of the Barque Lone Star
    (scion) 53
Crime: bibliography: Catalogue by
    Barzun and Taylor (review) 44-8
-- perfect, and Holmes: Levy 40-3;
    not suspected: Lowndes 120

i